Best Hikes Albuquerque

T0352064

HELP US KEEP THIS GUIDE UP TO DATE

Every effort has been made by the author and editors to make this guide as accurate and useful as possible. However, many things can change after a guide is published—trails are rerouted, regulations change, techniques evolve, facilities come under new management, etc.

We appreciate hearing from you concerning your experiences with this guide and how you feel it could be improved and kept up to date. While we may not be able to respond to all comments and suggestions, we'll take them to heart and we'll also make certain to share them with the author. Please send your comments and suggestions to the following address:

Globe Pequot Press
Reader Response/Editorial Department
246 Goose Lane, Suite 200
Guilford, CT 06437

Thanks for your input, and happy trails!

Best Hikes Albuquerque

The Greatest Views, Wildlife, and Forest Strolls

Second Edition

Stewart M. Green

GUILFORD, CONNECTICUT

FALCONGUIDES®

An imprint of The Rowman & Littlefield Publishing Group, Inc.
4501 Forbes Blvd., Ste. 200
Lanham, MD 20706
www.rowman.com
Falcon and FalconGuides are registered trademarks and Make Adventure Your Story is a trademark
of The Rowman & Littlefield Publishing Group, Inc.

Distributed by NATIONAL BOOK NETWORK

Copyright © 2013 The Rowman & Littlefield Publishing Group, Inc.
This FalconGuide edition 2020

Photos by Stewart M. Green unless otherwise noted
Maps by Melissa Baker

British Library Cataloguing in Publication Information available

Library of Congress Control Number: 2020942028

ISBN 978-1-4930-4622-5 (paper : alk. paper)
ISBN 978-1-4930-4623-2 (electronic)

∞™ The paper used in this publication meets the minimum requirements of American National
Standard for Information Sciences—Permanence of Paper for Printed Library Materials, ANSI/NISO
Z39.48-1992.

Contents

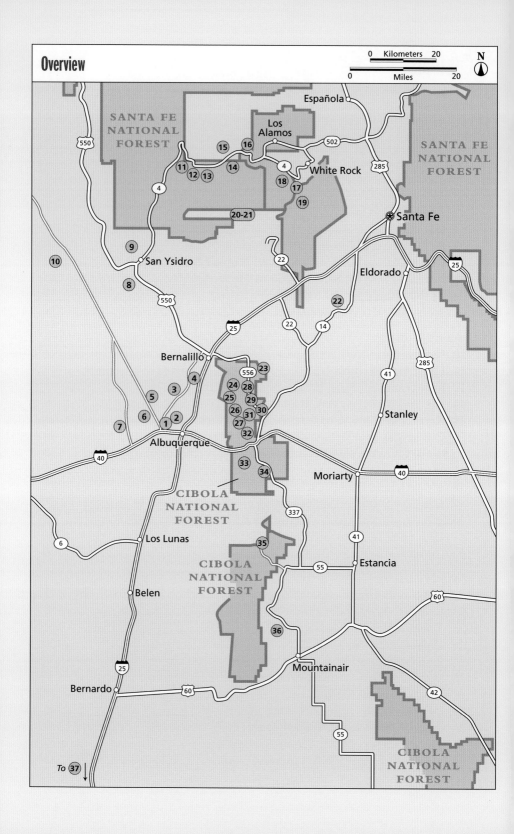

The Cerro la Jara Trail crosses grassy meadows in Valle Grande.

Introduction

Albuquerque, surrounded by towering mountains and scenic canyons, is an outdoor-oriented city. Hundreds of miles of trails surround the city, offering quick foot escapes for both resident and visiting hikers. The weather also cooperates, with plentiful sunshine and generally light rainfall and snow allowing year-round hiking adventures. *Best Hikes Albuquerque* describes the finest hikes and trails for hikers within an hour or so drive of the city.

Whether you're on a tight schedule and want a quick outdoor outing or need a full day to wander up a rocky canyon, the hikes in this book allow you to find a day hike suitable for your abilities and time constraints. The hikes include easy nature strolls for families and kids and barrier-free trail sections that are wheelchair accessible. All of the trailheads are easily reached by vehicle and have designated parking lots. Some trailheads offer hiker facilities, including drinking water and restrooms. The hikes are also rated by difficulty from easy to strenuous. Check the Trail Finder to help you decide which trail is best for your hiking party.

One of the best ways to enjoy, understand, and appreciate Albuquerque and New Mexico is by exploring its diverse terrain on foot. Trails take you away from busy highways and city roads and into ancient landscapes preserved in dry, rarified air; past alpine ponds ringed by windswept grass; up canyons below shining mountains; and to the summits of high peaks with views that stretch to distant horizons. Out there on the trail, hikers learn about New Mexico's rich Native American heritage

Looking north from JA Volcano to Black Volcano in Petroglyph National Monument.

at archaeological sites, discover the state's fascinating geologic story, and enjoy varied ecosystems from arid deserts and cliff-lined canyons to wetlands teeming with wildlife and subalpine forests atop mountain ranges.

Best Hikes Albuquerque is about walking for pleasure—about the joy of lacing up your boots, shouldering a pack, and setting off down a trail into the natural world. Pick a trail and follow your feet. You'll find you can go just about anywhere in New Mexico.

Albuquerque Weather

Albuquerque, one of America's sunniest cities, receives 310 days of sunshine each year. The area's mild climate and low humidity offers perfect conditions for hiking adventures, but be prepared for dramatic temperature changes between daylight and nighttime.

Summer days are usually in the 90s in the lower elevations and the 70s and low 80s atop the Sandia Crest. Heavy thunderstorms accompanied by dangerous lightning regularly occur during the monsoon season in July and August when moist air pushes north from Mexico. The shoulder seasons in spring and autumn are ideal for hiking, with warm, dry days, although spring afternoons are often windy. Albuquerque winters are mild, with daytime temperatures in the upper 40s and 50s and low snowfall. The surrounding mountains, however, are a different story, with snow and ice encasing

A rare winter snowfall blankets yucca along the Domingo Baca Trail.

the upper-elevation trails until the temperature warms and the snow melts in April.

LIGHTNING SAFETY

Stay safe from lightning strikes by following the 30/30 rule. Take shelter indoors or move to a safe location away from tall trees, fences, and power poles if there are less than 30 seconds between the time that you hear thunder and see lightning. Assume the safe lightning position, squatting or sitting with your arms wrapped around your legs, and wait for 30 minutes after the last lightning flash.

Practice Zero-Impact Philosophy

Albuquerque, surrounded by towering mountains and scenic canyons, is simply one of the best cities in the American West to get outside and enjoy wild nature. With all the hikers and outdoor enthusiasts in the Albuquerque region, it's important to practice a zero-impact philosophy so that the area's natural resources and its trails are protected from overuse and a positive outdoor experience is maintained for all back-country visitors. Use the following zero-impact suggestions to make both your own as well as everyone else's hike enjoyable and to protect New Mexico's spectacular natural world.

Zero-impact is about responsible outdoor ethics, including staying on the trail, not cutting switchbacks, packing out litter, keeping your dog leashed and picking up its poop, disposing properly of human waste, and leaving the environment as pristine as possible. Mountain, prairie, and desert ecosystems and environments are fragile and sensitive to human use. The marks of humans, including social trails carved by inconsiderate hikers and land damage from ATVs and motorcycles, linger for years on this arid landscape.

Tall cottonwoods line the bosque on the River Loop Trail at the Albuquerque Open Space Visitor Center Trails.

FALCONGUIDES PRINCIPLES OF ZERO IMPACT

Always stay on the trail. Cutting switchbacks or traveling cross-country causes erosion and destroys plants. Popular hiking areas are often braided with social trails from careless hikers going off-trail or shortcutting. Try to always follow the main route whenever possible. The mountains, especially steep and rocky slopes, are susceptible to erosion caused by unthinking off-trail hiking.

Pack it in—pack it out. Everything you carry and use, including food wrappers, orange peels, cigarette butts, plastic bottles, and energy-bar wrappers, needs to come out with you and be deposited in a trash can. Carry a plastic bag for picking up other trash along the trail. Also, remember to pick up your dog's waste and pack it out in a reclosable bag for proper disposal. Many bad dog owners leave their pet's feces in the middle of the trail. That's just gross.

Respect public and private property, including livestock fences, mining claims, and archaeological and historic sites. Federal laws protect all archaeological and historic antiquities, including Native American artifacts, projectile points, ancient ruins, petroglyphs and other rock art sites, fossilized bone and petrified wood, and historic sites, including old cabins and corrals. Don't carve your name on a rock surface or a tree. Leave natural features, like flowers and rocks, where you found them. Enjoy their beauty but leave them for the next hiker.

Properly dispose of human waste. Pooping outside is harmful to water sources and fragile desert and mountain environments as well as being unsightly and stinky. Carry a WAG bag, a self-contained poop unit to collect and carry your waste in the backcountry, on all of your hikes. Each puncture-resistant unit contains a NASA-developed solidifying agent, hand sanitizer, powder to hide odors, and toilet paper. Just squat, poop, seal the pouch, and dispose at the trailhead. The solidifier breaks down and deodorizes the waste, allowing you to safely toss the used WAG bag in the trash. In an emergency, dig a cat hole about 6 inches deep and at least 300 feet from water sources and dry washes. Do not burn or bury toilet paper. Instead, pack it out in a reclosable baggie and dispose of it later. The best thing to do, of course, is to use the public restrooms that are found at many of the trailheads before or after your hike.

Take only photographs and good memories. We can easily avoid leaving any evidence of our passage across Albuquerque's gorgeous and delicate desert and mountain environments. With care and sensitivity, we as hikers can do our part to keep central New Mexico and Albuquerque beautiful, clean, and pristine. Don't pick flowers, pick up rocks, or take anything with you when you leave. If everyone took just one item, it wouldn't be long before nothing special was left. Leave your souvenirs for other hikers to enjoy on their hike.

Every hiker should adopt a zero-impact ethic to minimize his or her impact on this beautiful land. It's our responsibility to pay attention to our effect on the environment so that we can ensure that all these fabulous trails will remain as wild refuges from the urban environment.

Be Prepared for Hiking Adventures

Hiking, while immensely rewarding, also comes with hazards and inherent risks, especially for those who come unprepared. Respect the mountain and desert environments and be prepared for emergencies, and you'll be safe. Remember that many dangers are found in the greater Albuquerque area.

You must assume responsibility for your actions and the safety of yourself and your hiking party. Be aware of your surroundings and dangers, including drop-offs, cliffs, and loose rock; the weather; and the physical condition of both your party and you. Never be afraid to turn around if conditions aren't right. Pay attention to those bad feelings—they keep you alive.

Here are a few suggestions to be prepared for emergencies on your hike:

- Bring extra clothes and a raincoat, especially in the mountains. The weather can change in an instant. Heavy thunderstorms regularly occur on summer afternoons and cold, wet clothing can lead to hypothermia.
- New Mexico has the eighth-most lightning strikes of any state in the United States, with almost 800,000 each year. Severe thunderstorms fed by moist tropical air during the monsoon season in July and August guarantee lightning almost every day. Pay attention to the weather and get off high places before a storm arrives. If you can hear thunder, you're probably not safe.
- The New Mexican air is thin, and the sun is bright. Summer temperatures are usually hot. Use sunscreen to avoid damaging sunburns and wear a hat.
- Carry plenty of water and sports drinks for electrolyte replacement due to sweating. Don't drink any water from streams unless you treat and purify it.
- If you're coming from a lower elevation, watch for symptoms of altitude sickness, including headache, nausea, and loss of appetite. The best cure is to lose elevation.
- Allow enough time for your hike. If you start in the late afternoon, bring a headlamp or flashlight so you can see the trail in the dark.

NEW MEXICO'S HIGHS AND LOWS

New Mexico's lowest point is a mere 2,842 feet above sea level in the southeastern part of the state, at the northern end of Red Bluff Reservoir on the Pecos River. The state's highest point is 13,161-foot Wheeler Peak, a snowcapped mountain in the Sangre de Cristo Mountains northeast of Taos.

Volcanic tuff cliffs tower above the Main Loop Trail and the ruins of Tyuonyi at Bandelier National Monument.

- Bring plenty of high-energy snacks for the trail and treats for the youngsters.
- Wear comfortable hiking shoes and good socks. Your feet will thank you for that. To avoid blisters, break in your shoes before wearing them in the backcountry.
- Enjoy wildlife you see along the trail, but keep your distance and treat the animals with respect. Cute little animals can bite and spread diseases like rabies. Watchful mother animals, including mule deer and black bears, are protective of their babies. Rattlesnakes are often found on low-elevation trails. Watch where you place your hands and feet. Don't feed wildlife to avoid disrupting their natural eating habits.
- Carry a day pack to tote all your trail needs, including a raincoat, food, water bottle, first-aid kit, flashlight, matches, and extra clothes. A whistle, GPS unit, topo map, binoculars, camera, pocketknife, and FalconGuides identification book for plants and animals are all handy additions. And don't forget your *Best Hikes Albuquerque* book!

THE TEN ESSENTIALS

The Ten Essentials are easy to carry and will help you survive. The purpose of carrying the Ten Essentials is twofold: to allow you to respond positively to an accident or emergency and to allow you to survive one or more nights outside. It's best to carry most of the Ten Essentials in your hiking pack on a major trek like the Pino Trail or Domingo Baca Trail up the western flank of the Sandia Mountains so that you will be prepared for any emergency.

These are the essential items to carry:

1. **Navigation.** Bring a map, compass, GPS unit, and extra batteries.
2. **Sun protection.** Sunscreen is essential to protect from the burning rays of the high-altitude sun as well as lip balm and either baby powder or Gold Bond powder for chafing.
3. **Insulation.** Bring plenty of clothing and dress in layers. Waterproof outer gear is essential.
4. **Illumination.** Bring a headlamp and extra batteries in case you have to hike down in the dark.
5. **First-aid supplies.** A small first-aid kit with bandages, Band-Aids, and basic medical supplies is important.
6. **Fire.** Bring a lighter and box of matches to start a fire for warmth if you are benighted.
7. **Repair kit and tools.** A multiuse tool or pocketknife along with some duct tape can repair torn gear.
8. **Nutrition.** Pack plenty of food. Bring extra energy bars to stash in your pack. You may need them if you get lost.
9. **Hydration.** Bring plenty of water. In summer bring a minimum of three quarts of water. You can substitute a sports drink for one of them or bring powder to mix in water. You can refill your water bottles or CamelBak at many trailheads.
10. **Emergency shelter.** It's easy to pack a lightweight space blanket or ultralight tarp for shelter from the storm.

The Slot Canyon Trail squeezes between sculptured walls at Kasha-Katuwe Tent Rocks National Monument.

How to Use This Guide

Take a close enough look, and you'll find that this guide contains just about everything you need to choose and enjoy a hike near Albuquerque. Here's an outline of the book's major components.

Each hike starts with a summary of the hike's highlights. These quick overviews give you a taste of the hiking adventures to follow. You'll learn about the trail terrain and what surprises each route offers.

Following the overview, you'll find the hike specs: quick, nitty-gritty details of the hike. These specs include: **Distance:** The total distance of the recommended route—one way for a loop hike or round-trip for an out-and-back or lollipop hike. Options are additional.

Hiking time: The average time it will take to cover the route. It is based on the total distance, elevation gain, and condition and difficulty of the trail. Your fitness level will also affect your time.

Difficulty: Each hike has been assigned a level of difficulty. The rating system was developed from several sources and personal experience. These levels are meant to be a guideline only and may prove easier or harder for different people depending on ability and physical fitness.

Easy—Five miles or less total trip distance in one day, with minimal elevation gain and paved or smooth-surfaced dirt trail.

Moderate—Up to 10 miles total trip distance in one day, with moderate elevation gain and potentially rough terrain.

Strenuous—More than 10 miles total trip distance in one day, with strenuous elevation gain and/or rough or rocky terrain.

Best seasons: General information on the best time of year to hike.

Schedule: Days and hours the trail and visitor center, offices, etc., are open to the public. Unless restrictions are stated, the trail is open 24 hours, and if the park is open, the trails are open.

Other trail users: Such as horseback riders, mountain bikers, inline skaters, trail runners, etc.

Canine compatibility: Know the trail regulations before you take your dog hiking with you. Dogs are not allowed on several trails in this book.

Fees and permits: Whether you need to carry any money with you for park entrance fees, parking, and permits.

Maps: A list of other maps to supplement the maps in this book. USGS maps are the best source for accurate topographical information, but the local park map may show more recent trails. Use both.

Trail contact: This is the location, phone number, and website URL for the local land manager(s) in charge of the trails within the selected hike. Get trail access information before you head out, or contact the land manager after your visit if you see problems with trail erosion, damage, or misuse.

Stop at the sculpture garden at the start of the Pino Trail before heading into the Sandias.

Special considerations: This section calls your attention to specific trail hazards, like hunting seasons or a lack of water, and other safety information.

Finding the trailhead: Gives you dependable driving directions to where you'll want to park, as well as GPS coordinates for the start of the hike.

The Hike is the heart of the chapter. Detailed and honest, it's a carefully researched impression and description of the trails on the hike. It also often includes lots of area history, both natural and human.

Under **Miles and Directions,** mileage cues identify all turns and trail name changes, as well as points of interest.

Options and **Extra Credit** hikes are also given for many trails to make your journey shorter or longer depending on your time limitations. Don't feel restricted to the routes and trails that are mapped here. Be adventurous and use this guide as a platform to discover new routes for yourself.

How to Use the Maps

Overview map: This map shows the location of each hike in the Albuquerque area by hike number.

Route map: This is your primary map and guide to each hike. It shows all of the access roads and trails, points of interest, water, landmarks, and geographical features. It also distinguishes trails from roads and paved roads from unpaved roads. The selected route is highlighted, and directional arrows point the way.

Petroglyphs along the Piedras Marcadas Canyon Trail depict Kokopelli, the ancient flute player of the Ancestral Puebloans.

Map Legend

Municipal

≡(25)≡ Freeway/Interstate Highway

≡(550)≡ US Highway

≡(14)≡ State Road

≡279≡ County/Paved/Improved Road

= = = : Unpaved Road

├──┼──┤ Railroad

──── Leader Line

Trails

------ Featured Trail

- - - - Trail or Fire Road

Water Features

⬭ Body of Water

〜 River/Creek

〜 Intermittent Stream

ơ Spring

≋ Waterfall

Land Management

⬛ National Park/Forest

⬜ State/County Park

Symbols

〜 Bridge

■ Building/Point of Interest

▲ Campground

∩ Cave

•─• Gate

→ Hike Arrow

▲ Mountain/Peak

🅿 Parking

🛆 Picnic Area

🚻 Restroom

🔲 Scenic View/Overlook

||||||| Steps/Boardwalk

→ To Text

○ Towns and Cities

㉑ Trailhead

❓ Visitor/Information Center

⬛ National Monument/
Wilderness Area

Albuquerque Area

A pond reflects the sky and the Sandia Mountains at Rio Grande Nature Center State Park.

1 Rio Grande Nature Center Trails

Rio Grande Nature Center State Park provides an escape to nature in the heart of Albuquerque. This 1.35-mile-long loop hike passes through cottonwoods along the Rio Grande and offers scenery and good bird watching.

Distance: 1.35-mile lollipop
Hiking time: About 1 hour
Difficulty: Easy
Best seasons: Spring and fall are best. Winters can be cold but dry. Summer is hot.
Schedule: Open daily 8 a.m. to 5 p.m. Closed Thanksgiving, Christmas, and New Year's Day.
Other trail users: Bicyclists on first trail section
Canine compatibility: No dogs allowed
Fees and permits: Fee per vehicle; free to walk or bike into park
Maps: USGS Los Griegos; trail map available at visitor center and on website

Trail contact: Rio Grande Nature Center State Park, 2901 Candelaria Rd. NW, Albuquerque 87107; (505) 344-7240; www.emnrd.state .nm.us/spd/riograndenaturecenterstatepark .html
Special considerations: Trails are accessed from Candelaria Road outside the park entrance before and after park hours. Park on the street where legal and walk west on the trail to a canal. Parking lot gates are locked at 5 p.m. and vehicles left in the lot are locked in overnight. If you plan on being on the trail after 5 p.m., park outside the gate.

Finding the trailhead: From I-40 in Albuquerque, take exit 157A to Rio Grande Boulevard. Turn right (north) onto Rio Grande Boulevard NW and drive 1.4 miles to Candelaria Road NW. Turn left (northwest) onto Candelaria Road NW and drive 0.6 mile to the park entrance. Turn right onto a park road and drive 500 feet to a large parking area east of the visitor center (GPS: 35.129682 N / -106.682616 W). Start from a trailhead on the west side of the parking lot (GPS: 35.129551 N / -106.682995 W), and hike 400 feet to a trail junction with a short trail to the visitor center. Begin the hike on the west side of the center.

The Hike

The 38-acre Rio Grande Nature Center State Park lies along the east bank of the Rio Grande northwest of downtown Albuquerque. The park offers a fun family-friendly trail system that weaves through open woods along the river. The park and trails are on the Rio Grande flyway, a well-used migration route for birds and waterfowl. Bring binoculars and a bird book to spot some of the 250 different species of birds that live in or migrate through Albuquerque. The trail passes through a bosque, or riverside forest, which offers tall cottonwood trees that shade hikers and provide valuable habitat for riparian wildlife, including sandhill cranes, beavers, porcupines, coyotes, turtles, roadrunners, great blue herons, and bald eagles in winter.

North of the parking lots and visitor center is a wildlife preserve with Observation Pond and Candelaria Wetlands that attract migratory waterfowl. The area is closed to public visitation, but three wildlife viewing areas allow visitors to see birds. Wildlife

Rescue of New Mexico has a wildlife rehab center on the south side of the park. The visitor center, with hands-on exhibits, workshops, seminars, educational programs, and wildlife presentations, is the perfect place to learn about the bosque and the Rio Grande. Visit the center either before or after your hike.

Hikers also park vehicles at the nature center to access other trails along the Rio Grande, including the multiuse Paseo del Bosque and Aldo Leopold Trails, which pass through the state park. The popular and paved Paseo del Bosque Trail runs from north to south for 16 miles along the Rio Grande through Albuquerque, and the 1.26-mile Aldo Leopold Trail (Hike 2), named for a famous conservationist, heads north through the bosque from the state park. These are part of Albuquerque's 400-mile multiuse trail system.

Hikers pause on the bank of the Rio Grande on the River Loop Trail at Rio Grande Nature Center State Park.

Begin the hike at a trailhead on the west side of the parking lot. Follow a trail for 400 feet to a junction, with a right turn going through a culvert tunnel into the park visitor center. The hike continues west on the marked trail for 400 feet to a bridge across Riverside Drain, a canal east of the river. Cross the bridge to a set of stairs and the junction of the Paseo del Bosque Trail and the Aldo Leopold Trail, which heads right.

Climb the stairs and cross the paved Paseo del Bosque Trail, then descend a short hill to a trail junction at 0.1 mile. The hike makes two loops from this junction, following the 0.64-mile Bosque Loop Trail and the 0.55-mile River Loop Trail before returning to this junction.

The first 400-foot segment turns right (north) at the junction on the Bosque Loop Trail. Hike to a bridge over the Silvery Minnow Channel and continue to another trail junction at 0.25 mile from the visitor center. Go right (north) at the junction on the River Loop Trail.

Hike northwest on the dirt trail for 0.2 mile through a shady cottonwood forest to a sharp bend above the Rio Grande. Step west to the riverbank for a good view across the Rio Grande's broad muddy channel. At the elbow bend 0.35 mile from the visitor center, make a left turn and head southwest along the riverbank, going up and down wooden stairs. After hiking 0.2 mile along the river from the elbow bend,

Hikers walk on the sandy River Loop Trail through the bosque along the Rio Grande.

the trail reaches an open area with spacious views of the brown river. The trail turns left here and heads southeast for 0.1 mile to the junction of the River Loop Trail and Bosque Loop Trail. Turn right (south) onto the Bosque Loop Trail, the final hike segment.

The hike goes south through the open bosque woodland and after 0.2 mile from the junction reaches a bridge over the Silvery Minnow Channel, a usually dry overflow channel for the Rio Grande that fills with water during spring runoff and flooding for the endangered silvery minnow fish. Continue another 0.1 mile to a trail junction, where a short path goes right to the riverbank. The hike bends left (east) at the junction on the Bosque Loop Trail and heads northeast.

You reach the original junction at the end of the Bosque Loop Trail at 1.25 miles. Turn right (east) to return to the Rio Grande Nature Center State Park visitor center in 0.1 mile for a 1.35-mile round-trip hike.

Miles and Directions

0.0   Leave the trailhead at the parking lot (GPS: 35.129551 N / -106.682995 W) and walk west for 400 feet to a trail junction. Go right to the Rio Grande Visitor Center if desired. The hike goes west. Walk another 400 feet to a bridge over the Riverside Drain. Continue to the junction with the Paseo de Bosque Trail (GPS: 35.130965 N / -106.684966 W).

0.1   Reach the junction of the Bosque and River Loop Trails. Turn right (north) on the Bosque Loop Trail.

0.2   Cross a bridge over Silvery Minnow Channel to a junction. Go right (north) on the River Loop Trail.

0.4   The trail makes a sharp left turn and heads southwest near the riverbank.

0.6   The trail reaches a river overlook and makes a sharp left (southeast) turn.

0.7   Reach the junction with the Bosque Loop Trail. Turn right and hike southwest on the Bosque Loop Trail.

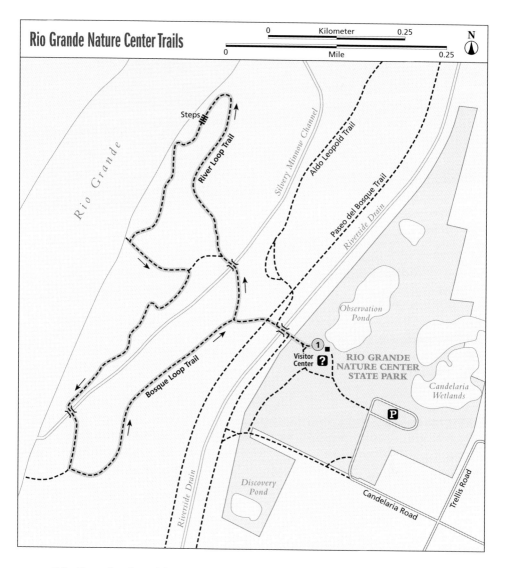

0.9 The trail makes a left turn and crosses a bridge over Silvery Minnow Channel.

1.0 Reach a trail junction. Go left on the Bosque Loop Trail. The trail to the right leads west to a viewing area of the Rio Grande.

1.25 Reach the trail junction and end of the Bosque Loop Trail. Go right and hike east back to the visitor center.

1.35 Arrive back at the west side of the visitor center.

Area Info

Friends of the Rio Grande Nature Center, 2901 Candelaria Rd. NW, Albuquerque; (505) 344-7240; www.emnrd.state.nm.us/spd/riograndenaturecenterstatepark.html

2 Aldo Leopold Trail

The Aldo Leopold Trail, beginning at Rio Grande Nature Center State Park, is an out-and-back hike that explores the cottonwood bosque on the eastern bank of the Rio Grande, offering scenic views and wildlife observation northwest of downtown Albuquerque.

Distance: 2.8 miles out and back with loop at end
Hiking time: About 1.5 hours
Difficulty: Easy
Best seasons: Spring and fall are best. Winters can be cold but dry. Summer is hot.
Schedule: Open daily 8 a.m. to 5 p.m. year-round
Other trail users: Mountain bikers
Canine compatibility: No dogs allowed
Fees and permits: State park fee per vehicle; walk or bike in for free from nature center
Maps: USGS Los Griegos; trail map available at nature center

Trail contacts: Albuquerque Parks & Recreation, (505) 768-5353; Open Space Visitor Center, 6500 Coors Blvd. NW, Albuquerque 87120; (505) 897-8831; www.cabq.gov/parksandrecreation/open-space/open-space-visitor-center
Special considerations: Reach the trail from the Candelaria Road access path outside the state park entrance before and after designated park hours. Parking lot gates are locked at 5 p.m. and vehicles left in the lot are locked in overnight. Park outside the gate if you plan on being on the trail after 5 p.m.

Finding the trailhead: From I-40 in Albuquerque, take exit 157A to Rio Grande Boulevard. Turn right (north) on Rio Grande Boulevard NW and drive 1.4 miles to Candelaria Road NW. Turn left (northwest) onto Candelaria Road NW and drive 0.6 mile to the entrance to Rio Grande Nature Center State Park. Turn right into the park and drive 500 feet north to a large parking area and the trailhead on the west side of the lot. GPS: 35.129551 N / -106.682995 W.

The Hike

This easy 2.8-mile trail celebrates Aldo Leopold, a leader in the twentieth-century American conservation movement. Acknowledged as the father of modern-day wildlife conservation, Leopold was a conservationist, forester, writer, and outdoor enthusiast. He is well known for his collection of essays, first published in 1949, titled *A Sand County Almanac: And Sketches Here and There*. In this slender book, Leopold discusses many of his ideas about conservation, including the "land ethic."

Leopold, born in 1887 in Burlington, Iowa, developed an interest in nature at a young age, exploring the natural world that surrounded his boyhood home. This passion for the outdoors led him to the Yale Forest School, where he joined the first generation of professional foresters, graduating with a master's degree in 1909. He then pursued a career with the newly established USDA Forest Service in Arizona and New Mexico. Within a few years, Leopold was promoted to supervisor for the Carson National Forest in New Mexico. He left behind an impressive environmental legacy in New Mexico, including the creation of the Gila Wilderness Area, the first designated wilderness in the United States.

Leopold had a special place in his heart for Albuquerque and advocated for its responsible growth. He married his wife, Estella, in 1912 and lived near the Rio Grande. Serving as the secretary of Albuquerque's chamber of commerce, Leopold promoted the creation of a parkland that became Rio Grande Valley State Park. His vision and efforts also led to the creation of the Rio Grande Zoological Park, Rio Grande Botanic Gardens, Rio Grande Nature Center, and the Albuquerque Wildlife Federation.

Access the Aldo Leopold Trail from the northwest side of the parking lot at Rio Grande Nature Center State Park northwest of downtown Albuquerque. The first section of the hike is the same as Hike 1.

The Aldo Leopold Trail, named for a famed conservationist, threads along the Rio Grande.

From the parking lot, follow a gravel trail west past the state park visitor center and across a bridge over Riverside Drain. After crossing the bridge, turn immediately right and hike 240 feet north to the paved Paseo del Bosque Trail, a 16-mile multiuse trail that runs through Albuquerque along the Rio Grande from Alameda Boulevard to Rio Bravo Boulevard. The trail runs along the top of a flood-control levee.

Cross the wide trail and start the Aldo Leopold Trail to the west. The trail initially passes through a maze of jetty jacks, or flood control fences, placed by the U.S. Army Corps of Engineers. Past the jacks, the trail bends north on the asphalt trail, passing through an open woodland of spreading cottonwood trees, the dominant tree on the Rio Grande bosque. Farther north the trail leaves state park land and enters the 53-acre Aldo Leopold Forest, a strip of land between the Paseo del Bosque Trail and the Rio Grande.

GREEN TIP
Did you know that it can take a plastic water bottle up to 500 years to decompose? Solution: Invest in a refillable water bottle and faucet filter, and save lots of money and the environment at the same time.

Stately cottonwood trees line the Aldo Leopold Trail.

Arrive at a wooden bench after 0.3 mile and continue hiking north on the asphalt path. Another bench is at 0.5 mile. Past the second bench, the trail curves to the left (northwest) and a sandy path splits off to the right (north). A sign here designates the trail as the Aldo Leopold Forest Trail. Go right on this short path to see the river.

The trail reaches the east bank of the Rio Grande at 0.7 mile and follows the river north. Stop and read several interpretive signs along this trail segment about the life and work of Aldo Leopold. This is a productive spot for bird watching, particularly waterfowl. Look for sandhill cranes, Canada geese, and several duck species during the winter months. Roadrunners, raccoons, beavers, and coyotes are also seen.

THE ENDANGERED BOSQUE

Bosque, a Spanish word meaning "woods" and pronounced BOHS-kay, is a forested riparian ecosystem on a river's floodplain in a desert. Bosques are found primarily in the American Southwest, mostly along the Rio Grande, which bisects New Mexico from the Colorado state line to El Paso, Texas. The Rio Grande sustains the bosque ecosystem and its habitat of cottonwood trees, providing critical habitat for over 500 animals. The state's bosque environments are endangered due to farming, irrigation diversions, flood-control projects, water storage, and urban development.

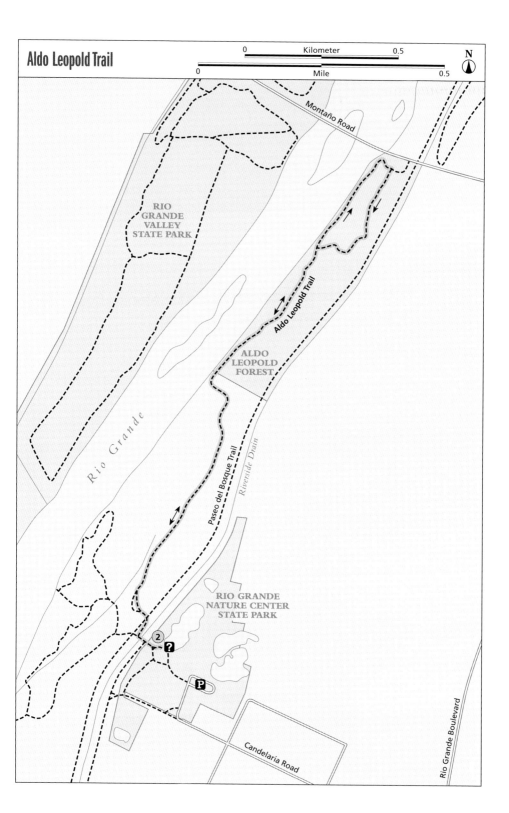

0   Kilometer   0.5

0   Mile   0.5

N

Montaño Road

RIO
GRANDE
VALLEY
STATE PARK

Aldo Leopold Trail

ALDO
LEOPOLD
FOREST

Rio Grande

Paseo del Bosque Trail

Riverside Drain

RIO GRANDE
NATURE CENTER
STATE PARK

2

?

P

Candelaria Road

Rio Grande Boulevard

At 0.8 mile the trail becomes sandy and continues north through big cottonwoods. Reach a main fork in the trail at 1.1 miles and the start of a 0.6-mile loop at the north part of the hike. Take the left trail and head toward the river. Hike north near the riverbank for 0.3 mile and at 1.4 miles make a sharp right turn to the east before reaching Montaño Boulevard's bridge. Hike east to a paved spur of the Paseo del Bosque Trail that goes south from the bridge. Before reaching the paved trail, go right and follow a sandy trail south beneath shady cottonwoods and parallel to the Paseo del Bosque Trail.

At 1.7 miles return to the junction at the start of the loop segment. Continue straight on the trail to the asphalt trail section. At 2.2 miles reach the asphalt trail and follow it back to the Paseo del Bosque Trail. Cross the bridge over Riverside Drain, pass the visitor center, and return to the state park parking lot after 2.8 miles.

Miles and Directions

0.0 Begin at the trailhead on the west side of the Rio Grande Nature Center State Park parking area (GPS: 35.129559 N / -106.683019 W). Follow the gravel trail west past the visitor center and reach a bridge.

0.15 Go right on the west side of the bridge on an asphalt trail and hike north for 240 feet to the paved Paseo del Bosque Trail (GPS: 35.131431 N / -106.684470 W).

0.2 Cross the paved trail and go through cottonwoods and past jetty jacks for 200 feet to a junction. Go right.

0.3 Reach a wooden bench and continue northeast on the asphalt path.

0.5 The trail reaches the Rio Grande and enters Aldo Leopold Forest.

1.1 Come to a fork in the trail (GPS: 35.141949 N / -106.678458 W). Take the left trail toward the river for a loop at the north end of the hike.

1.4 Reach the south side of the Montaño Bridge and turn right (east). Hike east a couple hundred feet to an asphalt spur of the Paseo del Bosque Trail (GPS: 35.144379 N / -106.675260 W) and go right (south) on the dirt trail parallel to the paved trail.

1.7 Reach the junction at the start of loop. Continue straight on the main Aldo Leopold Trail.

2.2 Return to the asphalt trail and keep right.

2.8 Cross the bridge and arrive back at the Rio Grande Nature Center State Park visitor center and parking lot.

Area Info

Rio Grande Nature Center State Park, 2901 Candelaria Rd. NW, Albuquerque; (505) 334-7240; www.emnrd.state.nm.us/spd/riograndenaturecenterstatepark.html

GREEN TIP
Carpool or take public transportation to the trailhead.

3 Albuquerque Open Space Visitor Center Trails

The Albuquerque Open Space Visitor Center offers a network of trails that explore the Rio Grande bosque, with excellent viewing of sandhill cranes in fall and winter. This 2-mile hike connects three trails that loop through the bosque ecosystem. Shorten the hike by doing only one trail.

Distance: 2-mile lollipop
Hiking time: About 1.5 hours
Difficulty: Moderate
Best seasons: Spring and fall are best. Winters can be cold but dry. Summer is hot.
Schedule: Open Tues through Sun 9 a.m. to 5 p.m. year-round. Closed Thanksgiving, Christmas, New Year's Day, and Fourth of July.
Other trail users: Bikers and trail runners
Canine compatibility: Leashed dogs allowed

Fees and permits: None
Maps: USGS Los Griegos; trail map available at Open Space Visitor Center
Trail contact: Open Space Visitor Center, 6500 Coors Blvd. NW, Albuquerque 87199; (505) 897-8831; www.cabq.gov/parksandrecreation/open-space/open-space-visitor-center
Special considerations: Reach the trails from the Sagebrush Community Church public parking area before and after visitor center hours.

Finding the trailhead: From I-40 in Albuquerque, take exit 155 onto Coors Boulevard North. Drive north on Coors Boulevard for 4.7 miles to the entrance to the Open Space Visitor Center on the right. Turn right onto Bosque Meadows Road and drive 0.1 mile to the parking area. GPS: 35.165459 N / -106.673391 W

The Hike

The Albuquerque Open Space system preserves, maintains, and manages cultural and natural resources in the Albuquerque area. The open space program also provides outdoor education and recreational opportunities, including hiking. The Albuquerque Open Space Visitor Center is the hub for over 29,000 acres of open space managed by the City of Albuquerque. The Open Space Division educates both residents and visitors about the importance of protecting and preserving natural areas around the city. The visitor center offers exhibits, year-round educational programs, and an art gallery.

From the parking lot outside the visitor center, find the trailhead on the west side of the lot. Walk through an arched doorway and turn left (south). Hike south on the gravel Visitor Center Trail. This trail segment runs alongside La Orilla Channel for 0.2 mile before intersecting Roberson Lane. Cross the road and continue hiking south. After 0.3 mile the trail drops east from the channel onto a packed dirt trail. At the bottom of a hill, signs direct you to the Bosque Trails.

Hike east, following the signs for 0.1 mile, to a "Birds of the Bosque" kiosk and trail junction. Stay right (east) on the River Loop Trail. The trail to the left (north)

Hikers follow the River Loop Trail by the Rio Grande.

is your return trail. The trail is sandy in places and sometimes other hikers roam off trail, so pay attention to follow the main path. Keep hiking in a southeast direction and you'll be fine.

Reach a small loop section of the River Loop Trail at 0.6 mile and go right (south) onto the loop. At 0.7 mile the trail makes a sharp left (north) turn and runs along the brown Rio Grande for a short stretch. The loop, shaded by tall Rio Grande cottonwoods, a subspecies of the plains cottonwood, ends at 0.8 mile. At the junction the trail turns right (northeast) onto the Canopy Loop Trail.

Continue hiking northeast along the Canopy Loop Trail through a typical Rio Grande bosque, a river bottomland covered with cottonwoods and shrubs. Large metal structures called "jetty jacks" are scattered along the trail. Jetty jacks, composed of three steel beams bolted together and bound with wire, were built to slow floodwaters, causing the river to deposit sediment and stabilize the floodplain. About 29,000 Kellner jetty jacks were placed along the Rio Grande in the mid-twentieth century in an attempt to keep the river from expanding. The jacks, along with upriver dams, worked so well that the Rio's floodplain no longer floods, changing the bosque ecosystem, increasing fire danger, and slowly killing the cottonwood trees. Historically, the river would swell with snowmelt in the spring, spilling over its banks and flooding the bosque to create a moist bed for cottonwood seeds to sprout into trees. Over 10,000 of the jacks have been removed, and the remaining jacks are slowly being taken out. The next step is to begin planting young cottonwoods to replace the elderly trees towering above the trail and to figure out how to let the river flood the area.

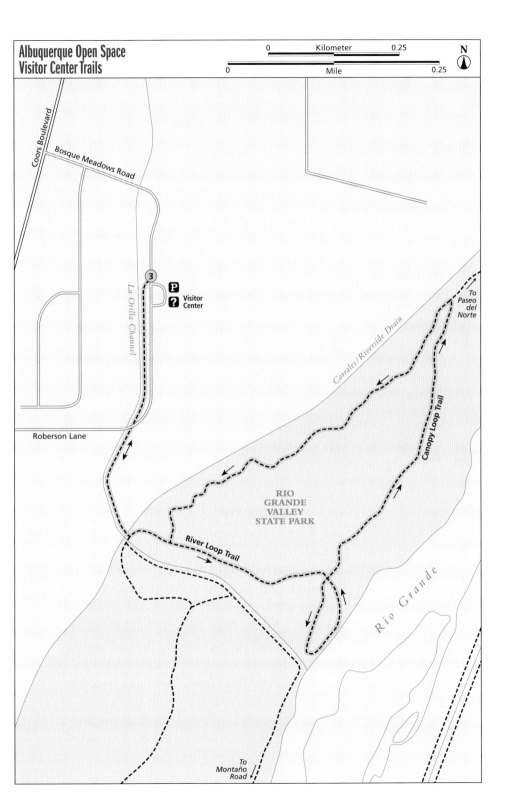

Albuquerque Open Space
Visitor Center Trails

0   Kilometer   0.25

0   Mile   0.25

N

Coors Boulevard

Bosque Meadows Road

La Orilla Channel

3

P

? Visitor
Center

Roberson Lane

Corrales/Riverside Drain

Canopy Loop Trail

To
Paseo
del
Norte

RIO
GRANDE
VALLEY
STATE PARK

River Loop Trail

Rio Grande

To
Montaño
Road

After 1.1 miles the trail makes a sharp left (southwest) turn. A trail to the right (northeast) leads to the Arboreal Dome. Stay left (southwest) on the Canopy Loop Trail and continue hiking southwest toward the River Loop Trail. The River Loop and Canopy Loop Trail junction is reached at 1.6 miles. Turn right (west) to return to the Open Space Visitor Center, trailhead, and parking area in 0.4 mile.

Miles and Directions

0.0   Leave the Open Space Visitor Center parking area from its west side to the trailhead at an arched doorway (GPS: 35.165265 N / -106.673729 W). Hike south on a gravel trail along La Orilla Channel.

0.2   Cross over Roberson Lane and continue south.

0.3   Follow the Bosque Access sign that directs hikers left (east) off the channel path onto a dirt trail that crosses over the Corrales/Riverside Drain canal. Continue hiking south to the River Loop Trail.

0.4   Reach a trail junction at the "Birds of the Bosque" kiosk (GPS: 35.160906 N / -106.673239 W) and stay right (east) on the River Loop Trail. The trail to the north is the Canopy Loop Trail.

0.6   Reach a junction with the Canopy Loop Trail to the left and the loop portion of the River Loop Trail (GPS: 35.160241 N / -106.669933 W). Turn right (south) to begin the loop.

0.7   The trail makes a sharp left to begin the hike north along the west bank of the Rio Grande.

0.8   The loop portion ends. Turn right (northeast) on the Canopy Loop Trail.

1.1   The trail makes a sharp left turn to lead hikers southwest back toward the River Loop Trail. A trail heading northeast from here leads to the Arboreal Dome.

1.6   The Canopy Loop Trail ends. Turn right to return to La Orilla Channel and the trailhead.

2.0   Arrive back at the Open Space Visitor Center parking area.

GREEN TIP

While it's cute to see a squirrel nibbling food left by hikers, it's important not to feed wild animals. Deer, squirrels, prairie dogs, and other animals don't need food from humans to survive, and foods like french fries and bread are actually unhealthy for them. Animals have specialized diets and can become malnourished or die if they eat the wrong foods. They also can't differentiate wrappers and foil from food and get sick eating them. Feeding wild animals makes them lose a fear of humans, so they become aggressive and must be destroyed. They also become a nuisance panhandling for food; young animals don't learn foraging skills; and they can transfer diseases like rabies and plague to humans. Keep wild animals wild by not feeding them.

Clouds hang over the Sandia Mountains and the Rio Grande on the River Loop Trail.

Area Info

ABQ BioPark Botanic Garden, 2601 Central Ave. NW, Albuquerque 87104; (505) 768-2000; www.cabq.gov/biopark/garden

ABQ BioPark Zoo, 903 Tenth St. SW, Albuquerque 87102; (505) 768-2000; www .cabq.gov/biopark/zoo

4 Paseo del Bosque Trail

The 16-mile-long Paseo del Bosque multiuse trail, called one of the best urban trails in the West, is enjoyed by hikers, bikers, in-line skaters, and joggers. Watch for wildlife, including beavers, birds, snakes, and turtles, along the hike.

Distance: 8.6-mile loop
Hiking time: About 4.5 hours
Difficulty: Strenuous due to length
Best seasons: Year-round. Summers are hot.
Schedule: Open daily year-round 7 a.m. to 9 p.m. Apr through Oct, 7 a.m. to 7 p.m. Nov through Mar
Other trail users: Bikers, horseback riders, in-line skaters, and joggers
Canine compatibility: Leashed dogs allowed
Fees and permits: None

Maps: USGS Los Griegos; detailed trail map and brochure available at Open Space Visitor Center
Trail contact: Open Space Division, Parks and Recreation, 3615 Los Picaros SE, Albuquerque 87105; (505) 452-5200; www.cabq.gov/openspace/riograndevalley.html
Special considerations: Pack out trash from picnic areas. Respect private property along the trail.

Finding the trailhead: From I-25 in Albuquerque, take exit 233. Turn left (west) on Alameda Boulevard NE / NM 528 and drive west for 3.4 miles to a Rio Grande Valley State Park parking area on the left just before the Rio Grande (GPS: 35.195095 N / -106.640044 W). The trailhead is at the northwest corner of the parking lot (GPS: 35.195429 N / -106.640266 W).

The Hike

The Paseo del Bosque Trail, also called the Riverside Bike Path, is the most popular and well-known trail in Albuquerque's city limits. The 16-mile-long multiuse trail, running along the Rio Grande through Albuquerque, offers seven main access points along with many secondary access points for hikers. The trail, uninterrupted by roads and highways, is regularly used by hikers, bicyclists, runners, in-line skaters, and equestrians. Public restrooms are at the Alameda parking lot.

The parking lot on the south side of Alameda Boulevard at Rio Grande Valley State Park is the starting point for this section of the Paseo del Bosque Trail. Don't be fooled by the name, since Rio Grande Valley State Park isn't actually a state park. While the parkland was established in 1983, the City of Albuquerque Open Space Division and the Middle Rio Grande Conservancy District manage the area. The Alameda Wetland on the south side of the parking lot is a constructed wetland on the Rio Grande floodplain. Stop by to observe ducks, geese, and other waterfowl.

From the parking area at Rio Grande Valley State Park, locate the paved Paseo del Bosque Trail at the northwest corner of the lot. Turn right (north) onto the trail and cross under Atrisco Alameda Boulevard NW, then turn left to cross the drainage at 0.05 mile. After crossing the bridge, bend left (south) on the trail. The paved Paseo del

Bosque Trail parallels the Rio Grande as it runs south. Look for many areas to stop and rest along the route. Tall cottonwoods growing in the bosque along the river offer plenty of shade for hot summer days.

After 1.1 miles the trail passes under Paseo del Norte NW and continues south. At 2.5 miles, the trail offers fine views of the Rio Grande through cottonwood trees to the west. Beyond the river, the Albuquerque Volcanoes in Petroglyph National Monument (see Hikes 5, 6, and 7) poke against the western sky. Continue hiking south on the paved trail and cross under Montaño Road NW at 4.3 miles. After passing under the road, turn left (east) and cross the Montaño Paseo del Bosque Trail Bridge over a channel, and then turn left (north) again and hike north on a narrow dirt trail that borders the east side of the channel.

Alternatively, turn around at the bridge and return north on the paved trail to the Alameda Trailhead for an 8.6-mile round-trip hike.

The dirt trail follows the channel for about a mile until it opens up at 5.4 miles. This trail section skirts the edge of several private properties and houses. After 7.5 miles the dirt trail briefly reconnects with the paved trail and passes under Paseo del Norte NW again. Under the bridge, the trails separate again, with the dirt return trail splitting east.

Return to the trailhead by hiking north to 27-acre Bachechi Open Space, a Bernalillo County parkland, on the right (east) at 8.3 miles. At 8.4 miles the dirt trail

A mallard duck swims in open water beside the Paseo del Bosque Trail.
EMILY RESSLER-TANNER

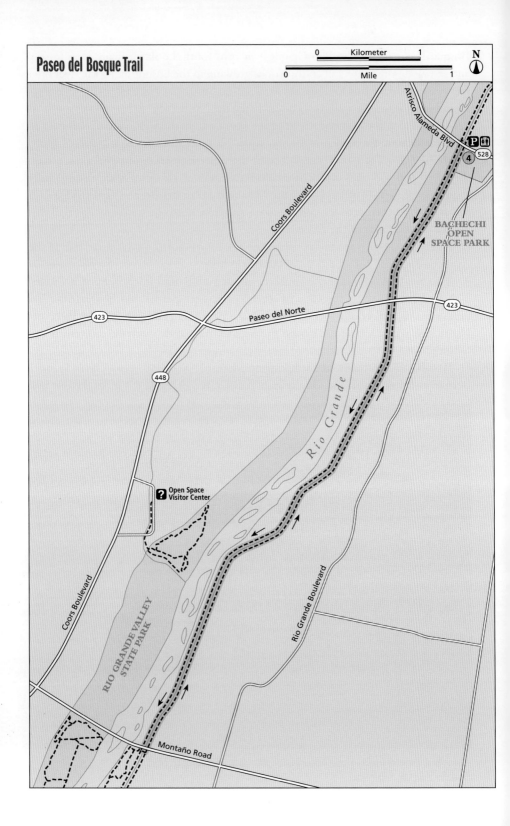

Paseo del Bosque Trail

0   Kilometer   1

0   Mile   1

N

Atrisco Alameda Blvd

BACHECHI
OPEN
SPACE PARK

Coors Boulevard

Paseo del Norte

423

423

448

Rio Grande

Open Space
Visitor Center

Rio Grande Boulevard

Coors Boulevard

RIO GRANDE VALLEY
STATE PARK

Montaño Road

Hikers and bicyclists share the 16-mile-long Paseo del Bosque along the Rio Grande.

meets the paved trail and follows it for the last 0.2 mile to the Alameda Trailhead at Rio Grande Valley State Park and the end of the hike at 8.6 miles.

Miles and Directions

0.0 Begin at the trailhead at the northwest corner of the Rio Grande Valley State Park parking area (GPS: 35.195429 N / -106.640266 W). Walk 20 feet west to the Paseo del Bosque Trail and turn left (south) on the wide paved trail split with a center line.

0.05 Turn left (west) and cross a bridge over a channel, then bend left (south) to continue on the trail.

1.1 The trail crosses under Paseo del Norte NW.

2.5 Arrive at a view of the Rio Grande and Albuquerque Volcanoes to the west.

4.3 The trail passes through shade under Montaño Road NW alongside a diversion channel and turns left (east) to cross the Montaño Paseo del Bosque Trail Bridge (GPS: 35.144388 N / -106.674812 W). Take another left (north) after crossing the bridge onto the dirt trail to begin the return hike. *Option:* Turn around at the bridge and return north on the paved trail to the Alameda Trailhead.

5.4 The narrow dirt trail opens up and widens.

7.5 The dirt trail briefly reconnects to the paved trail to cross under Paseo del Norte NW. Past the road, stay right (east) on the dirt trail.

8.3 Reach Bachechi Open Space Park on the right (east).

8.4 The dirt trail reconnects with the paved trail; continue north.

8.6 Arrive back at the Rio Grande Valley State Park parking area and trailhead.

Area Info

Rio Grande Nature Center State Park, 2901 Candelaria Rd. NW, Albuquerque 87107; (505) 344-7240; www.emnrd.state.nm.us/spd/riograndenaturecenterstate park.html

5 Piedras Marcadas Canyon Trail: Petroglyph National Monument

The 2-mile out-and-back Piedras Marcadas Canyon Trail offers a quick getaway from the city. It traverses a shallow canyon lined with the largest gallery of petroglyphs, or rock drawings, in Petroglyph National Monument.

Distance: 2.0 miles out and back
Hiking time: About 1.5 hours
Difficulty: Easy
Best seasons: Year-round. Summers are hot.
Schedule: Day use only. Parking lot open daily 8 a.m. to 5 p.m.; trail open sunrise to sunset.
Other trail users: Trail runners
Canine compatibility: Leashed dogs allowed (6-foot leash)

Fees and permits: None
Maps: USGS Los Griegos; detailed trail map and brochure available at visitor center
Trail contact: Petroglyph National Monument, 6001 Unser Blvd. NW, Albuquerque 87120; (505) 899-0205; www.nps.gov/petr
Special considerations: Watch for rattlesnakes along the trail in the warmer months. Carry plenty of water. No shade on the trail.

Finding the trailhead: From I-40 in Albuquerque, take exit 154 and turn right (north) onto NM 345 / Unser Boulevard. Drive 4.4 miles and turn right (east) onto Montaño Road, then drive 1.25 miles and turn left (north) onto Taylor Ranch Road. Continue 2.5 miles north as Taylor Ranch Road becomes Golf Course Road. At 2.5 miles turn left (northwest) onto Jill Patricia Street NW and then make a quick right into the Las Marcadas parking lot. GPS: 35.188820 N / -106.685804 W.

The Hike

The Piedras Marcadas Canyon Trail, located at the northernmost section of 7,236-acre Petroglyph National Monument, is an interesting 2-mile round-trip trail in a shallow canyon almost completely surrounded by suburbs. The mostly easy trail passes numerous volcanic boulders covered with petroglyphs pecked into the dark rock surface by ancient Native Americans. The trail, 6.5 miles from the park visitor center, is open daily from sunrise to sunset. The trailhead and parking area sit in a suburban area off Golf Course Road NW. The best way to reach it is to plug the trailhead's GPS coordinates (35.188820 N / -106.685804 W) into your vehicle's or phone's GPS system.

The hike follows an easy, sandy trail up Piedras Marcadas Canyon. No shade or water is found along the route, so carry water and wear a hat, especially in summer. The trail is not wheelchair or stroller accessible, and bicycles are not allowed. Dogs are permitted but must be on a 6-foot leash. Pick up all dog waste and deposit it in the trash bin at the trailhead.

Petroglyph National Monument, established in 1990, protects a spectacular outdoor gallery of Native American rock art on a 17-mile-long volcanic escarpment on the western edge of Albuquerque. The monument preserves over 24,000 rock art images, mostly petroglyphs; hundreds of archaeological sites; and a chain of five extinct volcanoes. The parkland has a visitor center and four major areas, including Piedras Marcadas Canyon, for visitors to hike and explore. The monument is managed jointly by the National Park Service and the City of Albuquerque. Since it is next to a major city, the park faces numerous issues, including vandalism and destruction of the petroglyphs and archaeological sites. Urban sprawl and highways also impact the national parkland and the preservation of its unique cultural resources.

The Piedras Marcadas Canyon Trailhead is located in an urban area, behind an oil change shop and restaurant on Golf Course Road NW. The trailhead has a trail map and information and trash cans, but no restrooms. From the Las Marcadas parking lot, hike northwest on a paved trail passing between houses. After a couple hundred feet, the trail turns to dirt and veers left (southwest). Follow signs for wide Piedras Marcadas Canyon, which means "canyon of marked rocks."

Reach a trail junction after 0.25 mile and go right (northwest) on the main trail to see the area's best petroglyphs panels on black boulders on the canyon's northern edge. The wide trail heads north across the sandy canyon floor and reaches the first petroglyphs after 0.26 mile.

The sandy Piedras Marcadas Trail edges below basalt bluffs on the west side of Albuquerque.

About 400 separate rock art images are on the scattered boulders below the rocky escarpment. These petroglyphs, created by Ancestral Puebloan people between AD 1300 and 1600, were created by using a hammer stone to chip, or peck, off the dark patina on the weathered surface of the boulders, revealing the light-colored field-stone beneath. Look for images of geometric and abstract shapes, people, animals, and masks.

Protect the rock art by only looking at the images and taking photographs, staying on the trail, and not climbing on the boulders. Learn more about petroglyphs in the book *Rock Art: The Meanings and Myths Behind Ancient Ruins in the Southwest and Beyond* (2018) from FalconGuides.

Continue hiking on the trail as it winds along the northern edge of the canyon, reaching the second signed petroglyph-viewing area at 0.4 mile on the west side of the trail. At 0.47 mile are more petroglyphs in a large area with scattered volcanic boulders. A short side trail goes west a hundred feet to petroglyph-covered boulders. Hike south past a 30-foot-high cliff to the fourth petroglyph on to the right (north) at 0.5 mile.

The rocks found in both Piedras Marcadas and nearby Rinconada Canyon are composed of vesicular basalt, a volcanic rock that flowed from five fissure volcanoes

A petroglyph of a human-like figure adorns a boulder above the Piedras Marcadas Trail.

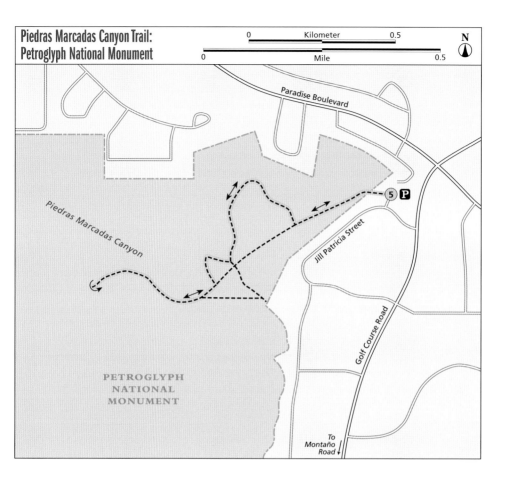

that lie west of Albuquerque. The rocks were originally light gray until a layer of desert varnish, a thin dark patina, darkened them. The light gray fieldstone that was revealed by Native Americans pecking petroglyphs on the dark brown patina surface makes a visually stunning sight.

The next trail segment begins at 0.52 mile, where you go right on the trail rather than straight. The trail arcs beneath the escarpment, passing more petroglyphs and dipping across a couple sandy washes. The trail reaches the main canyon trail at 0.62 mile. Go right (southwest) on the sandy trail.

Follow the trail up the broad canyon. Keep left at a trail junction at 0.85 mile and pass another signed petroglyph site with big boulders at 0.98 mile. The trail ends in the canyon floor at 1.0 mile from the trailhead. Two signs with arrows direct hikers to return to the trailhead on the Piedras Marcadas Canyon Trail. Turn around here and return to the parking area by following the trail along the floor of the canyon for 0.75 mile or by following the outer trail past the petroglyphs for a 2-mile round-trip hike.

Miles and Directions

0.0 Hike west for 200 feet from the trailhead and parking area (GPS: 35.188820 N / -106.685804 W) between houses and turn left (southwest) into the canyon.

0.25 Reach a trail junction (GPS: 35.187932 N / -106.689286 W). Go right toward black boulders.

0.26 Reach the first group of boulders covered with petroglyphs. Continue hiking on the trail below the escarpment on the north side of the canyon.

0.4 Reach the second group of petroglyph-covered boulders. Follow the trail as it turns southwest.

0.52 Come to the fourth group of boulders with petroglyphs and a connecting trail on the left (south). Go right (northwest) on the main trail (GPS: 35.187070 N / -106.691648 W).

0.57 Reach the fifth signed petroglyph site. Follow the trail along the edge of the escarpment past petroglyphs.

0.62 Reach the main canyon trail (GPS: 35.186201 N / -106.692191 W). Go right (southwest) and continue up Piedras Marcadas Canyon.

0.98 Reach the final petroglyph site noted in the park trail guide.

1.0 The hike ends in the canyon, with two arrows directing hikers to return to the trailhead on the Piedras Marcadas Canyon Trail (GPS: 35.186040 N / -106.697043 W). Follow the trail back to the trailhead and parking area. ***Option:*** Shorten the hike by 0.25 mile by following the trail along the canyon floor back to the trailhead.

2.0 Arrive back at the trailhead and parking area.

Area Info

Albuquerque Open Space Visitor Center, 6500 Coors Blvd. NW, Albuquerque 87120; (505) 897-8831; www.cabq.gov/openspace/visitorcenter.html

Petroglyph National Monument Visitor Center, 6001 Unser Blvd. NW, Albuquerque 87120; (505) 899-0205, ext. 335; www.nps.gov/petr

GREEN TIP

Harness the power of the sun with a portable solar panel to recharge batteries for electronic units like mobile phones in the backcountry. Pick a flexible panel that can be rolled or folded up for easy transport or a smaller rigid panel that can be attached to your pack, bike, or tent.

6 Rinconada Canyon Trail: Petroglyph National Monument

The 2.2-mile-long Rinconada Canyon Trail loops through a wide canyon with boulders covered with rock art images in Petroglyph National Monument on the northwestern edge of Albuquerque.

Distance: 2.2-mile loop
Hiking time: About 1.5 hours
Difficulty: Moderate due to length
Best seasons: Year-round
Schedule: Main parking lot open daily 8 a.m. to 5 p.m.; trail open sunrise to sunset. Park outside the gated lot for after-hours hiking.
Other trail users: Trail runners
Canine compatibility: Leashed dogs allowed (6-foot leash)
Fees and permits: None

Maps: USGS Los Griegos; detailed trail map and brochure available at visitor center and on website
Trail contact: Petroglyph National Monument, 6001 Unser Blvd. NW, Albuquerque 87120; (505) 899-0205, ext. 335; www.nps.gov/petr
Special considerations: Rattlesnakes are present in the canyon in the warmer months. Lock your vehicle at the parking lot and don't leave valuables. Bring plenty of water. No shade on trail. Not suitable for dogs in summer.

Finding the trailhead: From I-40 in Albuquerque, take exit 154 and turn right (north) onto NM 345 / Unser Boulevard. Drive 2.3 miles and turn left into the Rinconada Canyon Trail parking area. GPS: 35.127024 N / -106.725218 W

The Hike

The 2.2-mile-long Rinconada Canyon Trail is a loop hike in broad Rinconada Canyon in Petroglyph National Monument on the northwest edge of Albuquerque, 1.2 miles southwest of the national monument visitor center off Unser Boulevard NW. Besides passing petroglyphs on volcanic boulders, the trail provides a quick escape from Albuquerque's busy streets and suburbs with quiet, fun hiking and scenic views. Allow at least an hour and a half to hike the moderately difficult trail and observe several rock art sites.

The trailhead area offers interpretive signs, restrooms, plenty of parking spaces, and a shaded ramada. Leashed dogs are permitted, but owners must pick up their waste. Deposit it in a trash can at the trailhead. The parking and trailhead lie directly west of the intersection of Unser Boulevard NW and St. Joseph's Avenue NW. Plug in the parking lot's GPS coordinates (35.127024 N / -106.725218 W) to easily find the trailhead.

The hike offers mostly easy walking on a wide, sandy trail with minimal elevation gain on three slight inclines and spectacular petroglyphs in a wild setting. Bring binoculars to spot some of the 300 petroglyphs along the trail and on the hillside above.

Petroglyphs were pecked on a basalt boulder by Ancestral Puebloans near the Rinconada Canyon Trail.

The trail is not wheelchair or stroller accessible, and bicycles are not allowed. Wear a hat, use sunscreen, and carry water, especially in summer. No shade is found along the trail, and there is only one bench for resting. To preserve the desert environment, do not leave the trail or climb on boulders off the trail.

The floor of Rinconada Canyon is composed of the Santa Fe Formation, a thick layer of gravel and sand that washed off nearby mountains into the Rio Grande Valley. Geologists estimate that some parts of the Santa Fe Formation are up to 25,000 feet

PETROGLYPH NATIONAL MONUMENT

Petroglyph National Monument, one of the largest petroglyph sites in North America, protects basalt-rimmed canyons, open plains, and five volcanic cinder cones on the western edge of Albuquerque. A petroglyph, a type of rock art created by aboriginal peoples, is an image, symbol, or design that was engraved, pecked, carved, or sculpted on a natural rock surface with a hammer stone. The national monument preserves petroglyphs made over the last 700 years by Native Americans and early Spanish settlers. The petroglyphs still have deep meanings to Native peoples who live in the area and continue to practice traditional ceremonies. It's important that visitors respect these sacred images and rock art sites by not vandalizing or attempting to remove them from the parkland.

thick. The rocky escarpment on the western side of the canyon is formed by basalt from lava flows that spewed from several volcanoes on the western side of Petroglyph National Monument. The last eruption occurred almost 200,000 years ago.

Begin at the Rinconada Canyon Trailhead at the northwest corner of the parking area and hike west on the signed Rinconada Canyon Trail. After 0.15 mile, the trail reaches a Y-junction where the loop portion of the hike begins. The left fork is the return trail. Go right at the junction and hike northwest along the southern edge of a basalt escarpment toward the main petroglyph sites.

The first petroglyphs are found at 0.2 mile on the right (north) side of the trail. From this point forward you can view petroglyphs that have been carved on boulders along the volcanic escarpment. After 0.5 mile the trail angles southwest and continues into western Rinconada Canyon. Follow the obvious main trail. Several social trails made by rogue hikers venturing off the designated trail are scattered throughout the canyon. The park administration asks visitors to stay on the main trail to maintain and preserve the natural setting and avoid eroding the fragile desert ecosystem.

Reach the final petroglyph panel at 1.2 miles near the west end of the canyon and the escarpment. After 1.3 miles, the trail reaches the end of the canyon and bends left. Follow the return trail east back toward the trailhead and parking area. The trail

The Rinconada Canyon Trail follows the southern edge of a basalt escarpment.

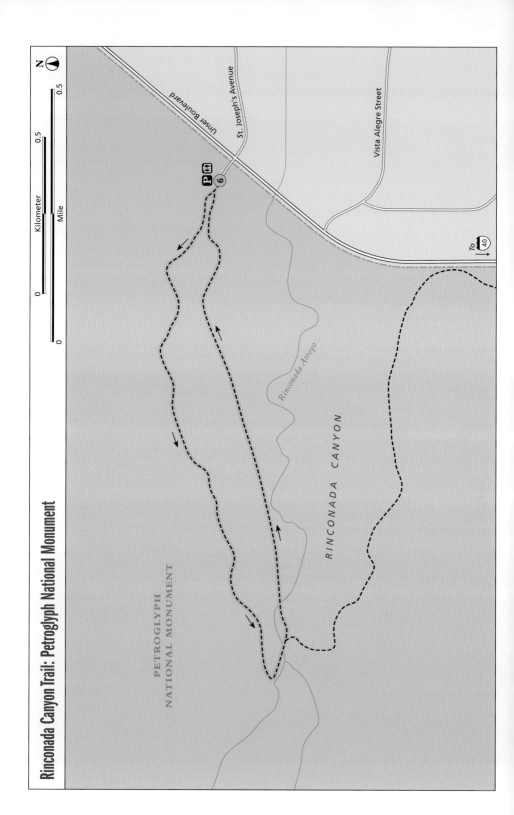

Rinconada Canyon Trail: Petroglyph National Monument

crosses an open area composed of the sandy Santa Fe Formation, away from the volcanic escarpment and petroglyphs sites. For about 0.75 mile you hike across sand dunes and through a typical central New Mexico desert with scrubby brush. Watch for collared lizards and desert millipedes on the ground and turkey vultures soaring above the canyon as you hike back to the sounds of civilization.

After 2.05 miles the trail reaches the end of the loop portion of the hike. Bear right (east) onto the final 0.15-mile trail segment that returns to the trailhead.

Miles and Directions

0.0 Start at the trailhead (GPS: 35.127211 N / -106.725264 W) on the northwest corner of the parking lot. Head west on the trail.

0.15 Reach a Y-junction and the start of the loop portion of the trail (GPS: 35.127520 N / -106.727031 W). Go right (northwest) to begin the loop.

0.2 Reach the first of eleven petroglyphs that are shown on the park's trail map.

0.5 The trail heads southwest into Rinconada Canyon.

1.2 Reach the final petroglyph panel on the park's trail map.

1.3 The trail bends and heads east on the canyon floor toward the trailhead (GPS: 35.125313 N / -106.742528 W).

2.05 The loop portion of the trail ends at the first junction. Keep right (east) and return to the trailhead.

2.2 Arrive back at the trailhead and parking lot.

Area Info

Petroglyph National Monument Visitor Center, 6001 Unser Blvd. NW, Albuquerque 87120; (505) 899-0205, ext. 335; www.nps.gov/petr

GREEN TIP

When hiking with your dog, stay in the center of the trail and keep Fido close and on a leash. Dogs that run loose harm fragile desert soils and spread pesky weeds by carrying seeds in their fur.

7 Volcanoes Trail: Petroglyph National Monument

The 2.8-mile Volcanoes Trail makes a loop hike around three of the Albuquerque Volcanoes on the western edge of Petroglyph National Monument west of the city. This fine hike explores the barren landscape, crossing a flat plain and threading through basalt boulders beneath the dark volcanoes. The hike can be easily shortened.

Distance: 2.8-mile loop

Hiking time: About 2 hours

Difficulty: Moderate

Best seasons: Year-round. Summers are hot.

Schedule: The Volcanoes Day Use Area is open daily from sunrise to sunset, the parking lot is open 9 a.m. to 5 p.m., park outside the gated parking lot for after- or before-hours access. Trail may close early due to severe weather.

Other trail users: None

Canine compatibility: Leashed dogs allowed (6-foot leash)

Fees and permits: None

Maps: USGS The Volcanoes; trail map and brochure available at visitor center and on website

Trail contact: Petroglyph National Monument, 6001 Unser Blvd. NW, Albuquerque 87120; (505) 899-0205, ext. 335; www.nps.gov/petr

Special considerations: Watch for thunderstorms with lightning on summer afternoons and rattlesnakes during warmer months. No shade on trail except at ramadas. Bring water. Lock your vehicle and don't leave any valuables to avoid car break-ins.

Finding the trailhead: From Albuquerque, take I-40 west to exit 149. Turn right (north) onto Atrisco Vista Boulevard and drive 4.8 miles north to the Volcanoes Access Road. Turn right (east) on the road and drive 0.3 mile to the Volcanoes Day Use Area parking lot and trailhead. GPS: 35.130517 N / -106.780109 W

The Hike

The Volcanoes Day Use Area in Petroglyph National Monument offers a unique opportunity to explore a barren, sagebrush-covered landscape and three extinct volcanoes west of Albuquerque. The area was once used for military bombing practice, cattle ranching, illegal dumping, and off-road vehicle use. After being designated as a national monument and managed by the National Park Service, the area's rugged beauty and rich history was revealed and preserved.

Depending on how far you go on the three trails—the Volcanoes Trail, the Vulcan Volcano Loop Trail, and the JA Volcano and Albuquerque Overlook trail segment—allow an hour to two and a half hours to hike the moderately difficult trail system. Most of the hiking is easy but rated moderate due to length.

The parking lot area offers vault toilets and a shaded ramada. Leashed dogs are allowed on the trails, but owners must scoop their waste. Deposit it in a trash can at the trailhead.

Vulcan Volcano rises above windswept grass along the Volcanoes Trail.

The hike is hot in summer and may be windy in winter and spring. During the warm months, wear a hat, use sunscreen, and carry plenty of water, including extra for your dog. There is no shade along the trail, but shaded benches are found on the first half-mile trail section to a scenic overlook. Hikers must follow designated trails only to preserve the fragile desert environment, so don't leave the trail or hike cross-country. Native peoples revere the ancient volcanoes, locally called the Three Sisters, and believe that climbing to their summits desecrates this holy land. Respect their beliefs. No petroglyphs are found along the trails.

The Rio Grande Rift, one of the few active rift zones in the world, stretches down the Rio Grande Valley through New Mexico from Colorado to Mexico. Molten magma, or liquid rock, beneath the North American continent pushed the earth's crust upward, causing numerous cracks and fractures in it. These cracks and fractures weakened the Rio Grande Rift valley, causing it to collapse. The Sandia Mountains, rising east of Albuquerque, mark the eastern edge of the rift zone.

Five volcanic cones sit on West Mesa on the western side of the rift zone. Geologists say that volcanic fissures occurred first, creating lava flows that left behind the volcanic escarpments on the sides of Piedras Marcadas and Rinconada Canyons (see Hikes 5 and 6). Later eruptions that formed the volcanic cones are still visible west of Albuquerque.

Begin at a trailhead on the southeast corner of the Volcanoes Day Use Area parking lot. Hike southeast on a paved walkway that becomes dirt after 75 feet. JA Volcano rises to the east. Reach a shaded rest and viewing area after 0.14 mile on the right (south). Continue hiking southeast toward JA Volcano. At 0.41 mile the Black Volcano return loop trail intersects from the left (north). Continue straight (east), passing a shaded ramada at 0.44 mile, and hike below the northern flank of 5,944-foot JA Volcano to a scenic overlook with a shaded ramada at 0.51 mile. The overlook offers a spacious view across the Rio Grande Valley and Albuquerque to the distant Sandia Mountains. Turn around here and hike back to the parking lot for an easy 1-mile out-and-back hike, which is ideal for families.

At the scenic overlook, turn left for the next trail segment and hike north on the Black Volcano loop trail for 0.4 mile to the north side of Black Volcano. The land appears barren, but if you look around and study the area, you see desert life everywhere, including lichens on the dark basalt rocks. Sagebrush and other shrubs offer food and shelter for mammals, including rock squirrels, kangaroo rats, deer mice, and coyotes; reptiles like New Mexico whiptail lizards and three species of rattlesnakes; and many birds, including Gambel's quails, roadrunners, curve-billed thrashers, turkey vultures, cactus wrens, and western meadowlarks.

After circling around the north side of 5,985-foot Black Volcano, the trail curves northwest and reaches a junction with the Black Volcano return trail at 0.95 mile. This trail section heads south for 0.4 mile back to the first hike segment north of JA Volcano. Take it if you want a shorter, 1.75-mile round-trip hike back to the trailhead.

Continue the hike by keeping right and hiking north on the Vulcan Volcano loop trail. At 1.1 miles, the trail passes the east side of a small volcanic cone. Continue hiking to a trail junction at 1.2 miles with a connector trail that heads northeast, but

The Volcanoes Trail passes below JA Volcano, one of three extinct volcanoes at Petroglyph National Monument.

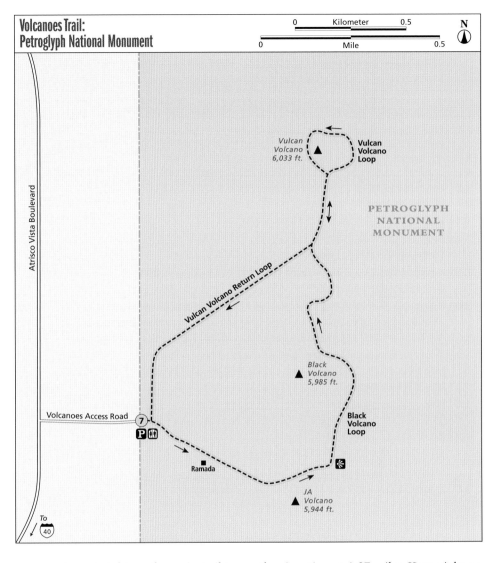

continue straight on the main trail to another junction at 1.27 miles. Keep right on the well-trod trail and begin the loop hike around 6,033-foot Vulcan Volcano. The trail to the left heads southwest and is the return route to the parking area. You'll take this trail after circling Vulcan Volcano.

From the trail junction, the trail heads northeast across dry slopes to the east side of Vulcan Volcano. The trail around Vulcan is well traveled and easy to follow. After 1.5 miles the trail reaches a junction on the southeast side of Vulcan with a back-country trail that heads north for a mile to Bond Volcano and Butte Volcano on the northern edge of the national monument. Continue straight on the main trail around Vulcan Volcano. The trail scrambles across rough, rocky slopes along the side of the volcano, reaching its northernmost point at 1.7 miles. The trail then heads around to the western slopes and bends south to the start of the Vulcan loop path south of the volcano at 2.1 miles.

From this major junction, go right and hike southwest across gentle terrain on the Vulcan Volcano return trail back to the trailhead. Follow the wide trail southwest for 0.6 mile to a fence along the western boundary of Petroglyph National Monument. At 2.65 miles the trail bends south and follows the boundary fence for 0.15 mile to a trailhead on the north side of the parking area at 2.8 miles.

Miles and Directions

0.0 Leave the parking lot at the main signed trailhead (GPS 35.130517 N / -106.780109 W). Hike southeast.

0.14 Reach a rest/viewing area on the right (south).

0.41 Reach the Black Volcano return loop to the left (GPS: 35.128655 N / -106.773503 W). Continue hiking straight (east).

0.51 Reach the scenic overlook and ramada (GPS: 35.128998 N / -106.771880 W). Turn left on the Black Volcano Trail and hike north.

0.95 Reach a junction with the Black Volcano return trail north of Black Volcano (GPS: 35.134167 N / -106.772497 W). Keep right and hike north on the Vulcan Volcano loop. A left turn on the Black Volcano loop trail goes south for 0.4 mile to an overlook trail.

1.2 Arrive at a four-way junction with the Vulcan Volcano loop trail and the trail that returns to the trailhead (GPS: 35.137844 N / -106.772754 W). Go right (north) on the loop trail around Vulcan Volcano.

1.5 Arrive at a junction with the trail that heads right to Bond Volcano and Butte Volcano (GPS: 35.139721 N / -106.769927 W). Go straight and continue hiking around Vulcan Volcano.

1.7 Reach the north side of Vulcan Volcano.

2.1 Return to the four-way junction and the end of the Vulcan Volcano loop. Go right and hike southwest to the parking area and trailhead.

2.8 Arrive back at the trailhead on the north side of the parking lot.

Area Info

Petroglyph National Monument Visitor Center, 6001 Unser Blvd. NW, Albuquerque 87120; (505) 899-0205, ext. 335; www.nps.gov/petr

Shooting Range Park, 16001 Shooting Range Access NW, Albuquerque 87120; (505) 836-8785; www.cabq.gov/parksandrecreation/open-space/facilities/shooting-range-park/shooting-range-park

GREEN TIP

Be careful to preserve New Mexico's natural, cultural, and historical sites and areas, including petroglyphs, pictographs, and artifacts, so that future generations can also enjoy and appreciate them.

8 Perea Nature Trail

The 0.9-mile Perea Nature Trail makes a loop in a riparian wetland along the Rio Salado south of the village of San Ysidro. This short, fun hike is a good introduction to New Mexico riparian zones and offers views of the Jemez Mountains and Blanco Mesa.

Distance: 0.9-mile loop
Hiking time: About 1 hour
Difficulty: Easy
Best seasons: Year-round
Schedule: No restrictions
Other trail users: None
Canine compatibility: Leashed dogs allowed
Fees and permits: None
Maps: USGS San Ysidro; trail map available at trailhead

Trail contact: BLM Rio Puerco Field Office, 100 Sun Ave. NE, Ste. 330, Albuquerque 87109; (505) 761-8700; www.blm.gov/nm/st/en/prog/recreation/rio_puerco/perea_nature_trail.html

Special considerations: Stay on the trail to preserve the sensitive riparian wetland along the Rio Salado. Practice Leave No Trace principles to lessen your impact.

Finding the trailhead: From Albuquerque, drive north on I-25 to exit 242 toward US 550 / Bernalillo. Turn left (west) onto US 550 and drive northwest for 22 miles. After crossing the Rio Salado Bridge, turn left (west) and drive 70 feet to a large parking area and trailhead for the Perea Nature Trail. GPS: 35.545779 N / -106.781866 W

The Hike

The Perea Nature Trail, one of the shortest hikes in this guide, offers fun hiking through a riparian wetland along the Rio Salado, a trickling stream that begins on mesas to the northwest. Riparian wetlands, composing about 2 percent of New Mexico, are the state's most species-rich ecosystem, with abundant wildlife and diverse plants and trees that flourish with both surface and subterranean water. Vegetation along the trail includes towering cottonwood trees, a sure sign of underground water, as well as four-wing saltbush, arrowgrass, cattails, yerba mansa, and sedges. The Rio Salado marsh here often dries up between November and March, but overflow irrigation water from the nearby Rio Jemez and floodwaters on the Rio Salado keep it moist through summer.

The hike offers more than just wildlife and vegetation, however. North of the trail are scenic views of the dark Jemez Mountains, the remains of a massive collapsed volcano that also forms the southern end of the Rocky Mountains, the Valles Caldera National Preserve in the Jemez Mountains and the San Ysidro Fault. Distinctive Blanco Mesa rises southwest of the Perea Nature Trail. The white-surfaced mesa is often used as a stunning background for photographs, movies, and commercials.

One-seed junipers line the Perea Nature Trail. EMILY RESSLER-TANNER

The dirt-surfaced trail is easy to follow and makes a great hike for kids and hikers who want to explore a unique environment. There are no facilities at the trailhead, but restrooms, water, and visitor services are in San Ysidro, including a service station, grocery store, and post office. Bring binoculars to use at bird blinds to spot humming-birds, kingfishers, Brewer's blackbirds, northern orioles, rufous-sided towhees, scrub jays, western meadowlarks, and other species. Watch for turkey vultures and hawks wheeling overhead in the sky or great horned owls in the trees.

From the trailhead on the northwest side of the parking area, hike north on the packed dirt trail. Reach a Y-junction and the start of the trail's loop section after 0.04 mile, or 220 feet. Go right (northwest) to begin the loop.

The trail heads northwest through the riparian zone along the north bank of the mostly dry river. Look for plentiful wildlife, including coyotes, deer, and smaller mammals along with numerous species of birds, that frequent the area. At 0.3 mile reach a blind on the left (west) side of the trail that looks across a small pond. Continue hiking to a quiet sitting area on the right (east) side of the trail before crossing a bridge to the left (west) at 0.44 mile. After the bridge, turn left (south) and continue hiking.

Reach another rest bench at 0.5 mile on the left (east) side of the trail. To the right (west) are excellent views of Blanco Mesa. Past the bench is another observation blind on the left (east) side of the trail at 0.6 mile. Continue hiking south. Look for animal tracks in the soft, damp ground alongside the trail. At 0.8 mile turn left and hike southeast across two elevated walkways above the wetland. After crossing the bridges, reach the end of the hike's loop portion at 0.86 mile. Turn right and hike southeast for 220 feet to the trailhead and parking area for a 0.9-mile-long hike.

Miles and Directions

0.0 Leave the trailhead from the northwest corner of the parking lot (GPS: 35.545779 N / -106.781866 W).

0.04 Arrive at a junction and the start of the loop (GPS: 35.546335 N / -106.782060 W). Go right to begin the loop.

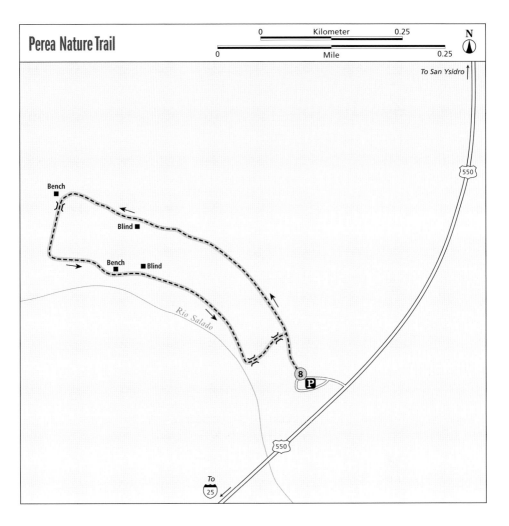

0.3 Reach the first observation blind on the left (west) and continue hiking northwest.

0.4 The trail turns left (west) and crosses a bridge. After crossing the bridge, turn left (south).

0.5 Reach a bench on the left (east).

0.6 Reach an observation blind on the left (east).

0.8 Turn left (northeast) to cross two more bridges.

0.86 The loop section of the trail ends. Turn right (south) to return to the trailhead and parking lot.

0.9 Arrive back at the trailhead and parking lot.

Area Info

Jemez Hot Springs, 040 Abousleman Loop, Jemez Springs 87025; (575) 829-9175; www.jemezhotsprings.com

Ponderosa Valley Vineyards, 3171 NM 290, Ponderosa 87044; (575) 834-7487; www.ponderosawinery.com

9 San Ysidro Trials Area Trail

The San Ysidro Trials Area Trail offers beautiful hiking except for a few days each year when the New Mexico Trials Association (NMTA) holds motocross events. This 5.1-mile lollipop hike explores narrow canyons and slickrock flats.

Distance: 5.1-mile lollipop
Hiking time: About 3 hours
Difficulty: Moderate
Best seasons: Spring and fall
Schedule: Open year-round
Other trail users: Mountain bikers, horseback riders, and off-road vehicles
Canine compatibility: Leashed dogs allowed
Fees and permits: None
Map: USGS San Ysidro
Trail contact: BLM Rio Puerco Field Office, 100 Sun Ave. NE, Ste. 330, Albuquerque

87109; (505) 761-8700; www.blm.gov/visit/san-ysidro-trials-area
Special considerations: A locked gate blocks motorized access to the main parking area north of the highway. To shorten the hike by 2.4 miles, you can pick up a key for the gate by contacting the BLM office in Albuquerque. The area may be closed to hikers during motorcycle trial periods. Check www.nmtrials.org for a schedule of events.

Finding the trailhead: From Albuquerque, take I-25 north to exit 242 toward US 550 / Bernalillo. After exiting, turn left (west) onto US 550. Drive 25 miles on US 550 to the village of San Ysidro. From the junction of US 550 and NM 4 in San Ysidro, drive northwest for 1.6 miles to a right (north) turn into the signed San Ysidro Trials Area parking lot. GPS: 35.554855 N / -106.806956 W

The Hike

The San Ysidro Trials Area Trail offers hikers a unique opportunity to hike a lollipop trail at the southern end of the Rocky Mountains. Both the Nacimiento Mountains here and the Sangre de Cristo Mountains above Santa Fe are considered the southern tip of the Rocky Mountains, which begin in British Columbia. The area also forms the southeastern edge of the Colorado Plateau.

The Trials Area hosts five or six dirt bike races each year, but don't be fooled by these events. Other than those few races, motorized vehicles are not allowed in the area. As you hike, it's difficult to tell that dirt bikes race through the area on the trails.

GREEN TIP
Pass your environmental ethics down—the best way to instill good green habits in your children is to set a good example by recycling, reusing, and following Leave No Trace principles when hiking, camping, and traveling.

Water pools in slickrock along the San Ysidro Trials Area Trail.
EMILY RESSLER-TANNER

Mountain bikers often use the trails because many hikers don't want to walk the extra 1.2 miles up the road to the main Trials Area parking lot. If you are willing to hike to the parking, you will find that the area offers gorgeous scenery and fun hiking.

From the Trials Area parking lot on the north side of US 550, pass a locked gate and hike north on the dirt and sand road that begins at the northwest corner of the lot. Follow the road as it climbs and turns slightly northwest. Pass a fence at 0.5 mile with a sign for the San Ysidro Trials Area. Continue hiking northwest and north to the main Trials Area parking lot.

At mile 1.2, in the middle of the dirt parking area, is an information kiosk. Directly behind the kiosk (east) is where the singletrack trail begins. Cross a dry wash and hike

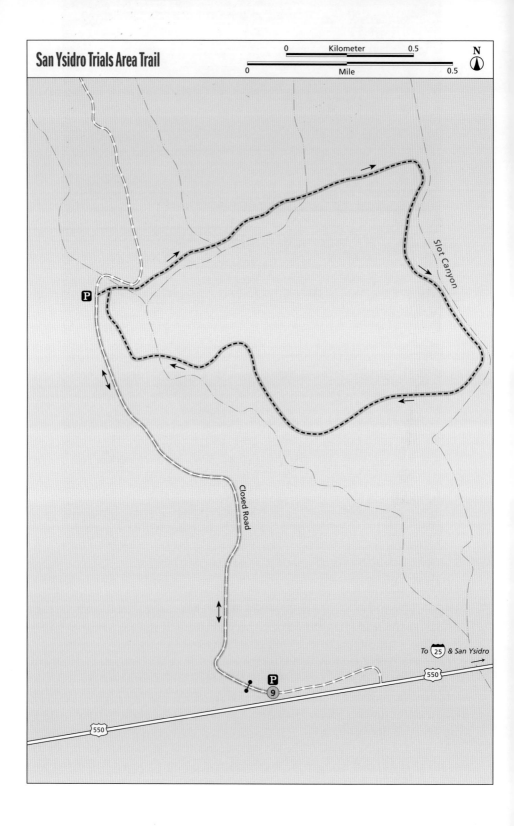

San Ysidro Trials Area Trail

northeast on the trail. This area can be confusing, as the sandy trail blends into the surrounding landscape. If you head in a northeasterly direction, you will be fine.

Reach a fork at 1.65 miles. Stay left (northeast) at the fork and continue to the "Grand Canyon." Reach the canyon at 2.0 miles and turn right (south) and follow the trail parallel to the canyon. There are places along the trail to climb down into the slot canyon. If you climb down and hike through the canyon, watch for numerous pools of water that require wading, depending on the water level. Hikers that hike above the slot canyon follow a well-worn trail, marked with rock cairns along the edge of the canyon.

At 2.5 miles the canyon opens up and the trail drops into the canyon for a short distance. The trail makes a sharp right (southwest) out of the canyon at 2.6 miles and crosses several hills to a wash at 3.1 miles, and then traverses slickrock areas. After 3.9 miles the trail returns to the main Trials Area parking lot. Turn left (west) onto the dirt road and return to the roadside Trials Area parking lot and trailhead at 5.1 miles.

Miles and Directions

0.0 Begin at the Trials Area parking area on US 550 (GPS: 35.554855 N / -106.806956 W). From the northwest corner of the lot, hike north up a dirt road.

0.5 Reach a fence with a sign for the San Ysidro Trials Area.

1.2 Reach the main Trials Area parking lot and locate the singletrack trail behind an information kiosk.

1.65 At a fork in the trail, stay left (northeast) and hike to the Trials Area Trail.

2.0 Reach a canyon, dubbed the "Grand Canyon" by mountain bikers. Turn right (south) and hike along the western side of the canyon.

2.5 The canyon opens up as the trail descends into the canyon.

2.6 The trail makes a right (southwest) turn out of the canyon.

3.1 Cross a dry wash and hike northwest.

3.9 Return to the main Trials Area parking lot. Turn left (west) onto the dirt access road and follow it to the parking area by the highway.

5.1 Arrive back at the Trials Area parking lot and trailhead.

Area Info

Valles Caldera National Preserve, 18161 NM 4, Jemez Springs 87025; (505) 661-3333; www.vallescaldera.gov

Jemez Mountains

The East Fork of the Jemez River meanders across Valle Grande near the Cerro la Jara Trail.

10 Cabezon Peak Trail

The Cabezon Peak Trail offers a rugged hike around the base of the massive plug of an extinct volcano, one of central New Mexico's most recognizable landmarks.

Distance: 2.5-mile lollipop
Hiking time: About 2.5 hours
Difficulty: Strenuous, with steep terrain
Best seasons: Spring and fall. Winters may be snowy and summers are hot.
Schedule: Open year-round
Other trail users: None
Canine compatibility: Leashed dogs allowed
Fees and permits: None

Maps: USGS Cabezon Peak; trail map available at trailhead
Trail contact: BLM Rio Puerco Field Office, 100 Sun Ave. NE, Ste. 330, Albuquerque 87109; (505) 761-8700; www.blm.gov/visit/cabezon-wsa
Special considerations: Roads to the trailhead may be muddy and impassable due to heavy rain or snow.

Finding the trailhead: From Albuquerque, take I-25 north to exit 242 toward US 550 / Bernalillo. Turn left (west) onto US 550 and drive north for 41 miles to a junction with CR 279. Turn left (west) onto CR 279 (signed San Luis and Cabezon Peak) and drive west and southwest for 12.2 miles, passing through the tiny village of San Luis, to a Y-junction. Keep left (southwest) at the Y on BLM 1114, a dirt road. Drive 2.8 miles on BLM 1114 to a junction with an unnamed road on the left (east) with a sign pointing to Cabezon Peak. Turn left (east) and drive 1 mile to the trailhead and parking area. GPS: 35.596927 N / -107.105251 W

The Hike

Cabezon Peak towers above the Rio Puerco Valley like a gigantic burnt tree stump. The 7,785-foot mountain, lined with vertical columns of basalt, is similar in appearance to Devils Tower National Monument in Wyoming. Cabezon is a volcanic plug, or neck, which formed when molten magma hardened in the throat of a volcano. Subsequent erosion later removed the surrounding softer rock, including sandstone and shale, leaving only the resistant basalt plug. It is the tallest of about fifty volcanic plugs scattered along the Rio Puerco Valley northwest of Albuquerque.

The Rio Puerco necks, part of the Mount Taylor volcanic field, are considered some of the best examples in the world of volcanic plugs. These small volcanoes erupted during late Pliocene times between 2.5 and 3 million years ago. The basalt on Cabezon Peak is about 2.6 million years old. These plugs are the remnants of cinder cones that began when underground magma pushed up through fissures in the surface. Pyroclastic material ejected into the atmosphere fell back to the surface and built a cone around the vent. Later that material and lava formed the hard plug in the vent.

The name Cabezon, meaning "big head," derives from the Spanish word for head, *cabeza*. The Navajo legend about the formation of Cabezon Peak begins with a fierce battle between the Twin War Gods and a giant on Mount Taylor. The Twin War Gods

Cabezon Peak is the largest volcanic peak in the Rio Puerco Valley.
EMILY RESSLER-TANNER

killed the giant and severed its head, causing a river of blood to flow across the land. The giant's head became Cabezon Peak, and the blood river solidified as black lava flows near Grants to the west.

The approach drive to Cabezon Peak is open all year, but the dirt roads deteriorate rapidly in bad weather and may be impassable during wet or snowy conditions. The worst road section is the short segment leading from BLM Road 1114 to the trailhead parking area. Check the road before driving it after thunderstorms or snow, and if it is muddy, park off BLM 1114 near the sign for Cabezon Peak and walk the last mile to the trailhead. This road can be slippery and muddy, and it's difficult to turn around on it.

The 2.5-mile Cabezon Peak Trail is a lollipop-loop hike that circumnavigates the cliff-walled mountain, climbing steep slopes to a bench below the steep cliffs. The peak, lying in the BLM's 8,159-acre Cabezon Peak Wilderness Study Area, is a wild and remote region with a harsh climate and distant views. The trail is hard to follow at times, crosses numerous dry washes, and threads through a couple jumbled boulder fields. It's best to hike the trail counterclockwise.

Be prepared for hot weather in summer, little shade, uneven footing, route-finding, and rattlesnakes. Carry plenty of water, use sunscreen, and wear a hat. The trail is unsuitable for small children. The area is often busy on weekends, with hikers using the first trail section to reach the scrambling route up Cabezon Peak, so come on weekdays for solitude. Primitive camping is found at the trailhead and on nearby BLM public lands. Use a Leave No Trace ethic by packing out trash, burying or preferably packing out human waste, and lessening your impact on this desert environment.

The 6,480-foot-high trailhead is at the end of the rough access road and east of the small parking area. Follow the rocky trail east and immediately begin to gain elevation. After 0.5 mile of moderately steep hiking, the trail levels out and begins to

EXTRA CREDIT HIKE: CLIMB CABEZON PEAK

Most hikers head to Cabezon Peak to climb to its flat summit. While the summit view is spectacular, the hands-and-feet ascent is not for everyone. The route generally does not require technical rock-climbing skills and equipment, but make no mistake—this is a climbing route. The route is rated Class 3 so you need to be comfortable climbing moderate terrain, and it's strenuous and requires route-finding skills. Dogs and children are not recommended for the ascent. Bring climbing helmets, a short climbing rope, a belay device, a few slings for anchors, and sturdy footwear.

The easiest ascent up Cabezon Peak is a scrambling route on the southeast flank of the mountain. Allow 4 to 6 hours to do the 2.6-mile round-trip ascent and descent, gaining 1,305 feet from trailhead to summit.

From the trailhead, hike east on the described trail for 0.75 mile to a bench below the southeast flank of the peak. Cairns mark the start of the summit route. Scramble up braided trails on a steep scree slope to the base of an obvious shallow gully.

Climb white rock in the lower gully (Class 3) to easier scrambling to a narrower upper gully. Climb the steep gully, passing the hardest section of the route (Class 3), until it ends on steep slopes broken by cliff bands. Some climbers, especially if they're inexperienced, may want to be belayed on a rope both climbing up and descending.

From the top of the gully, follow a rough trail past occasional cairns, scrambling over broken cliff bands to a weathered old juniper tree. Pay attention to the next route section, since it's easy to get off route. Traverse a trail for about 100 feet and then climb a fun wall with juggy handholds (Class 3) to the top of the cliffs. Continue up a trail for a few hundred more feet to the broad summit and a windbreak with a register waiting for your autograph and the date.

Reverse the route to return to the base of the peak. Again, some climbers may like the protection of a rope when they downclimb the exposed cliff sections.

circle Cabezon. Cross an old barbed-wire fence at 0.6 mile and continue hiking east. On the southeast side of the peak at 0.75 mile, a pile of stacked rocks, or cairn, marks the start of the summit trail, which goes left and climbs north, heading toward the climbing route (see Extra Credit Hike sidebar for route description).

Continue hiking northeast from the start of the summit trail. As you hike, look for wildlife along the trail. Common birds include meadowlarks, quail, red-tailed hawks, golden eagles, and ferruginous hawks, while mammals consist of mule deer, pronghorns, coyotes, badgers, kangaroo mice, and prairie dogs. Watch where you place your hands and feet, since this high desert is ideal rattlesnake habitat. In the warmer

YOSEMITE DECIMAL SYSTEM

The Yosemite Decimal System (YDS) is a numbered system that rates the difficulty of walks, hikes, and climbs. It is the rating system most commonly used in the United States and Canada.

> **Class 1:** Trail hiking.
>
> **Class 2:** Hiking over rough ground such as scree and talus. May include the use of hands for stability.
>
> **Class 3:** Scrambling with the use of hands and feet. Contains short, steep sections where falls could result in severe injury.
>
> **Class 4:** Scrambling over steep and exposed terrain. The climbing is relatively simple, but a fall could result in severe injury or death. Use of climbing rope is encouraged.
>
> **Class 5:** Climbing on steep mountain terrain where an unroped fall would result in injury or death.

months, you may encounter a snake along the trail. Give it a wide berth and continue on your way. Dryland shrubs and grasses dominate the lower elevations, while cholla and prickly pear cacti are replaced by a pygmy woodland of piñon pine and juniper near the base of the peak.

The trail becomes faint as you cross through a boulder field on the north side of the peak at 1.0 mile. Look for cairns and pay attention to your direction of travel. It's difficult to get lost—just keep the peak and cliffs to your left. Reach a saddle at 1.7 miles and continue south. At 2.0 miles is the junction with the approach trail and the end of the loop portion of the hike. Turn right and hike west for 0.5 mile to return to the trailhead at 2.5 miles round-trip.

A sign marks the turnoff to the Cabezon Peak Trailhead. Park here to avoid getting stuck if the road is muddy. EMILY RESSLER-TANNER

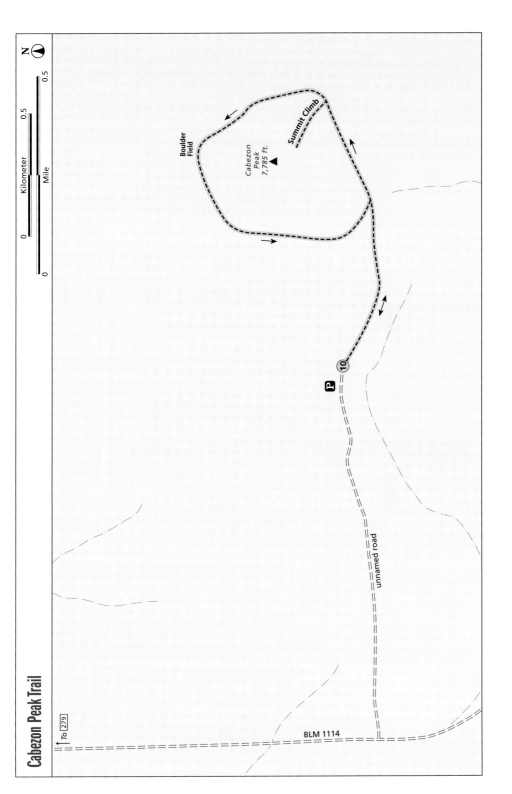

Cabezon Peak Trail

To 279

Boulder Field

Cabezon Peak
7,785 ft.

Summit Climb

10

P

unnamed road

BLM 1114

N

Kilometer
0   0.5

Mile
0   0.5

Miles and Directions

0.0 The trail begins east of the parking area (GPS: 35.596927 N / -107.105251 W). Hike east on the rocky trail to ascend a slope to the peak base.

0.5 Reach the top of the slope. The trail levels out as it begins to circumvent the tower; continue east.

0.6 Cross an old barbed-wire fence and continue east.

0.75 Reach a cairn, or rock pile, marking the popular scrambling route to Cabezon's summit (GPS: 35.597391 N / -107.093459 W). Continue northeast to hike around the tower.

1.0 Reach a boulder field on the north side of the peak. Scramble across to the trail and continue west.

1.7 Reach a saddle; continue hiking south.

2.0 Return to the junction with the approach trail. Hike west on the trail to return to the trailhead.

2.5 Arrive back at the trailhead and parking area.

Area Info

Ojito Wilderness Area, Cabezon Road west of San Ysidro; BLM Rio Puerco Field Office, 100 Sun Ave. NE, Ste. 330, Albuquerque 87109; (505) 761-8700; www.blm .gov/visit/ojito-wilderness

Walatowa–Pueblo of Jemez, Pueblo of Jemez Welcome Center, 7413 NM 4, Jemez Pueblo 87024; (575) 834-7235; www.jemezpueblo.com

HIKING TIP

Hiking is the best way to get in condition for hiking, but a strong core takes you a long way. Start with lunges, sit-ups, and push-ups to build core strength. Consult FalconGuides' *Outdoor Fitness* by Tina Vindum for a well-rounded approach to conditioning for outdoor adventures.

11 East Fork Trail: Battleship Rock to Jemez Falls

The East Fork Trail is a wonderful hike on the western flank of the Jemez Mountains in Santa Fe National Forest. The trail section from Battleship Rock to Jemez Falls is a popular destination for hikers and backpackers. McCauley Hot Springs along the trail provides a place to relax.

Distance: 7.2 miles out and back
Hiking time: 5 to 6 hours
Difficulty: Strenuous due to length and elevation gain
Best seasons: Apr through Oct. May and June are the best months.
Schedule: Parking area open daily sunrise to sunset
Other trail users: Mountain bikers
Canine compatibility: Leashed dogs allowed
Fees and permits: Day-use permit must be purchased to park.

Map: USGS Jemez Springs
Trail contact: Santa Fe National Forest, PO Box 150, Jemez Springs 87025; (575) 829-3535; www.fs.usda.gov/santafe
Special considerations: Trail may be snowy and icy in winter. Poison ivy and water hemlock are present in the area. No camping within a quarter mile of the Jemez Falls Trailhead. Drop-offs below cliffs at overlook and slick rocks below the falls.

Finding the trailhead: From Albuquerque, drive north on I-25 to exit 242 toward US 550 / Bernalillo. Turn left (west) onto US 550 and drive north for 22.8 miles to the town of San Ysidro and the turn for NM 4. Turn right (northeast) onto NM 4 and continue 23.1 miles to the Battleship Rock Trailhead and parking area on the right (south). The parking area is about 5 miles north of the village of Jemez Springs. GPS: 35.828046 N / -106.643958 W

The Hike

The Battleship Rock to Jemez Falls section of the East Fork Trail (#137) offers hikers a challenging uphill climb with a rewarding view of 70-foot-high Jemez Falls. The hike back is an easier downhill journey with the option to rest your weary legs in McCauley Hot Springs.

Battleship Rock, a 200-foot-high landmark, towers above the picnic area and trailhead. The jutting rock, resembling the bow of an old warship, is a layer cake of cliffs composed of compacted ash, or welded tuff (technically called welded ignimbrite), ejected from massive volcanic eruptions that occurred a couple million years ago. The formation rises above the confluence of the East Fork of the Jemez River and San Antonio Creek, forming the Jemez River.

Battleship Rock Picnic Area, with thirty-three picnic sites, is located before the day-use parking area and Battleship Rock Trailhead. A day-use fee is charged to park

Battleship Rock towers over the trailhead for the East Fork Trail.

at the trailhead and picnic area. Water is available at the picnic area, so fill up your water bottles or CamelBak here before starting the hike.

From the Battleship Rock parking area, find the trailhead behind the pit toilets and hike south through the picnic area to the tumbling East Fork of the Jemez River. The trail runs along the river for 0.2 mile before climbing the north side of the canyon above the river. The trail switchbacks up the steep slope and then begins a long and steady ascent. After 1.1 miles the trail levels out at an ideal spot for a break and snack.

Continue hiking southeast through a pine forest on the packed dirt trail to another good rest area at 1.7 miles with large boulders off the trail. After hiking another 0.8 mile, or almost 2.5 miles from the trailhead, you reach McCauley Hot Springs at 7,350 feet. The crystal-clear springs, on a bench high above the East Fork of the Jemez River, are a popular soaking spot, with a large, shallow pool filled with 80- to 90-degree water and a couple smaller and deeper hot pots. The springs bubble out of the hillside above and run into the large pool, before trickling down to stone-lined pools below.

The warm springs are often empty on weekdays but are usually filled with soakers on weekends. While national forest regulations prohibit nudity, many soakers dip in the pools sans clothing, so visitors should be comfortable around bare people. Backpackers often camp near McCauley Hot Springs and day-soakers trek up to the springs, but after soaking, put your boots on and start hiking to the trail's best wonder—Jemez Falls.

East Fork Trail: Battleship Rock to Jemez Falls

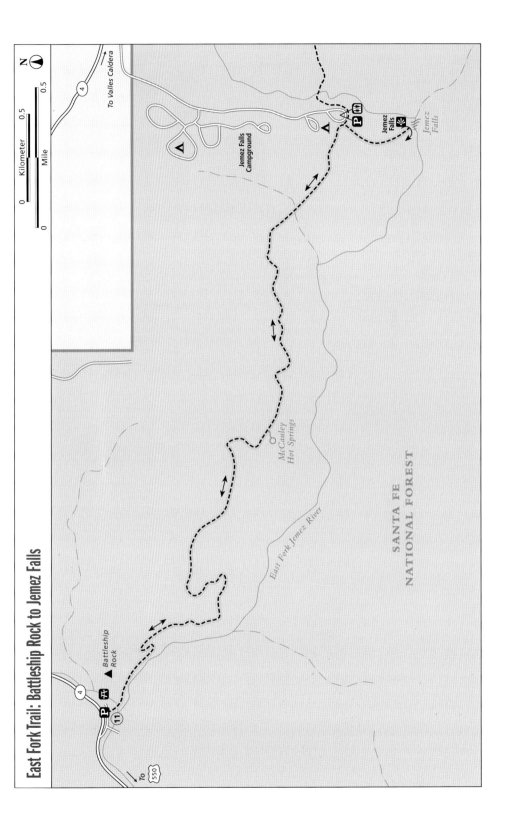

To Valles Caldera

To 550

Battleship Rock

McCauley Hot Springs

East Fork Jemez River

Jemez Falls Campground

Jemez Falls

SANTA FE NATIONAL FOREST

N

Kilometer
Mile

The East Fork Trail passes beneath Battleship Rock before climbing steep slopes.

The East Fork Trail continues east, threading across the mountainside and slowly gaining elevation. At about 3.0 miles the trail intersects an unnamed trail. Continue straight (southeast) on the East Fork Trail until you reach a spur trail to Jemez Falls Campground on a gentle sloping mesa. Continue east on the main trail to another trail junction at 3.3 miles. Go right (south) at the junction on the Jemez Falls Trail and hike 0.3 mile to the Jemez Falls overlook. The lovely 70-foot waterfall gushes through a rocky gap, plunging into a shallow pool rimmed by cliffs. The best view is from the fenced overlook.

The waterfall is the turn-around point for the hike. Return downhill to the Battleship Rock Trailhead on the East Fork Trail for a 7.2-mile round-trip hike.

Miles and Directions

0.0 From the parking area, locate the trailhead behind the pit toilets (GPS: 35.828245 N / -106.644002 W). Hike east on the East Fork Trail between Battleship Rock and the river.

0.2 The trail climbs away from the East Fork of the Jemez River.

1.1 Reach a good rest area after a moderate ascent.

1.7 Reach another good rest spot.

2.5 Arrive at McCauley Hot Springs (GPS: 35.820061 N / -106.627231 W).

3.0 The East Fork Trail intersects an unsigned trail. Continue straight (southeast).

3.3 Reach the Jemez Falls Trail. Turn right (south) onto the spur trail and hike 0.3 mile to the waterfall.

3.6 Arrive at Jemez Falls and a fenced overlook (GPS: 35.812611 N / -106.607054 W). Return to Battleship Rock on the same route.

7.2 Arrive back at Battleship Rock and the trailhead parking area.

Area Info

Jemez Springs Bath House, 62 Jemez Springs Plaza, Jemez Springs 87025; (575) 829-3303; www.jemezspringsbathhouse.com

Jemez Historic Site, 18160 NM 4, Jemez Springs 87025; (575) 829-3530; www.nmmonuments.org/jemez

Walatowa–Pueblo of Jemez, Pueblo of Jemez Welcome Center, 7413 NM 4, Jemez Pueblo 87024; (575) 834-7235; www.jemezpueblo.com

GREEN TIP

Consider the packaging of products you bring on your hike. It's best to properly dispose of packaging at home before you hit the trail. If you're on the trail, pack the packaging and all trash out with you.

12 Jemez Falls Trail: Santa Fe National Forest

The Jemez Falls Trail is a short, easy hike from the southern edge of Jemez Falls Campground to a 70-foot-high waterfall that tumbles off a basalt cliff. The hike is the best easy day hike in New Mexico to a gorgeous waterfall.

Distance: 0.7 mile out and back

Hiking time: About 30 minutes

Difficulty: Easy, with 125 feet of elevation loss and gain

Best seasons: May and June are best months to see falls.

Schedule: Day use only. Access road is closed in winter, so trail is usually open Apr through Oct.

Other trail users: None

Canine compatibility: Leashed dogs allowed

Fees and permits: None

Map: USGS Redondo Peak

Trail contact: Santa Fe National Forest, PO Box 150, Jemez Springs 87025; (575) 829-3535; www.fs.usda.gov/santafe

Special considerations: No camping within a quarter mile of trailhead. Drop-offs below cliffs at overlook and slick rocks below the falls.

Finding the trailhead: From Albuquerque, drive north on I-25 to exit 242 toward US 550 / Bernalillo. Turn left (west) onto US 550 and drive north for 22.8 miles to the town of San Ysidro and the turn for NM 4. Turn right (northeast) onto NM 4 and continue 30 miles, passing Battleship Rock, to a right (south) turn on Jemez Falls Road. Drive 1.5 miles past Jemez Falls Campground to a loop with parking at road's end. GPS: 35.816085 N / -106.606570 W

The Hike

Jemez Falls, plunging almost 70 feet off a basalt cliff, is reached by the 0.35-mile Jemez Falls Trail in the heart of the rugged Jemez Mountains northwest of Albuquerque. The wide trail is generally open from April through October, although the road past Jemez Falls Campground may be closed until after the snow melts. May and June are the best months to hike the trail, since the waterfall is usually a rushing torrent of white water. The flow lessens later in the summer and autumn.

The Jemez Falls Trailhead is located at the southern end of a loop road at the Jemez Falls Group Picnic Area just south of Jemez Falls Campground. The trailhead lies along the East Fork Trail (Hike 13), which begins 4 miles to the west at Battleship Rock and heads east to Las Conchas Trailhead. The trailhead area has paved parking and vault toilets but no drinking water. The area is day use only, with no overnight camping within a quarter mile of the trailhead. The fifty-two-site campground makes a perfect base camp for hiking to the falls as well as exploring nearby Valles Caldera National Preserve and the Jemez Mountains.

A short hike leads to Jemez Falls, one of the highest waterfalls near Albuquerque.

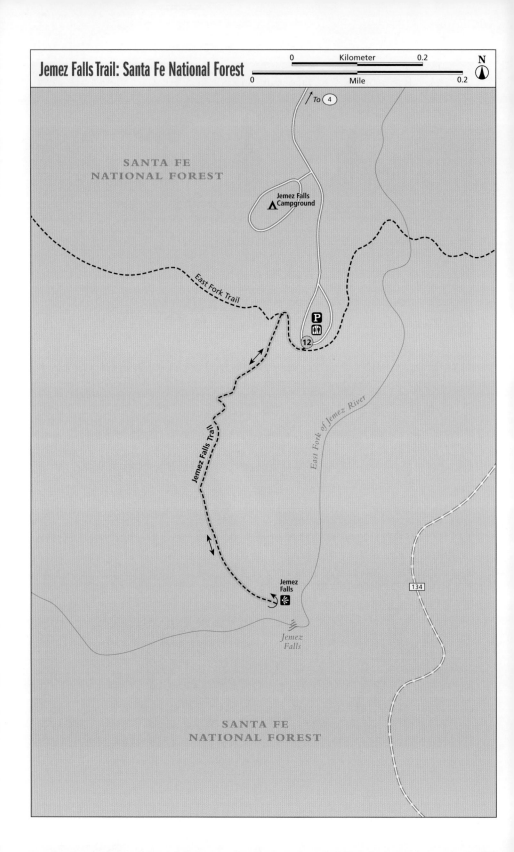

Jemez Falls Trail: Santa Fe National Forest

0 Kilometer 0.2

0 Mile 0.2

N

To 4

SANTA FE
NATIONAL FOREST

Jemez Falls
Campground

East Fork Trail

P

12

Jemez Falls Trail

East Fork of Jemez River

Jemez
Falls

134

Jemez
Falls

SANTA FE
NATIONAL FOREST

The popular trail is busy in the summer, so plan on getting to the trailhead early on weekends to avoid crowds. Take your time hiking the trail if you're visiting from a lower elevation, since Jemez Falls lies at 7,500 feet above sea level and you might get out of breath when hiking back up to the trailhead from the waterfall.

Start the hike at the trailhead next to the vault toilet at the south end of the parking lot. While some folks descend a social trail that heads south on a blunt ridge, it's not the actual trail and it steepens at the end of the ridge above the falls. Instead, go right and follow the Jemez Falls Trail north down a hillside. The left side is fenced to discourage trail-cutting and erosion. After a couple hundred feet, the trail makes a sharp bend left, passes its junction with the East Fork Trail, and contours across a slope above a dry wash. Towering ponderosa pines shade the wide trail.

After 0.3 mile, the trail bends left and descends a rocky slope, reaching the stonewall-lined Jemez Falls overlook 0.35 mile from the trailhead. This spectacular viewpoint perches above a compact horseshoe-shaped amphitheater ringed with dark basalt cliffs. The East Fork of the Jemez River plunges over the cliff into a punchbowl below. Pine, spruce, and fir blanket the mountainsides above the waterfall, while willows clot the riverbanks above the falls. Upper Jemez Falls, not seen from the overlook, lies about a hundred yards upriver, while several cascading falls are found downriver from Jemez Falls.

After admiring the waterfall, retrace your steps back up the trail for a 0.7-mile round-trip hike.

Miles and Directions

0.0 Begin at the trailhead at the southern end of a loop road at Jemez Falls Campground (GPS: 35.816085 N / -106.606570 W). Go right from the restrooms down the trail.

0.35 Reach the overlook above Jemez Falls (GPS: 35.812611 N / -106.607054 W). Follow the trail back to the parking lot and trailhead.

0.7 Arrive back at the parking lot and trailhead.

Area Info

Bandelier National Monument, 15 Entrance Rd., Los Alamos 87544; (505) 672-3861, ext. 517; www.nps.gov/band

Valles Caldera National Preserve, PO Box 359, Jemez Springs 87025; Valle Grande Visitor Center, (575) 829-4100, ext. 3

Walatowa–Pueblo of Jemez, Pueblo of Jemez Welcome Center, 7413 NM 4, Jemez Pueblo 87024; (575) 834-7235; www.jemezpueblo.com

13 East Fork Trail: East Fork Trailhead to Las Conchas Trailhead

The East Fork Trail is an excellent out-and-back hike through ponderosa pine woodlands, aspen groves, and wildflower-strewn meadows on rounded ridges and along the East Fork of the Jemez River in the Jemez Mountains

Distance: 9.6 miles out and back
Hiking time: 5 to 6 hours
Difficulty: Moderately strenuous
Best seasons: Spring, summer, and fall
Schedule: Parking area open daily sunrise to sunset; overnight parking available
Other trail users: Mountain bikers and rock climbers
Canine compatibility: Leashed dogs allowed

Fees and permits: None
Map: USGS Jemez Springs
Trail contact: Santa Fe National Forest, 051 Woodsy Lane, PO Box 150, Jemez Springs 87025; (505) 829-3535; www.fs.usda.gov/santafe
Special considerations: Trail is snowy and icy in winter. Poison ivy and water hemlock are present.

Finding the trailhead: From Albuquerque, take I-25 north to exit 242 toward US 550 / Bernalillo. Turn left (west) on US 550 and drive north for 22.8 miles to San Ysidro and a turn onto NM 4. Turn right (northeast) onto NM 4 and drive 32.6 miles to the trailhead parking area on the right (south) side of the highway (GPS: 35.820850 N / -106.591071 W). The hike's turn-around point, or end if you choose to do the hike 4.8 miles one way, is the Las Conchas Trailhead (GPS: 35.815156 N / -106.532960 W).

The Hike

The East Fork of the Jemez River, beginning to the northeast in Valle Grande, passes through the heart of the Jemez Mountains on its way west to a confluence with San Antonio Creek at Battleship Rock, forming the Jemez River. The East Fork Trail passes through a conifer forest, aspen groves, and grassy meadows before dropping down to the banks of this National Wild and Scenic River.

The trailhead is at 8,082 feet on the northeast side of the trailhead parking area past an outhouse. A large Santa Fe National Forest sign greets hikers, and beyond that the trail begins. There is a large interpretive map of the East Fork Trail here. The

EXTRA CREDIT HIKE

A fabulous alternative out-and-back hike is to park at the Las Conchas Trailhead and hike 1.6 miles up the Jemez River to the trail's exit from the canyon. Turn around here and return to the trailhead for a 3.2-mile round-trip hike.

obvious trail leads east through a ponderosa pine forest. Several undesignated trails cross the area and the trail occasionally meets up with a rough forest road, which can be confusing. Continue hiking northeast on the main trail, which is occasionally marked with white triangles, and you'll be fine.

At 0.4 mile the trail leaves a forest road on the left (northeast) and farther along passes white-trunked aspen trees. A spur trail joins from the right at 0.85 mile, but continue east on the main trail / forest road. At 0.9 mile the East Fork Trail breaks off the forest road again. Look for the wooden trail sign marked 137.

At 1.1 miles arrive at the spur trail that accesses "the box," a steep-sided box canyon. Down in the depths of the box canyon north of the trail is East Fork Jemez Box Falls (GPS: 35.826026 N / -106.569826 W), a double-tiered waterfall reached by descending into the steep canyon. Continue hiking right (east) on the East Fork Trail (#137) toward the Las Conchas Trailhead. At 1.4 miles the trail rejoins a forest road for about 0.1 mile before breaking off left (east) again.

Recross the forest road at 2.0 miles and continue southeast. The singletrack trail winds through aspens here. Look for wildflowers like Indian paintbrush in summer and for golden aspen leaves in late September and October. This is a good place to see butterflies in the late spring, so watch for the striking yellow and black western tiger swallowtail.

The trail begins to descend a ridge to the Jemez River valley below at 2.6 miles. During the summer, look for red and yellow shooting star columbine along the trail's rocky shoulder. Cross through a hikers' maze at 3.0 miles and continue to descend the ridge into the canyon.

Footbridges cross the placid East Fork of the Jemez River on the East Fork Trail. JD TANNER

East Fork Trail: East Fork Trailhead to Las Conchas Trailhead

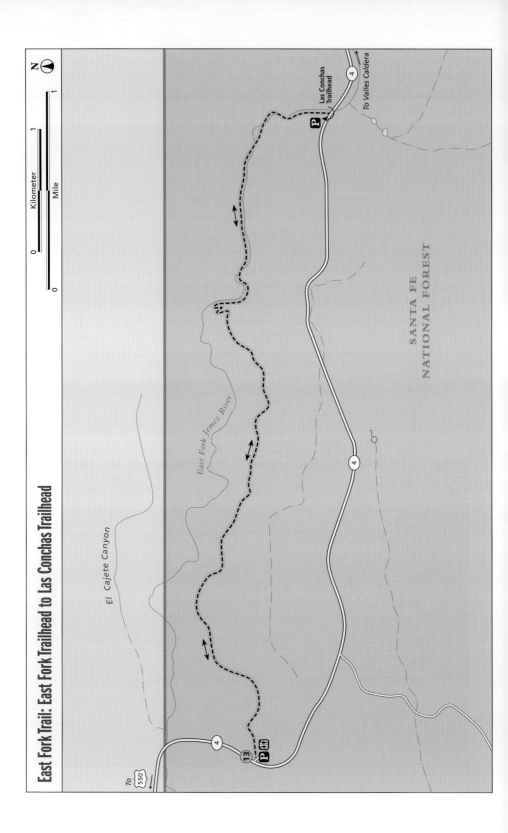

After 3.2 miles the trail reaches the East Fork of the Jemez River. This 11-mile river segment is a designated National Wild and Scenic River. After reaching the river, look left (west) for a great view of the river's deep box canyon. The trail continues east along the river. At 3.3 miles is the first of seven wooden footbridges that cross the Jemez River and muddy sections of the trail.

This beautiful river section, with the stream meandering through grassy meadows, is a popular fishing area with a healthy population of rainbow trout. The lower canyon is also the popular Las Conchas rock-climbing area, with bolted sport-climbing routes on numerous cliffs including Chilly Willy Wall, Gallery Wall, The Sponge, and Leaning Tower. Consult *Rock Climbing New Mexico* (FalconGuides) for detailed climbing information.

Reach the Las Conchas Trailhead at 8,411 feet on NM 4 after 4.8 miles. Unless you have set up a car shuttle or left a vehicle at this trailhead, you need to turn around and return 4.8 miles to the East Fork Trailhead via the same route. The Las Conchas Day Use Area, with picnic tables, vault toilets, and fishing access, is 0.9 mile east of the Las Conchas Trailhead on the north side of NM 4.

Miles and Directions

0.0 Begin at the trailhead on the northeast side of the roadside parking lot (GPS: 35.820850 N / -106.591071 W). Hike east on an obvious dirt trail.

0.4 The trail leaves the forest road; continue northeast.

0.85 Reach a spur trail. Continue east on the main trail / forest road.

0.9 The East Fork Trail leaves the forest road. Watch for a wooden trail sign marked 137.

1.1 Reach the spur trail to "the box." Continue right (east) on the East Fork Trail (#137) toward the Las Conchas Trailhead.

1.4 Return to the forest road for about 0.1 mile. Watch for the trail to break left (east).

2.0 Cross the forest road and hike southeast.

2.6 The trail descends a steep ridge.

3.0 Arrive at a hikers' maze; continue to descend the ridge.

3.2 Reach the East Fork of the Jemez River (GPS: 35.824269 N / -106.550414 W). Go right and hike east along the south bank of the river.

3.3 Cross the first of seven wooden footbridges and continue east along the river.

4.8 Reach the Las Conchas Trailhead on the north side of NM 4 (GPS: 35.815156 N / -106.532960 W). Turn around and return to the trailhead via the same route.

9.6 Arrive back at the East Fork Trailhead.

GREEN TIP
Seeing colorful summer wildflowers is a highlight of every backcountry hike. Take pictures of these beauties instead of picking them.

KEEP YOUR PACK PACKED

Attention weekend warriors: Between work, family, and your packed schedule, it can be hard to go hiking, especially during the workweek. To minimize the time you spend getting gear ready for a hike, do a gear check after each hike and leave your "go-to" gear already packed for the next spur-of-the-moment trek. Keep the pack and gear in an easy-to-reach location like your car's trunk so you can just grab it and go!

Area Info

Valles Caldera National Preserve, PO Box 359, Jemez Springs 87025; Valle Grande Visitor Center (575) 829-4100, ext. 3; www.nps.gov/vall

Fenton Lake State Park, 455 Fenton Lake Rd., Jemez Springs 87025; (575) 829-3630; www.emnrd.state.nm.us/SPD/fentonlakestatepark.html

Bandelier National Monument, 15 Entrance Rd., Los Alamos 87544; (505) 672-3861, ext. 517; www.nps.gov/band

Walatowa–Pueblo of Jemez, Pueblo of Jemez Welcome Center, 7413 NM 4, Jemez Pueblo 87024; (575) 834-7235; www.jemezpueblo.com

GREEN TIP
Question: What are the most commonly found
pieces of litter at fishing areas?
Answer: Fishing line and bait cups.
Issue: Besides being an eyesore, animals can get tangled in fishing
line. The pungent smell of bait cups attract animals and pests
to the area, which is unhealthy for both anglers and animals.

14 Cerro la Jara Trail: Valles Caldera National Preserve

The Cerro la Jara Trail, beginning at the Valles Caldera National Preserve visitor center, makes an easy loop around a volcanic dome in Valle Grande, crossing flower-studded meadows below high, wooded mountains.

Distance: 1.5-mile loop
Hiking time: About 1 hour
Difficulty: Easy, with 55 feet of elevation gain
Best seasons: Late spring through fall
Schedule: Open daily sunrise to sunset
Other trail users: Horseback riders
Canine compatibility: Dogs allowed but must be under control and on a leash shorter than 6 feet
Fees and permits: Park entry fee
Map: USGS Bland

Trail contact: Valles Caldera National Preserve, PO Box 359, Jemez Springs 87025; Valle Grande Visitor Center, (575) 829-4100, ext. 3; www.nps.gov/vall
Special considerations: The Valle Grande Entrance Station is open daily from May 15 to Oct 31 from 8 a.m. to 6 p.m. and from Nov 1 to May 14 from 9 a.m. to 5 p.m. (closed Thanksgiving and Christmas). Best cell phone service is at the entrance station area, but not all carriers have a signal. Most of the back-country has no cell service.

Finding the trailhead: From Albuquerque, drive north on I-25 to exit 242 toward US 550 / Bernalillo. Turn left (west) onto US 550 and drive northwest for 22.8 miles to the town of San Ysidro and the turn for NM 4. Turn right (northeast) on NM 4 and drive 41 miles to a left (north) turn on the Valles Caldera National Preserve entrance road #01 at mile marker 39.2. Drive 1.9 miles on the dirt road (impassable when wet) to a large parking lot on the east side of the Valle Grande Entrance Station (GPS: 35.856914 N / -106.491075 W). The trailhead is on the west side of the road by a cattle guard. GPS: 35.856306 N / -106.490625 W

The Hike

The 1.5-mile Cerro la Jara Trail is a superb short hike that loops around 8,745-foot Cerro la Jara, a rounded volcanic dome directly west of the Valle Grande Entrance Station in the middle of broad Valle Grande, the largest of four valleys in Valles Caldera National Preserve. The easy singletrack trail, beginning at the entrance station, navigates open grasslands north of the placid East Fork of the Jemez River with minimal elevation gain and wide views across Valle Grande, one of New Mexico's hidden beauty spots.

Summer is the best season to hike the trail, with warm, sunny days. Watch for heavy afternoon thunderstorms accompanied by lightning in July and August. If you're hiking during a storm, take cover and keep a low profile to avoid lightning strikes on the open trail. Autumn is also gorgeous, with groves of quaking aspen

The East Fork of the Jemez River meanders across Valle Grande near the Cerro la Jara Trail.

painting golden tapestries across the mountainsides above the trail. The trail is open in winter for cross-country skiing and snowshoeing. Call the preserve ahead of time to make sure that the access road to the trailhead at the Valle Grande Entrance Station is open and passable during the winter.

Start the hike at the entrance station at the end of the public access road. The road into the rest of the preserve is gated here and is closed much of the year. Ask at the station about opening and closing dates for facilities in the preserve and how to obtain a backcountry vehicle permit if you want to hike, fish, mountain bike, or watch wildlife. Up to thirty-five backcountry vehicle permits are allotted each day during the summer.

Cross the dirt road from the entrance station to the signed La Jara Trailhead by a cattle guard. The easy hike, with only 55 feet of elevation gain, heads southwest paralleling the park road on the left. The narrow trail is easy to follow but is overgrown with grass in a few places. Pay attention to markers along the trail to keep on course.

After 0.2 mile the trail passes through a large colony of Gunnison's prairie dogs, one of five species of prairie dogs. The buff-toned rodents, living only in the Four Corners region, are active during the day, munching on grasses and herbs. Prairie dogs boast one of the most advanced natural animal languages, with a complex system of vocal communication, including barks that warn of nearby predators like soaring hawks. Watch your step as you pass through the prairie dog town so that you don't inadvertently step in an entrance hole.

The trail bends right at 0.3 mile and begins skirting the southwestern flank of Cerro la Jara. The low-browed mountain pushed up after the collapse of the extinct volcano that formed the 13.7-mile-wide Valles Caldera about 1.5 million years ago. The eruption, one of the most powerful in earth's history, dwarfed the 1980 Mount St. Helens eruption, ejecting over 150 cubic miles of debris and an ash field that extended to Iowa. Cerro la Jara along with other mountains in the caldera are called resurgent lava domes. Note the eroded basalt boulders and low cliffs on Cerro la Jara's steep slopes.

The Cerro is closed to hikers to protect its untrampled habitats, particularly for the second-largest elk herd in New Mexico. Other animals seen here include mule deer, coyotes, black bears, and badgers. Some of the preserve's 115 recorded bird species are mountain bluebird, downy woodpecker, Stellar's jay, ruby-crowned kinglet, and raptors including golden eagle, great horned owl, and red-tailed hawk. The caldera also boasts a breeding population of eastern meadowlark. Other unique species are the Rio Grande cutthroat trout and the lungless Jemez Mountains salamander.

At 0.65 mile the trail, on the south side of Cerro la Jara, jogs right and crosses a wide, grassy wash before bending northwest and at 0.7 mile reaches a picnic bench tucked among three boulders. This is a good stop to enjoy gorgeous views northwest across open meadows to 11,254-foot Redondo Peak, the highest mountain in the national preserve, and southwest down the East Fork of the Jemez River's broad valley to rounded hills on the edge of the caldera.

Continue on the good path around the northwest edge of Cerro la Jara, slowly gaining elevation. At 1.1 miles the trail reaches a Y-junction near the park road. Take the right fork and hike east across dry slopes studded with sagebrush and reach the road at 1.4 miles. Finish by walking east on the road for 0.1 mile back to the entrance station and parking lot for a 1.5-mile hike.

A hiker leads a leashed dog along the Cerro la Jara Trail.

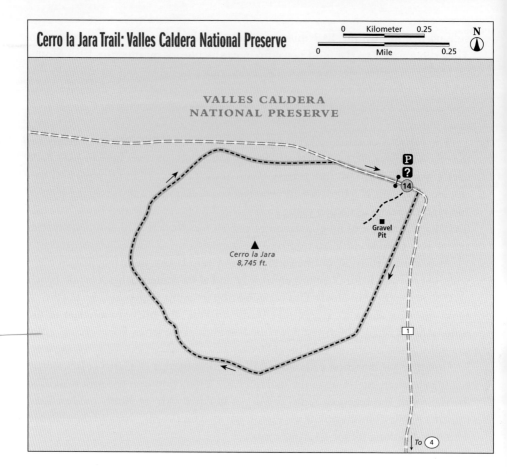

0   Kilometer   0.25

0   Mile   0.25

N

VALLES CALDERA
NATIONAL PRESERVE

Gravel
Pit

Cerro la Jara
8,745 ft.

To 4

Miles and Directions

0.0 Start at the trailhead on the park road southwest of the Valle Grande Entrance Station (GPS: GPS: 35.856306 N /-106.490625 W). Hike southwest on the singletrack trail.

0.2 Pass through a prairie dog town.

0.3 The trail bends right below the southwestern flank of Cerro la Jara.

0.65 Go right across a grassy wash.

0.7 Reach a picnic bench among boulders.

1.1 Reach a Y-junction near the park road. Go right (east) on the singletrack trail paralleling the road.

1.4 Reach the closed park road. Go right and walk on the road to the entrance station.

1.5 Arrive back at the entrance station and parking lot.

Area Info

Bandelier National Monument, 15 Entrance Rd., Los Alamos 87544; (505) 672-3861, ext. 517; www.nps.gov/band

The Cerro la Jara Trail crosses thick grass in Valle Grande.

Walatowa–Pueblo of Jemez, Pueblo of Jemez Welcome Center, 7413 NM 4, Jemez Pueblo 87024; (575) 834-7235; www.jemezpueblo.com

White Rock Visitor Center, 115 NM 4, Los Alamos 87547; (505) 672-3183, (800) 444-0707; www.visitlosalamos.org

15 Coyote Call Trail: Valles Caldera National Preserve

The moderate Coyote Call and Rabbit Ridge Trails offer a great hike for gorgeous views and exploring the Valles Caldera National Preserve in the Jemez Mountains. Elk in the caldera regularly graze near the roadside trailhead. Bring binoculars!

Distance: 5.4-mile loop with out and back
Hiking time: 2 to 3 hours
Difficulty: Moderate
Best seasons: Late spring through early fall
Schedule: Open daily sunrise to sunset
Other trail users: None
Canine compatibility: Dogs allowed on Coyote Call Trail (not Rabbit Ridge Trail) but must be under control and on a leash shorter than 6 feet
Fees and permits: None

Maps: USGS Bland; trail map available on park website and at Valle Grande Visitor Center
Trail contact: Valles Caldera National Preserve, PO Box 359, Jemez Springs 87025; Valle Grande Visitor Center, (575) 829-4100, ext. 3; www.nps.gov/vall
Special considerations: Sign in and out at the trailhead register. Best cell phone service is at the Valle Grande Visitor Center area, but not all carriers have a signal. Most of the backcountry has no cell service.

Finding the trailhead: From Albuquerque, drive north on I-25 to exit 242 toward US 550 / Bernalillo. Turn left (west) onto US 550 and drive northwest for 22.8 miles to the town of San Ysidro and the turn for NM 4. Turn right (northeast) on NM 4 and drive 43 miles to the trailhead parking area on the left (north) side of the highway (GPS: 35.848535 N / -106.465089 W). The parking area is 1.7 miles northeast of the Valle Grande main entrance at mile marker 39.2 on NM 4. Cross the road to the trailhead on the south side of NM 4. GPS: 35.848111 N / -106.46528 W

The Hike

The 5.4-mile loop Coyote Call and Rabbit Ridge Trails offer sweeping views of Valles Grande, a wide valley north of the trailhead that is protected in 88,900-acre Valles Caldera National Preserve. Valles Caldera, one of the largest dormant supervolcanoes in the world, is a 13.7-mile-wide collapsed volcanic crater, or caldera, which formed when the volcano collapsed after a catastrophic eruption about 1.2 million years ago. The caldera and its many peaks, including 11,254-foot Redondo Peak, are part of the Jemez Mountains.

The area's striking scenery offers open grasslands, meadows splotched with wildflowers, thick conifer forests, and crystal-clear rivers and streams. The floor of the caldera features rounded lava domes, hot springs, fumaroles, and natural gas seeps. The scenic preserve is home to almost 3,000 elk, the second-largest elk herd in New Mexico, and contains miles of pristine trout streams and several species of endangered plants and animals. In July 2000, 140 square miles of the area was purchased by the federal government to protect the historic Baca Ranch and create Valles Caldera National Preserve, a parkland administered by the National Park Service.

Park at a triangular pullout on the north side of NM 4. The trail begins at a short pullout on the south side of NM 4 at the Coyote Call Trailhead sign. Walk through a gate and register at a metal registration box. Follow the trail, an old ranch road, south for 100 feet to a Y-junction and keep right. The wide trail is faint in places, so watch for brown posts and blue or yellow trail markers that guide the way.

The trail heads south and gently ascends through a meadow and a mixed aspen and conifer forest. Near the top of a hill at 0.45 mile, the trail takes a sharp turn to the left (east). After a few yards is a wooden trail sign for the Coyote Call Trail (Meadow Walk) and Rabbit Ridge Trail (Scenic View) at a junction. The Rabbit Ridge Trail is a steep out-and-back spur trail that offers wide views across the Valles Caldera National Preserve. The following description includes directions and mileage for both the Rabbit Ridge Trail and the Coyote Call Trail.

Turn right (southeast) on the Rabbit Ridge Trail and continue climbing along a ridge. After about 1 mile of hiking, a long stretch of trail leads through the charred remains of the forest that was scorched during a huge wildfire in the summer of 2011. The area is slowly recovering, with new saplings and wildflowers pushing through the burn zone. The open trail offers spacious views across Valle Grande.

The Coyote Call Trail winds across meadows and through aspen groves above Valle Grande.

Aspens, their bark chewed by New Mexico's second-largest elk herd, line the Coyote Call Trail.

After 1.7 miles the trail reaches the end of the Rabbit Ridge Trail on the western boundary of Bandelier National Monument. Turn around here and return west to the junction with the Coyote Call Trail at 2.9 miles. Turn right (east) on the Coyote Call Trail (Meadow Walk).

The next trail segment is mostly flat, with a few gentle inclines. Watch for elk tracks, bits of black obsidian, and shooting star columbines along the trail. After 3.5 miles the trail reaches a brown post with "1 mi" carved into it. This is a trail marker for the Coyote Call Trail.

The trail turns left (northwest) after 4.1 miles and begins to switchback down a blunt ridge. Reach the trail's "2-mile" post at 4.5 miles and hike southwest on the grassy trail. Complete the loop and return to the trailhead after 5.4 miles.

Miles and Directions

0.0 Begin at the trailhead on the south side of NM 4 (GPS: 35.848111 N / -106.46528 W), and sign in at the hiker registration box. Hike south from the trailhead on the wide, grassy trail. In 100 feet reach a trail junction. Keep right on the trail.

0.45 The trail turns sharply to the left (east). At the sign for the Coyote Call Trail (Meadow Walk) and Rabbit Ridge Trail (Scenic View), turn right (southeast) on the Rabbit Ridge Trail. **Option:** You can shorten the hike to a 3-mile loop by avoiding the Rabbit Ridge Trail and turning left at the junction to continue on the Coyote Call Trail.

1.7 Reach the end of the Rabbit Ridge Trail at the Bandelier National Monument boundary line. Turn around and return to the Coyote Call Trail / Rabbit Ridge Trail junction.

2.9 Reach the trail junction. Turn right (east) onto the Coyote Call Trail.

3.5 Reach the Coyote Call Trail's brown "1-mile" post.

4.1 The trail turns left (northwest) and begins to descend a blunt ridge.

4.5 Reach the Coyote Call Trail's "2-mile" post. Hike southwest on the grassy trail to the first trail junction. Go right.

5.4 Arrive back at the trailhead.

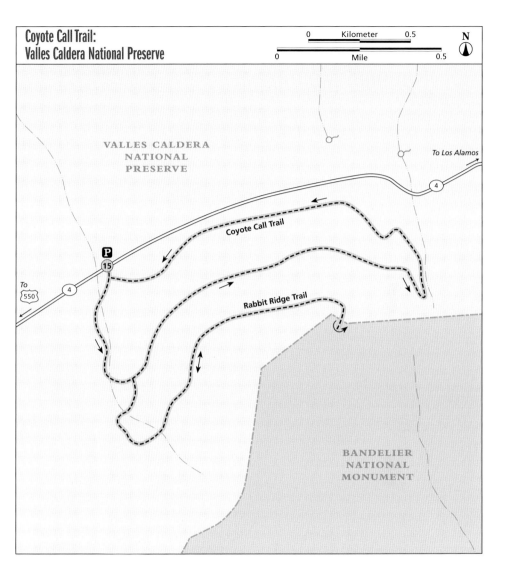

Area Info

Bandelier National Monument, 15 Entrance Rd., Los Alamos 87544; (505) 672-3861, ext. 517; www.nps.gov/band

Fenton Lake State Park, 455 Fenton Lake Rd., Jemez Springs 87025; (575) 829-3630; www.emnrd.state.nm.us/SPD/fentonlakestatepark.html

Walatowa–Pueblo of Jemez, Pueblo of Jemez Welcome Center, 7413 NM 4, Jemez Pueblo 87024; (575) 834-7235; www.jemezpueblo.com

White Rock Visitor Center, 115 NM 4, Los Alamos 87547; (505) 672-3183, (800) 444-0707; www.visitlosalamos.org

16 Cerro Grande Route: Bandelier National Monument

The 2.2-mile Cerro Grande Route in the northwest corner of Bandelier National Monument offers a beautiful hike to the park's highest point and breathtaking views of Valles Caldera National Preserve.

Distance: 4.4 miles out and back
Hiking time: 2 to 3 hours
Difficulty: Strenuous, with 1,250 feet of elevation gain
Best seasons: May through Oct
Schedule: Parking lot open daily dawn to dusk
Other trail users: None
Canine compatibility: No dogs allowed

Fees and permits: None
Map: USGS Bland
Trail contact: Bandelier National Monument, 15 Entrance Rd., Los Alamos 87544; (505) 672-3861; www.nps.gov/band
Special considerations: Thunderstorms and lightning pose a serious threat during the summer.

Finding the trailhead: From Albuquerque, take I-25 north to exit 242 toward US 550 / Bernalillo. Turn left (west) onto US 550 and drive north for 22.8 miles to the town of San Ysidro and the turn for NM 4. Turn right (northeast) onto NM 4 and continue 45.9 miles to the trailhead parking area on the left (north) side of the highway (GPS: 35.847738 N / -106.422054 W). Allow 2 hours to drive from Albuquerque to Bandelier National Monument.

The Hike

Most people visit Bandelier National Monument to see the ancient Native American ruins in the Frijoles Canyon area. However, a short drive from the main park entrance and the crumpled ruins is an excellent trail that climbs to the summit of 10,170-foot Cerro Grande, the highest point in the national monument. The mountain's high summit offers spacious views across Valles Caldera National Preserve to the west, the Sandia Mountains to the south, and the snowcapped Sangre de Cristo Mountains to the east.

The Cerro Grande Trailhead is located along scenic NM 4 but is not labeled as the Cerro Grande Route. A trailhead sign tells hikers that they are hiking in Bandelier National Monument, but at the time that this guide was written, there was no trailhead sign with the trail's name on it.

From the Cerro Grande parking area, locate the trailhead on the west side of the lot. The trail is marked with yellow diamonds. Begin hiking north through a meadow that is splashed with wildflowers during the summer. The trail winds through meadows and an open forest before heading northeast to the hike's uphill portion. After 0.45 mile begin ascending the dirt and rock trail. The trail levels out at 0.65 mile and then climbs again at 0.75 mile. Follow the climbing trail through a mixed forest of ponderosa pine, Douglas fir, white fir, and aspen to a meadow on the broad south ridge of the peak.

At 1.25 miles hike north through the high meadow to a series of switchbacks and the final approach to the summit. Be careful hiking in these open meadows during the summer. Thunderstorms accompanied by lightning are common in July and August and pose a dangerous threat to hikers, with no cover or shelter on the mountain's exposed upper slopes and summit.

Hike northeast on the first long switchback and continue up the yellow-blazed trail to the top. After 1.9 miles reach broad views of the rugged Sandia Mountains 50 miles to the southeast. At 2.0 miles are views of grassy Valles Grande and 11,254-foot Redondo Peak, the highest peak in Valles Caldera National Preserve. Finish up the last few switchbacks to the summit of Cerro Grande Peak at 2.2 miles. A rock pile marks the 10,170-foot summit.

While the trail ascends Cerro Grande's southeastern flank, which was untouched by the massive Cerro Grande Fire in 2000, the mountain's western, northern, and eastern slopes were devastated by the fire. The fire began on May 4 as a controlled burn high on Cerro Grande, but a combination of high winds and tinder-dry vegetation created a huge blaze that torched over 100,000 acres, burned 235 houses in Los Alamos to the east, and caused over $1 billion worth of damage. The fire was finally extinguished on July 20.

The summit offers spacious views across central New Mexico and of nearby Valle Grande and deep canyons that drain east through Bandelier National Monument to the Rio Grande in its deep gorge. After enjoying the views and a snack, retrace your

Many slopes on Cerro Grande were burned by the Cerro Grande Fire in 2000. JD TANNER

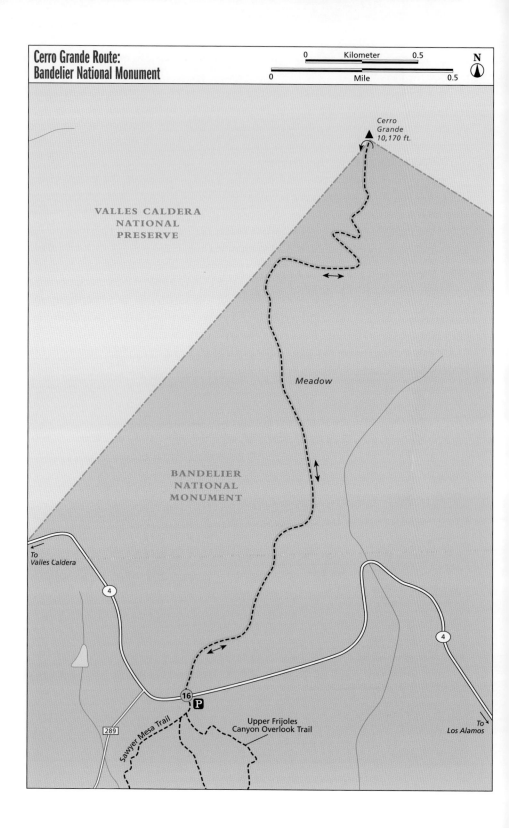

0   Kilometer   0.5

0   Mile   0.5

N

Cerro
Grande
10,170 ft.

VALLES CALDERA
NATIONAL
PRESERVE

Meadow

BANDELIER
NATIONAL
MONUMENT

To
Valles Caldera

4

4

16

P

Sawyer Mesa Trail

289

Upper Frijoles
Canyon Overlook Trail

To
Los Alamos

THE LAS CONCHAS FIRE

In the early afternoon of June 26, 2011, a fire exploded west of Bandelier National Monument after a 75-foot-high aspen fell onto a power line. The wildfire, driven by high winds, incinerated over 44,000 acres, including much of the national monument, in the next thirteen hours. The fire raced through tinder-dry forest, burning an acre of land per second, and eventually consumed over 156,293 acres of the Jemez Mountains. It became the largest wildfire in New Mexico history until the following year, when it was surpassed by the Whitewater-Baldy Complex Fire. The Las Conchas Fire devastated the old-growth ponderosa pine forest that blanketed most of Bandelier's mesas and canyons. Vegetation is now slowly reclaiming the burned areas, but with the warming and drying climate, it appears that the pines won't be returning to the Jemez Mountains.

steps down the trail to the trailhead and parking area on NM 4 for a 4.4-mile round-trip hike.

Miles and Directions

0.0 Start at the Cerro Grande Trailhead on the north side of NM 4 (GPS: 35.847738 N / -106.422058 W). Hike north on the Cerro Grande Trail blazed with yellow diamonds on trees.

0.45 The trail begins to climb a steep slope.

0.65 The trail levels out for a short distance.

0.75 Begin climbing another moderate ascent.

1.25 The trail leads into an open meadow and curves northeast toward Cerro Grande.

1.9 Reach views of the Sandia Mountains to the south.

2.0 Reach a view of Valles Caldera National Preserve to the west.

2.2 Reach the summit of Cerro Grande (GPS: 35.869438 N / -106.412846 W). Return down the trail to the trailhead.

4.4 Arrive back at the Cerro Grande Trailhead and parking area on NM 4.

Area Info

Puye Cliff Dwellings, NM 30 and NM 5 (Santa Clara Canyon Road); (505) 917-6650; www.puyecliffdwellings.com

Santa Clara Pueblo, PO Box 580, Española 87532; (505) 753-7326; www.new mexico.org/places-to-visit/native-culture/santa-clara-pueblo

Valles Caldera National Preserve, PO Box 359, Jemez Springs 87025; Valle Grande Visitor Center, (575) 829-4100, ext. 3; www.nps.gov/vall

White Rock Visitor Center, 115 NM 4, Los Alamos 87547; (505) 672-3183, (800) 444-0707; www.visitlosalamos.org

17 Main Loop Trail: Bandelier National Monument

The popular 1.25-mile Main Loop Trail is an easy hike past many archaeological sites, including Big Kiva, Tyuonyi, Talus House, and Long House, in Cañon de los Frijoles. The first trail section is wheelchair and stroller accessible.

Distance: 1.25-mile lollipop
Hiking time: About 1 hour
Difficulty: Easy
Best seasons: Spring, summer, and fall
Schedule: Trails are open daily dawn to dusk year-round. Frijoles Canyon Visitor Center is open daily spring and fall 9 a.m. to 5:30 p.m., summer 9 a.m. to 6 p.m., and winter 9 a.m. to 5 p.m.
Other trail users: None

Canine compatibility: No dogs allowed
Fees and permits: Entry fee per vehicle; National Park Passes accepted
Maps: USGS Frijoles; trail map available at visitor center
Trail contact: Bandelier National Monument, 15 Entrance Rd., Los Alamos 87544; (505) 672-3861; www.nps.gov/band
Special considerations: Fires and floods damaged the trail in 2011.

Finding the trailhead: From Albuquerque, take I-25 north for 45 miles to exit 282B toward US 285N / US 84W. Continue for 19.9 miles on US 285 / US 84 before exiting onto NM 502W. Drive west 9.9 miles on NM 502 and take the ramp toward NM 4W and White Rock. Continue 12.6 miles on NM 4 to Entrance Road and Bandelier National Monument on the left (southwest). Turn left (southwest) on Entrance Road and drive 3.1 miles to the Frijoles Canyon Visitor Center and parking area (GPS: 35.779001 N / -106.270733 W). Allow 2 hours to drive from Albuquerque to Bandelier National Monument.

Visitors are required to take a free shuttle bus from the White Rock Visitor Center to the main Bandelier visitor center and trailheads in Frijoles Canyon between 9 a.m. and 3 p.m. from mid-May to mid-October. Shuttles run every 30 minutes on weekdays and every 20 minutes on weekends. Park at a large lot at the White Rock Visitor Center (GPS: 35.827454 N / -106.211681 W) at 115 NM 4, White Rock, (505) 672-3183. For more information on the shuttle, visit www.nps.gov/band/planyourvisit/shuttle.htm.

The Hike

The 1.25-mile Main Loop Trail makes a lollipop loop hike through the richest archaeological area at 33,677-acre Bandelier National Monument. The trail explores many archaeological sites, passing the Big Kiva, the large ruin of Tyuonyi (pronounced chew-OHN-yee), Talus House, Long House, and many cavates, small alcoves chiseled into the soft cliff faces for living spaces.

An interpretive trail guide, available for purchase at the visitor center, is keyed to twenty-one numbered stops along the trail. The first 0.3-mile trail section to the west side of Tyuonyi is accessible to wheelchairs and strollers. The rest of the trail is rougher, skirting the cliff base on the canyon's north side and climbing stone stairways before descending to the valley floor and crossing the creek for the return leg. Allow an hour to hike the trail and explore its Ancestral Puebloan sites.

Bandelier National Monument, one of New Mexico's archaeological wonders, spreads across the rugged Pajarito Plateau on the eastern edge of the Jemez Mountains. The monument offers more than 70 miles of trails through canyons and over mesas. Many of the trails link to pathways in adjoining Santa Fe National Forest and Valles Caldera National Preserve.

The soft rock forming Bandelier's cliffs was deposited by two violent eruptions of the Jemez Volcano to the west over a million years ago. Ash and

Pinnacles frame Tyuonyi, the largest ruin on the Main Loop Trail.

cinders from the eruptions covered over 1,500 square miles, leaving a thousand-foot layer of ash between the volcano and the Rio Grande to the east. Geologists estimate that each eruption was about 600 times more powerful than the Mount St. Helens

HOW DID BANDELIER NATIONAL MONUMENT GET ITS NAME?

Adolph F. Bandelier (1840–1914), a Swiss anthropologist, first visited Frijoles Canyon with guides from Cochiti Pueblo on October 23, 1880, and discovered a trove of artifacts and sites on the fertile canyon floor. He later called it the "grandest thing I ever saw." Among the towering pines and pale volcanic cliffs, Bandelier found dwellings chiseled into soft rock at the base of the cliffs. He wrote: "There are some of one, two, and three stories. In most cases, the plaster is still in the rooms. . . . I found entire chimneys, metates, manos and a stone axe." Afterward, Bandelier tramped across the Southwest on foot, befriending Native peoples, observing rituals, recording myths and stories, and surveying archaeological sites. Considered the first archaeological scholar of the Southwest, it is fitting that the Pajarito Plateau and its rich Native American heritage was named for Adolph Bandelier after its 1916 designation as a national monument.

eruption in 1980. The volcano collapsed after the last eruption, forming today's Valles Caldera.

The pink rock lining the walls of Cañon de los Frijoles, often mistaken for sandstone, is compacted volcanic ash, a rock formation called tuff. The ancient people who inhabited the Bandelier area used harder hand stones like obsidian and basalt to enlarge openings and potholes in the tuff to create cavates. Some of the ruins are scattered along El Rito de los Frijoles, Spanish for "the little river of beans," one of the few water sources on the plateau that flows year-round. The ruins and creek, sometimes called Frijoles Creek, provide a beautiful setting for the Main Loop Trail. The popular trail is well worth the traffic to explore the ruins seen on the hike.

Locate the trailhead for the Main Loop Trail on the northwest side of the visitor center and hike northwest. Reach a trail junction after 0.15 mile. The loop portion of the hike begins here. Keep right (north) on the trail. The trail to the left (west) is the return trail. Follow the trail along the canyon floor past the 40-foot-wide Great Kiva, a subterranean ceremonial chamber, and reach the ruins of Tyuonyi Pueblo at 0.3 mile.

The paved trail passes through a break in Tyuonyi's east wall and bends north across its spacious central plaza. The semicircular pueblo, built around the plaza, contained

Hikers follow the Main Loop Trail through the ruins of Tyuonyi.

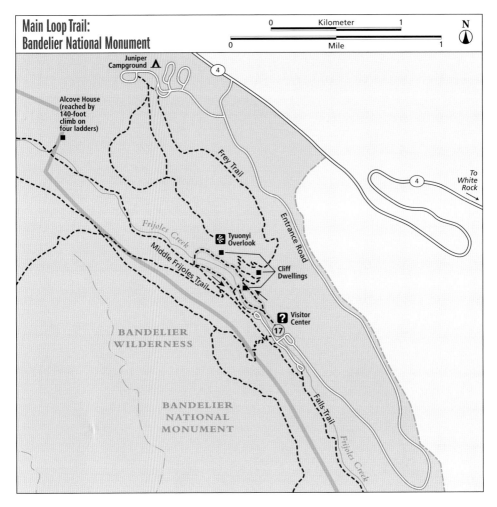

0   Kilometer   1

0   Mile   1

N

Juniper Campground

4

Alcove House
(reached by
140-foot
climb on
four ladders)

Frey Trail

4

To
White
Rock

Frijoles Creek

Tyuonyi
Overlook

Middle Frijoles Trail

Entrance Road

Cliff
Dwellings

Visitor
Center

17

BANDELIER
WILDERNESS

Falls Trail

Frijoles Creek

BANDELIER
NATIONAL
MONUMENT

about 400 rooms in two stories and housed between 100 and 200 residents. The scale of Tyuonyi is hard to appreciate as you walk through it, but views of the site from the canyon rim on either the Tyuonyi Overlook Trail on the north or the Frijolito Loop Trail on the south reveal the ruin's size. The pueblo was built using similar construction to sites in the Mesa Verde region of southwestern Colorado. Most of the rooms were probably used for food storage. Excavation of the site began in the summer of 1908 by a team led by archaeologist Edgar Hewett, who studied one of the three kivas in the plaza as well as the nearby Great Kiva. More excavations were made in the 1930s, and the exposed walls were stabilized to protect them from weathering.

Stay right (northeast) after passing the pueblo on the paved trail. A dirt trail to the left (northwest) heads into the middle of the canyon floor and away from the ruins. For the next 0.2 mile, explore the ancient ruins. A few ladders allow hikers to climb into some of the ruins. At 0.5 mile the Frey Trail leaves the Main Loop Trail to the right (north) and leads to Juniper Campground on the rim above. Stay left (west)

The Ancestral Puebloans lived in cavates, small caves carved in the soft tuff cliffs.

on the Main Loop Trail to view the archaeological sites. The trail makes a sharp left (southwest) turn at 0.75 mile and heads away from the ruins.

Follow the trail southwest away from the cliff dwellings and descend a gentle slope toward Rito de los Frijoles and the canyon floor. Cross the creek at 0.8 mile and turn left (southeast) to continue on the Main Loop Trail, the return loop to the trailhead area. In 2011 this trail section was severely damaged by spring floods. Hike 0.1 mile and turn left (northeast) again to cross back over the creek, then make a quick right (southeast) after the crossing to stay on the Main Loop Trail. After 1.1 miles reach the end of the loop portion of the hike and turn right (south) to return to the trailhead and visitor center at 1.25 miles.

Miles and Directions

0.0 Begin at the northwest side of the Frijoles Canyon Visitor Center (GPS: 35.779231 N / -106.271144 W). Hike northwest on the Main Loop Trail.

0.15 Reach a trail junction and the start of the loop portion of the hike. Stay right (north) on the trail that leads to cliff dwellings. The trail to the left (west) is the return trail.

0.3 Hike through Tyuonyi Pueblo ruins and keep right (northeast) on the main trail to the cliff dwellings. A social trail to the left (northwest) bypasses the cliff dwellings.

0.5 The Frey Trail to the right (north) leads to Juniper Campground on the mesa above (GPS: 35.783265 N / -106.274836 W). Stay left (west) on the Main Loop Trail.

0.75 The trail makes a sharp left turn to the southwest and leaves the dwellings.

0.8 Cross Frijoles Creek and turn left (southeast) on the Main Loop Trail. The trail to the right (northwest) leads to Alcove House.

0.9 Turn left (northeast) again to cross Frijoles Creek and make a quick right turn to the southeast after crossing the bridge.

1.1 Reach the end of the hike's loop portion. Turn right (south) to return to the trailhead and visitor center.

1.25 Arrive back at the trailhead and visitor center.

Area Info

Bradbury Science Museum, 1350 Central Ave., Los Alamos 87544; (505) 667-4444; www.lanl.gov/museum

Puye Cliff Dwellings, NM 30 and NM 5 (Santa Clara Canyon Road); (505) 917-6650; www.puyecliffdwellings.com

Valles Caldera National Preserve, PO Box 359, Jemez Springs 87025; Valle Grande Visitor Center, (575) 829-4100, ext. 3; www.nps.gov/vall

White Rock Visitor Center, 115 NM 4, Los Alamos 87547; (505) 672-3183, (800) 444-0707; www.visitlosalamos.org

18 Alcove House Trail: Bandelier National Monument

The Alcove House Trail in Bandelier National Monument is a 3-mile out-and-back hike that can be combined with the Main Loop Trail. The trail follows the floor of Cañon de los Frijoles to a cliff dwelling reached by a 140-foot climb up four ladders.

Distance: 3.0 miles out and back
Hiking time: About 2 hours
Difficulty: Strenuous, with a climb up 4 ladders to the ruin
Best seasons: Spring and fall
Schedule: Trails are open daily dawn to dusk year-round. Frijoles Canyon Visitor Center is open daily spring and fall 9 a.m. to 5:30 p.m., summer 9 a.m. to 6 p.m., and winter 9 a.m. to 5 p.m.
Other trail users: None

Canine compatibility: No dogs allowed
Fees and permits: Fee per vehicle; National Park Passes accepted
Maps: USGS Frijoles; trail map available at visitor center and on park website
Trail contact: Bandelier National Monument, 15 Entrance Rd., Los Alamos 87544; (505) 672-3861, ext. 517; www.nps.gov/band
Special considerations: Trail may be closed in winter if ladders are snowy and icy. Wildfire and flooding severely damaged the trails in 2011.

Finding the trailhead: From Albuquerque, take I-25 north for 45 miles to exit 282B toward US 285N/US 84W. Continue 19.9 miles on US 285/US 84 before exiting onto NM 502W. Drive west 9.9 miles on NM 502 and take the ramp toward NM 4W and White Rock. Continue 12.6 miles on NM 4 to Entrance Road and Bandelier National Monument on the left (southwest). Turn left (southwest) onto Entrance Road and drive 3.1 miles to the visitor center and parking area (GPS: 35.779001 N / -106.270733 W). Allow 2 hours to drive from Albuquerque to Bandelier National Monument.

Visitors are required to take a free shuttle bus from the White Rock Visitor Center to the main Bandelier visitor center and trailheads in Frijoles Canyon between 9 a.m. and 3 p.m. from mid-May to mid-October. Shuttles run every 30 minutes on weekdays and every 20 minutes on weekends. Park at a large lot at the White Rock Visitor Center (GPS: 35.827454 N / -106.211681 W) at 115 NM 4, White Rock, (505) 672-3183. For more information on the shuttle, visit www.nps.gov/band/planyourvisit/shuttle.htm.

The Hike

The 3-mile round-trip hike to Alcove House offers hikers a chance to visit a spectacular reconstructed cliff dwelling perched in a high alcove on the north side of Cañon de los Frijoles. Alcove House, sitting 140 feet above the canyon floor, is reached by climbing steps hacked into the soft stone and four wooden ladders attached to the cliff. While the ladder climb is not for acrophobic hikers and small children, the view into the canyon from the archaeological site is amazing and worth the effort.

A kiva, a sacred underground chamber, was the center of religious life at Alcove House.

After reaching the airy alcove, once called Ceremonial Cave, hikers can scramble down a set of wooden stairs into a reconstructed kiva, a round semi-subterranean structure used for rituals by the Ancestral Puebloans. When visiting the ancient site and entering the kiva, remember that this is still a sacred place to the Puebloan people and should be treated with respect. The kiva was reconstructed in 1910, stabilized in the 1930s, and then closed and restabilized in 2013. The site was weakened by decades of constant foot traffic on and around the kiva.

Before setting off on the hike, check Bandelier's website or ask a ranger at the visitor center for park alerts and access updates. After the massive Las Conchas wildfire in 2011, much of the national monument was closed because of fire, flood, and trail damage. In winter, the trail to the base of the ladders is usually open but the ladders

WHAT IS A KIVA?

Kiva is a term used to refer to a religious center for the Anasazi and Puebloan peoples. Kivas are typically round structures built into the ground.

Hikers make a 140-foot climb up four ladders to Alcove House.

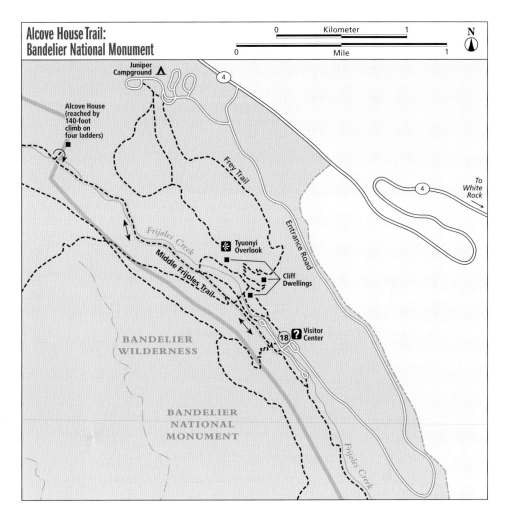

**Alcove House Trail:
Bandelier National Monument**

0   Kilometer   1

0   Mile   1

N

Juniper
Campground

Alcove House
(reached by
140-foot
climb on
four ladders)

Frey Trail

Frijoles Creek

Middle Frijoles Trail

Tyuonyi
Overlook

Entrance Road

Cliff
Dwellings

4

To
White
Rock

BANDELIER
WILDERNESS

18   Visitor
Center

BANDELIER
NATIONAL
MONUMENT

Frijoles Creek

and steps to Alcove House may be closed for weeks at a time due to dangerous ice and snow. A sign at the base of the ladders indicates if the site is closed.

Bandelier National Monument boasts a long human history that dates back over 10,000 years to some of the first Americans in the area now called New Mexico. These early nomads roamed across the Pajarito Plateau and the Rio Grande's deep canyons, camping seasonally, hunting animals, and gathering seeds, nuts, and edible plants. Later Ancestral Puebloans, possibly immigrants from the Four Corners region, began settling in fertile Frijoles Canyon around AD 1150. The cliff dwellings like Alcove House and large pueblos including Tyuonyi (pronounced chew-OHN-yee) near the visitor center were occupied from approximately AD 1200 to 1500. Archaeologists speculate that Alcove House housed as many as twenty-five people, probably a familial clan group. Besides the reconstructed kiva, the site has viga holes in the cliff walls where wooden beams were inserted for roofs and wall niches in areas where rooms once stood.

The hike begins at the east end of the parking lot immediately south of the visitor center. Hike northwest on the Nature Trail, passing an information sign and map, for 0.4 mile to a trail junction. Keep left (west), crossing Rito de los Frijoles on a foot bridge, and continue northwest on the Nature Trail. A right turn leads to the Main Loop Trail and the Tyuonyi and Long House ruins.

From this junction, the trail follows the creek to the base of the Alcove House ladders. After 0.7 mile the Nature Trail joins the Alcove House / Middle Frijoles Trail. Hike northwest on the trail, crossing the creek at 1.0 mile, 1.2 miles, and 1.3 miles. After the final creek crossing, follow the trail northeast to the base of the first of four wooden ladders that lead to Alcove House. Scramble up the ladders and chiseled stone steps in the cliff for 140 vertical feet, the equivalent of a modern fourteen-story building, to the shelter cave.

After exploring Alcove House, return down the trail to the visitor center and parking area for a 3-mile round-trip hike.

Miles and Directions

0.0 From the east end of the visitor center parking area (GPS: 35.779139 N / -106.271274 W), hike northwest on the Nature Trail past an information sign.

0.4 Reach a fork in the Nature Trail. Turn left (west), cross Frijoles Creek on a bridge, and continue northwest on the Nature Trail on the south side of the creek.

0.7 Turn northwest onto the Alcove House Trail.

1.0 Cross Frijoles Creek.

1.2 Cross Frijoles Creek.

1.3 Cross Frijoles Creek.

1.4 Reach the base of the cliff and ascend wooden ladders to Alcove House.

1.5 Reach Alcove House. Descend the ladders and return to the trailhead on the same trail.

3.0 Arrive back at the trailhead.

Area Info

Puye Cliff Dwellings, NM 30 and NM 5 (Santa Clara Canyon Road); (505) 917-6650; www.puyecliffdwellings.com

Santa Clara Pueblo, PO Box 580, Española 87532; (505) 753-7326; www.new mexico.org/places-to-visit/native-culture/santa-clara-pueblo

Valles Caldera National Preserve, PO Box 359, Jemez Springs 87025; Valle Grande Visitor Center, (575) 829-4100, ext. 3; www.nps.gov/vall

White Rock Visitor Center, 115 NM 4, Los Alamos 87547; (505) 672-3183, (800) 444-0707; www.visitlosalamos.org

19 Falls Trail: Bandelier National Monument

The Falls Trail to Upper Frijoles Falls in Bandelier National Monument is a spectacular 3-mile out-and-back hike that descends about 400 feet through a deep cliff-lined
canyon floored with a tumbling creek and towering ponderosa pine trees.

Distance: 3.0 miles out and back
Hiking time: 2 to 3 hours
Difficulty: Moderate due to climb back to
trailhead
Best seasons: Spring and fall. Summer days
can be hot.
Schedule: Trails are open daily dawn to dusk
year-round. Frijoles Canyon Visitor Center is
open daily spring and fall 9 a.m. to 5:30 p.m.,
summer 9 a.m. to 6 p.m., and winter 9 a.m. to
5 p.m.
Other trail users: None

Canine compatibility: No dogs allowed
Fees and permits: Fee per vehicle; National
Park Passes accepted
Maps: USGS Frijoles; trail map available at
visitor center and on park website
Trail contact: Bandelier National Monument,
15 Entrance Rd., Los Alamos 87544; (505)
672-3861; www.nps.gov/band
Special considerations: Fires and floods
severely damaged the trail in 2011. The trail
below the upper falls to the Rio Grande is
closed due to washout.

Finding the trailhead: From Albuquerque, take I-25 north for 45 miles to exit 282B toward
US 285N / US 84W. Continue 19.9 miles on US 285 / US 84 before exiting onto NM 502W. Drive
west 9.9 miles on NM 502 and take the ramp toward NM 4W and White Rock. Continue 12.6
miles on NM 4 to Entrance Road and Bandelier National Monument on the left (southwest). Turn
left (southwest) on Entrance Road and drive 3.1 miles to the visitor center and parking area (GPS:
35.779001 N / -106.270733 W). Allow 2 hours to drive from Albuquerque to Bandelier National
Monument.

Visitors are required to take a free shuttle bus from the White Rock Visitor Center to the main
Bandelier visitor center and trailheads in Frijoles Canyon between 9 a.m. and 3 p.m. from mid-May
to mid-October. Shuttles run every 30 minutes on weekdays and every 20 minutes on weekends.
Park at a large lot at the White Rock Visitor Center (GPS: 35.827454 N / -106.211681 W) at
115 NM 4, White Rock, (505) 672-3183. For more information on the shuttle, visit www.nps.gov/
band/planyourvisit/shuttle.htm.

The Hike

While many trails in Bandelier National Monument visit ancient ruins, the Falls Trail
explores one of the area's natural wonders. The trail leads hikers down Cañon de
los Frijoles (Frijoles Canyon) to the Upper Falls of the Rito de los Frijoles (Frijoles
Creek). The moderate 1.5-mile trail descends 400 feet in the steep-walled canyon east
of the monument visitor center to an unfenced overlook east of the waterfall. The
trail has steep drop-offs on its final section and two creek crossings on plank bridges.

Rito de los Frijoles plunges 80 feet off a cliff at the end of the Falls Trail.

Keep a watchful eye on small children on the hike. The trail is snowy and icy in winter and may be dangerous; use microspikes on your boots and trekking poles for traction and balance. Carry plenty of water in summer, and do not drink from the creek without treating the water first.

The trail once continued down the canyon from the Upper Falls to the Lower Falls and then to the west bank of the Rio Grande in White Rock Canyon, but major floods in 2011 and 2013 after wildfires erased the trail and limited hiker access to the gorge. For information about the trail and current conditions, ask at the visitor center or check the monument's website for park alerts.

Morning is the perfect time to hike the Falls Trail in summer, with cool air, pine shade, and birdsong filling the canyon. The upper falls, tucked in a narrow canyon, are in shadow most of the day. If you want to see the falls and take photos of sunlight on the water, plan your hike for midday, when the noon sun fills the canyon.

The Falls Trail begins on the southeast edge of the spur road that leads to overflow and backpacker parking on the south side of Frijoles Creek. From the visitor center, hike east from the shuttle stop on the south side of the parking area to a wooden footbridge that crosses Frijoles Creek. Cross the bridge and turn east onto the asphalt spur road, then walk 0.1 mile to the Falls Trailhead on the right.

The trail runs 100 feet to a junction with a trail that comes from the parking areas to the west and a kiosk with trail information and a map. Hike east on the wide trail, passing huge scrub oak trees on the left. The trail follows a bench above Frijoles Creek riffling over boulders in a box canyon below. After hiking 0.9 mile, the trail crosses Frijoles Creek on a plank bridge and continues through an open forest of tall ponderosa pines that fills the canyon floor. Some of the pines exceed 150 feet in height.

Cross Frijoles Creek again on a wooden bridge at 1.1 miles and continue hiking southeast on the right side of the creek. Look for strangely eroded tent rocks carved from soft pumice and ash on the canyon walls. These conical, teepee-shaped formations are formed primarily by water in the Bandelier Tuff Formation, a soft rock originally deposited as extensive ash falls and pyroclastic flows during volcanic eruptions from the nearby Valles Caldera supervolcano about 1.85 million years ago. Some geologists say the tent rocks are more resistant to erosion than the surrounding bedrock tuff because hot ash flowed over water, causing the ash to harden and be preserved as erosional remnants when the softer rock eroded away.

After crossing into the Bandelier Wilderness Area at 1.3 miles, the trail climbs gently high above the creek and a canyon. The sound of rushing water echoes from the narrowing canyon below the trail. The trail's last 0.1 mile edges across steep slopes above the deep canyon. Keep an eye on small children here, since a fall off the trail is fatal. After 1.5 miles the trail switchbacks down to an unfenced viewpoint above 80-foot-high Upper Frijoles Falls.

The waterfall funnels through a narrow gorge and plunges over a cliff composed of hard, erosion-resistant basalt. The basalt was deposited as a lava flow over two million years ago from a volcano in the Cerros del Rio volcanic field before the main eruption of today's Valles Caldera. The striking red layers below the trail, overlook, and basalt formation at Upper Frijoles Falls are called maar deposits. These formed in the volcanic field when molten magma interacted with water, probably from the ancestral Rio Grande. The deposits came from a 2-mile-wide maar volcano exposed in Frijoles Canyon above the falls.

A wooden plank bridge crosses Rito de los Frijoles.

A solitary ponderosa pine perches on a cliff edge above Upper Frijoles Falls.

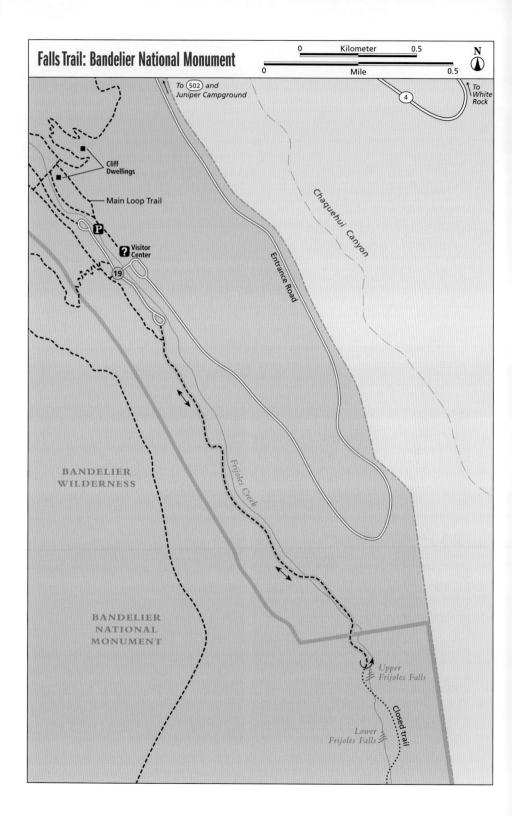

Falls Trail: Bandelier National Monument

Kilometer
0   0.5

Mile
0   0.5

N

To 502 and
Juniper Campground

To White
Rock

4

Chaquehui Canyon

Cliff
Dwellings

Main Loop Trail

Entrance Road

P

Visitor
Center

19

Frijoles Creek

BANDELIER
WILDERNESS

BANDELIER
NATIONAL
MONUMENT

Upper
Frijoles Falls

Closed trail

Lower
Frijoles Falls

After large wildfires decimated Bandelier National Monument, massive flooding in 2011 and 2013 altered Frijoles Canyon from the trailhead to the Rio Grande. The mile-long trail section from Upper Frijoles Falls to the river was destroyed in the flooding and has not been rebuilt due to unstable slopes and continuing erosion. Past the overlook, the trail remains closed to hikers.

The 2013 flash flood in the lower canyon completely changed the environment, gouging out cliffs and sweeping away trees and vegetation. Lower Frijoles Falls, a quarter mile below the Upper Falls, was redesigned from a 30-foot waterfall to a thin 90-foot plunge off an amphitheater of basalt cliffs. The Rito de los Frijoles went from its annual average of 1 CFS (cubic feet per second) to over 9,000 CFS, an astounding and epic amount of water, during the flood.

After admiring the view, return back up the Falls Trail for a 3-mile round-trip hike.

Miles and Directions

0.0 Begin at a trailhead at the first turn on the asphalt park road that leads to backpacker and overflow parking, 270 feet from Entrance Road (GPS: 35.776712 N /-106.269512 W).

0.06 Reach the junction of the Falls Trail and a trail that parallels the overflow parking road at an information kiosk (GPS: 35.775885 N /-106.269274 W). Hike southeast on a bench above Frijoles Creek.

0.9 Cross Frijoles Creek on a plank bridge and continue hiking southeast down the canyon on the left side of the creek.

1.1 Cross Frijoles Creek on another plank bridge (GPS: 35.765808 N /-106.261122 W) and follow the trail on the right bank of the creek.

1.4 Reach an exposed trail section above the deep canyon below.

1.5 Reach an unfenced viewpoint for Upper Frijoles Falls (GPS: 35.762656 N / -106.259794 W). The trail beyond here to the Rio Grande is closed. Return to the trailhead on the same route.

3.0 Arrive back at the trailhead.

Area Info

Bandelier National Monument, 15 Entrance Rd., Los Alamos 87544; (505) 672-3861; www.nps.gov/band

Puye Cliff Dwellings, NM 30 and NM 5 (Santa Clara Canyon Road); (505) 917-6650; www.puyecliffdwellings.com

Santa Clara Pueblo, PO Box 580, Española 87532; (505) 753-7326; www.newmexico.org/places-to-visit/native-culture/santa-clara-pueblo

Valles Caldera National Preserve, PO Box 359, Jemez Springs 87025; Valle Grande Visitor Center, (575) 829-4100, ext. 3; www.nps.gov/vall

White Rock Visitor Center, 115 NM 4, Los Alamos 87547; (505) 672-3183, (800) 444-0707; www.visitlosalamos.org

20 Slot Canyon Trail: Kasha-Katuwe Tent Rocks National Monument

The 1.5-mile Slot Canyon Trail is a spectacular hike up a slot canyon and past towering cliffs and strangely eroded tent rocks to an overlook with wide views of the national monument, the Jemez Mountains, and the distant Sandia Mountains.

Distance: 3.0 miles out and back
Hiking time: 2 to 3 hours
Difficulty: Strenuous, with 630 feet of elevation gain
Best seasons: Spring and fall. Summers are hot. Usually closed in winter due to snowfall.
Schedule: Open 8 a.m. to 5 p.m. daily, except for closure dates (Jan 1 and 6; Good Friday; Easter Sunday and following Monday; May 3; July 13, 14, and 25; Nov 1; Thanksgiving Day; Christmas). Gates are closed and locked at 5 p.m.
Other trail users: None

Canine compatibility: No dogs permitted on trail or in park, including in vehicles. Service animals are allowed.
Fees and permits: Fee per vehicle and for groups
Maps: USGS Canada; trail map available at trailhead and park entrance
Trail contact: BLM Rio Puerco Field Office, 100 Sun Avenue NE, Ste. 330, Albuquerque 87109; (505) 331-6259; www.blm.gov/visit/kktr
Special considerations: Park may be closed by the Pueblo de Cochiti tribal governor. No drinking water at the park. No cross-country hiking; only hike on designated trails. No rock scrambling or climbing off the trail.

Finding the trailhead: From Albuquerque, take I-25 north to exit 259. Turn left (northwest) toward the Santo Domingo / Cochiti Lake Recreation Area and drive northwest for 12.2 miles on NM 22. The road makes a left (southwest) turn to stay on NM 22 and continues 1.7 miles to Tribal Route 92. Turn right (northwest) onto Tribal Route 92 and reach the park entrance after 0.5 mile. From the fee station at the park entrance, drive 4.2 miles to a parking area on the right (north). The trailhead is on the northeast side of the lot. GPS: 35.657748 N / -106.411369 W

The Hike

The Tent Rocks National Recreation Trail in Kasha-Katuwe Tent Rocks National Monument is divided into two distinct segments: the 1.5-mile Slot Canyon Trail and the 1.2-mile Cave Loop Trail. The Slot Canyon Trail, gaining 630 feet of elevation, is a spectacular 3-mile round-trip hike that squeezes through a narrow slot canyon and then climbs steep slopes past gleaming white cliffs and bizarre tent rocks, eroded formations chiseled from soft volcanic tuff by wind and water. An additional mile-long loop trail is seasonally open at the Veterans' Memorial Scenic Overlook at the northwest corner of the monument.

A hiker enters the narrow slot canyon on the Slot Canyon Trail.

Kasha-Katuwe Tent Rocks, designated a 5,402-acre national monument in 2001, is jointly administered by the Bureau of Land Management (BLM) and Cochiti Pueblo. The historic village is occupied by Cochiti Puebloans, a recognized Native American tribe. The Cochiti people have inhabited this area, including the ancient villages at nearby Bandelier National Monument, for over 500 years. They call themselves

A swirl of thin volcanic ash layers line the walls of the slot canyon.

The twisting slot canyon at Tent Rocks is a highlight for Slot Canyon Trail hikers.

K'úutìim'é, or "People of the Mountains" in the Keresan language. The monument was created on Cochiti tribal land to preserve its unique geological features, wild character, and significance for the indigenous people.

Tent Rocks has become popular, partly because of social media, so the national monument takes preservation seriously. The only way to see the park is on the three designated foot trails, and no cross-country hiking is allowed since the volcanic rock and desert vegetation is fragile and easily damaged. The national monument is a day-use-only area, with no camping, fires, or cooking allowed. Restrooms and picnic areas are at the main trailhead and at the Veterans' Memorial Scenic Overlook parking area, 3.5 miles northwest of the trailhead on BLM Road 1011.

The monument has a carrying capacity equal to the number of vehicles parked in several small juniper-shaded lots by the trailhead. When the parking spots are filled, no one can enter the park until a car leaves it. Expect a 30- to 90-minute wait at the entrance gate. This approach keeps Tent Rocks from being overrun and crowded. Plan your hiking trip for weekdays and come early in the morning to ensure you find a parking spot.

Visitors can enter the park from 8 a.m. to 4 p.m. daily, although winter hours may vary. The park closes and gates are locked at 5 p.m. Come early to ensure you have enough time to do the hikes. Visitors must be out of the park and entrance station by closing time.

Dogs and other pets are banned from the national monument, meaning your dog cannot ride into the park or wait in your vehicle while you hike. Fines for bringing a dog into the park range from $350 to $1,000 plus possible jail time. If you have a dog and want to hike the trails, ask at the monument entrance station or the Cochiti Visitor Center on NM 22 for the names of local kennels and dog-sitters that will keep your animal for a fee while you visit Tent Rocks.

The Slot Canyon Trail climbs above a parade of pointed tent rocks.

A hiker passes below towering tent rocks on the Slot Canyon Trail.

The Slot Canyon Trail is usually closed in winter when snow fills the slot canyon. Check with the monument before your visit for closure information. The trail is hot in summer. Carry plenty of water and wear a hat and sunscreen. Watch for flash flooding on the entrance road and in the slot canyon after summer thunderstorms.

Begin the Slot Canyon Trail at the trailhead on the northeast side of the parking area. Follow the paved trail 80 feet to an interpretive sign with information about the national monument, the trails, human history, geology, birds, shrubs, and wildflowers. The first half-mile trail section to the junction of the Slot Canyon and Cave Loop Trails is wheelchair accessible.

The trail turns to packed dirt past the sign. Hike past a sculpture of two tent rocks and continue to the first junction of the two trails at 0.1 mile. Keep right on the Slot Canyon Trail. The trail to the left is the return section of the Cave Loop Trail. The trail heads northwest toward looming white cliffs, smoothed by erosion into rounded buttresses, deep crevices, and sharply pointed peaks. After 0.5 mile the trail reaches the second junction of the two trails. Stay to the right on the Slot Canyon Trail. The 1.2-mile Cave Loop Trail, making an open loop, goes left here and encircles a wide amphitheater before returning to the trailhead. This junction is the end of the wheelchair-accessible trail section.

The hike heads into a narrowing canyon flanked with high cliffs and several tall ponderosa pines, including a 100-foot tree with roots exposed by flash floods. Another pine grows against a massive block that slumped off the canyon wall. The deep canyon twists and turns through soft volcanic bedrock for the next 0.2 mile, passing through a 3-foot-wide corridor lined with sculpted rock layers. Exciting for both kids and adults, this tight slot canyon provides a unique hiking experience that isn't soon forgotten.

Past the slot, the canyon widens and the trail follows a dry, rocky creek bed, passing beneath two conical tent rocks topped by harder chunks of rock that slow erosion. The trail bends left and heads up an entrenched barren canyon below huge white cliffs and a collection of 90-foot-high tent rocks, the tallest in the national

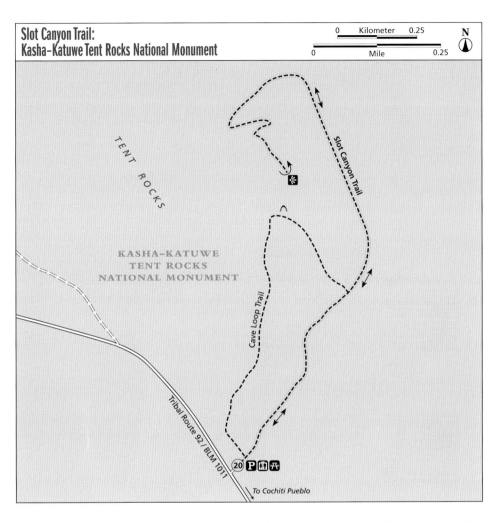

**Slot Canyon Trail:
Kasha-Katuwe Tent Rocks National Monument**

TENT ROCKS

KASHA–KATUWE
TENT ROCKS
NATIONAL MONUMENT

Slot Canyon Trail

Cave Loop Trail

Tribal Route 92 / BLM 1011

20 P

To Cochiti Pueblo

monument. Stop and catch your breath below these strange rock formations and let your imagination run wild. It's easy to see a parade of dunces with pointed hats, an army of soft-twist ice cream cones, a half-painted Christmas tree farm, or an encampment of Boy Scout tents.

The cliffs and tent rocks, called Kasha-Katuwe, or "white cliffs," in the Keresan language, are formed from volcanic rocks—pumice, ash, and tuff—deposited from volcanic eruptions from today's Valle Grande in the Jemez Mountains between six and seven million years ago. The 1,000-foot-thick layers were later exposed and shaped by water erosion, which fashioned the conical hoodoos, sharp canyons and arroyos, and tall fluted cliffs. The distinctive tapered shape of the tent rocks comes from a small caprock of harder volcanic material perched atop a narrow neck. After the tent rock loses its erosion-resistant cap, the summit quickly becomes a sharp point. Look at the tent rocks along the upper trail to see the various stages of erosion.

Water erosion shapes conical tent rocks above the Slot Canyon Trail.

After climbing through a rock forest of tent rocks, the trail begins steeply climbing out of the canyon on the northern slope of a broad ridge. Stay on the rocky trail and avoid shortcutting to lessen slope erosion. Near the top of the ascent is a rock step. Grab handholds and pull over a small overhang and then cruise up a couple more switchbacks to a high ridge at 1.2 miles. Continue up the trail to a rounded 6,381-foot summit with spacious views across the national monument to the distant Sandia Mountains to the south, the Sangre de Cristo Mountains above Santa Fe to the northeast, and the nearby Jemez Mountains, burned in the 2011 Las Conchas Fire, to the west. A park ranger is often on the top to answer visitor questions.

After enjoying the view, follow a trail southeast down a wide ridge for 500 feet to another spectacular overlook that perches directly above a high cliff and the amphitheater traversed by the Cave Loop Trail. Retrace your steps to the summit and follow the trail down to the trailhead for a 3-mile round-trip hike. It's easy on the way down to take a right turn on the Cave Loop Trail at its junction with the Slot Canyon Trail and hike 1.2 miles on it back to the trailhead (see Hike 21 for details).

Miles and Directions

0.0 Begin at the trailhead on the northeast side of the parking area (GPS: 35.657748 N / -106.411369 W).

0.1 Reach a junction with the Cave Loop Trail. Keep right on the Slot Canyon Trail.

0.5 Reach a second junction with the Cave Loop Trail, which goes left. Continue straight into the obvious slot canyon.

0.7 Leave the slot canyon.

1.2 Reach a ridgeline above the slot canyon.

1.5 End at a viewpoint on the summit of an unnamed mountain overlooking the national monument (GPS: 35.666027 N / -106.409580 W). Return to the trailhead on the same route.

3.0 Arrive back at the trailhead.

Area Info

BLM Rio Puerco Field Office, 100 Sun Avenue NE, Ste. 330, Albuquerque 87109; (505) 331-6259; www.blm.gov/visit/kktr

Cochiti Visitor Center, 1101 NM 22, Cochiti Pueblo 87072; (505) 465-8535

Bandelier National Monument, 15 Entrance Rd., Los Alamos 87544; (505) 672-3861; www.nps.gov/band

Tetilla Peak Recreation Area, 82 Dam Crest Rd., Pena Blanca 87401; (505) 465-0274

Turquoise Trail National Scenic Byway, NM 14 from Albuquerque to Santa Fe; Turquoise Trail Association, PO Box 303, Sandia Park 87047; (505) 281-5233; www.turquoisetrail.org

21 Cave Loop Trail: Kasha-Katuwe Tent Rocks National Monument

The easy Cave Loop Trail is a scenic hike below towering volcanic cliffs at Kasha-Katuwe Tent Rocks National Monument, a parkland co-managed by the Bureau of Land Management and Cochiti Pueblo north of Albuquerque.

Distance: 1.2-mile loop

Hiking time: About 1 hour

Difficulty: Easy; part of trail is ADA accessible

Best seasons: Spring and fall. Summers are hot. Often closed in winter due to snowfall.

Schedule: Open 8 a.m. to 5 p.m. daily, except for closure dates (Jan 1 and 6; Good Friday; Easter Sunday and following Monday; May 3; July 13, 14, and 25; Nov 1; Thanksgiving Day; Christmas). Gates are closed and locked at 5 p.m.

Other trail users: None

Canine compatibility: No dogs permitted on trail or in park, including in vehicles. Service animals are allowed.

Fees and permits: Fee per vehicle and for groups

Maps: USGS Canada; map available at trailhead and park entrance

Trail contact: BLM Rio Puerco Field Office, 100 Sun Avenue NE, Ste. 330, Albuquerque 87109; (505) 331-6259; www.blm.gov/visit/kktr

Special considerations: Park may be closed by the Pueblo de Cochiti tribal governor. No drinking water at the park. No cross-country hiking; only hike on designated trails. No rock scrambling or climbing off the trail.

Finding the trailhead: From Albuquerque, take I-25 north to exit 259. Turn left (northwest) toward the Santo Domingo / Cochiti Lake Recreation Area and drive northwest for 12.2 miles on NM 22. The road makes a left (southwest) turn to stay on NM 22 and continues 1.7 miles to Tribal Route 92. Turn right (northwest) onto Tribal Route 92 and reach the park entrance after 0.5 mile. From the fee station at the park entrance, drive 4.2 miles to a parking area on the right (north). The trailhead is on the northeast side of the lot. GPS: 35.657748 N / -106.411369 W

The Hike

The 1.2-mile Cave Loop Trail, part of the Tent Rocks National Recreation Trail, makes an easy loop hike in a huge amphitheater lined with towering white cliffs sculpted into flying buttresses, deep gullies, and strangely shaped hoodoos and tent rocks. The Cave Loop Trail is open year-round, except after heavy snow, while the Slot Canyon Trail is usually closed during the winter months. Allow an hour or so to hike the trail. If you hike the Slot Canyon Trail, follow the Cave Loop Trail from the slot entrance back to the parking lot to see all of the monument's natural wonders.

Kasha-Katuwe Tent Rocks National Monument, a parkland co-managed by the Bureau of Land Management (BLM) and the Pueblo of Cochiti, protects a compact

White cliffs, called Kasha-Katuwe in Keresan, loom above the Cave Loop Trail.

area of exposed volcanic cliffs that were deposited by massive eruptions in the Jemez volcanic field between six and seven million years ago. The 1,000-foot layers of ash and debris were compressed into soft tuff and pumice rocks, forming today's sheer cliffs.

The name Kasha-Katuwe, meaning "white cliffs" in the Pueblo language Keresan, was given by early Keresan-speaking people that were descended from the Ancestral Puebloans that first lived in the Four Corners region and later migrated to today's Bandelier National Monument before settling in several pueblos along the Rio Grande, including Cochiti. The pueblo co-manages Kasha-Katuwe Tent Rocks National Monument with the BLM since it lies on tribal land northwest of Cochiti Pueblo in Peralta Canyon on the southwestern edge of the Jemez Mountains. Most of the park rangers are from Cochiti, and the park can be closed at any time by the pueblo's governor. When you're hiking, remember that you are on tribal land, so don't disobey park rules like hiking off-trail or scrambling on the rock formations.

Visitation to the national monument is limited by the number of parking spaces in the parkland. Once the parking lot at the trailhead is filled, no more vehicles and people are allowed into the park until a vehicle departs. On weekends, holidays, and busy summer days, expect a wait of 30 to 90 minutes to enter the monument. It's best to hike on weekdays or to come early to ensure you can grab a parking spot. The gate at the monument's entrance station closes promptly at 5 p.m., so make sure that you hike and exit before closing time. Kasha-Katuwe is a day-use-only area, with a picnic area and restrooms at the trailhead but no camping, fires, or cooking allowed.

Dogs and other pets are banned in the monument. Your dog cannot ride into the park or wait in your vehicle while you hike. Stiff fines from $350 to $1,000 plus possible jail time await those who sneak their pets into the park. Ask at the entrance station or the Cochiti Visitor Center on NM 22 for local dog-sitters and kennels that will shelter your animal while you hike at Tent Rocks.

Start the hike at the trailhead on the northeast side of the parking area on the right side of BLM Road 1011. The first 0.5-mile trail section, shared with the Slot Canyon Trail, runs northeast on rolling slopes west of a dry wash. Walk 80 feet on the paved trail to an information kiosk with educational displays about the monument's geology, plant life, human history, and trails. Pick up a trail brochure here with interpretive details about Kasha-Katuwe.

Continue on a wide dirt trail past a couple of small sculptures of tent rocks and at 0.1 mile reach a Y-junction with the return loop of the Cave Loop Trail. While the trail can be hiked either direction, this description goes counterclockwise. Keep right at the junction signed Cave Loop and Slot Canyon Trail. Continue northeast on the trail, passing through a scrubby woodland of scattered junipers, toward the looming white cliffs and after 0.5 mile reach a junction. Go left on the signed Cave Loop Trail. The Slot Canyon Trail continues straight here up the slot canyon to an overlook atop the cliffs above the junction. If you hike the Slot Canyon Trail and want to return on Cave Loop, take a right here on your descent.

Teepee-shaped rocks line the Cave Loop Trail.

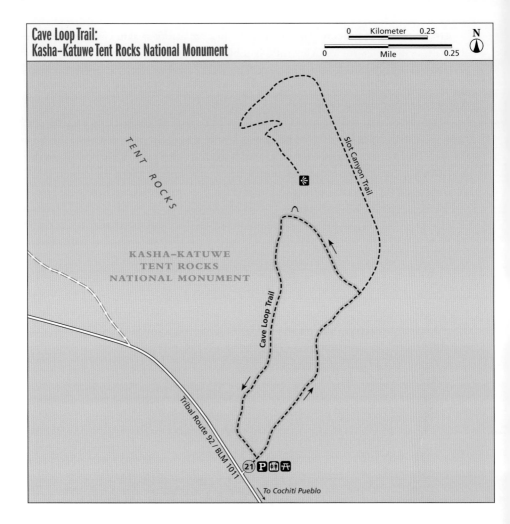

TENT ROCKS

Slot Canyon Trail

KASHA–KATUWE
TENT ROCKS
NATIONAL MONUMENT

Cave Loop Trail

Tribal Route 92 / BLM 1011

21

To Cochiti Pueblo

The next 0.7-mile section of the hike follows the Cave Loop Trail across dry slopes below the tuff cliffs in the amphitheater. The trail dips across shallow washes and rounded hills as it works west. This trail segment offers great views of the monument's iconic tent rock formations. Look across the slopes and cliffs above the trail to see tent-shaped rocks that range from a few feet tall to over 90 feet. Formations that have an erosion-resistant cap perched atop the softer tuff beneath are called hoodoos. Once the caprock topples off a hoodoo by centuries of erosion, wind and water attack the white tuff and sculpt the formation into a tent rock topped with a pointed cone. Erosion, usually quick runoff from heavy summer thunderstorms, shapes the tall cliffs into softly rounded buttresses creased by gullies. Note the thickness of various layers in the cliffs, with each representing a separate volcanic eruption. Geologists estimate about thirty-five eruptions deposited the striated tuff layers.

At 0.6 mile the trail reaches a shallow cave, properly called a cavate, tucked into a cliff face. The cavate was used by early Native Americans and was undoubtedly a warm refuge on cold days when a fire burned brightly inside, leaving soot on the cave roof, and a dry shelter during storms. The cave also offered protection from wild animals and views across the valley of possible enemy incursions. Note also the small size of the cavate entrance. The early inhabitants were shorter than people today, so they easily fit through the door and didn't mind the low ceiling inside the cave. Archaeological surveys indicate that Native peoples have lived in the Kasha-Katuwe area for at least 4,000 years. Later Keresan-speaking people built large pueblos, including today's Cochiti Pueblo and Katishtya, now called San Felipe, as well as abandoned Potrero Viejo to the northwest, over 500 years ago.

After exploring the cave, head down the trail, which bends left and runs south below tall white cliffs. After a mile, descend a hill past a forest of tent and teepee rocks. This a great photo stop, with the tent rocks framing the broad valley to the east. Continue downhill to the end of the loop at 1.1 miles at the first trail junction. Go right on the main trail and return to the trailhead, parking area, and restrooms at 1.2 miles.

Miles and Directions

0.0 Leave the Tent Rocks trailhead at the northeast side of the parking area. Hike on a paved trail northeast past interpretive signs to a wide, packed dirt trail.

0.1 Reach a Y-shaped trail junction and begin the loop portion of the hike. Keep right (northeast) on the marked Cave Loop and Slot Canyon Trails. The trail on the left is the return trail.

0.5 Reach a trail junction below cliffs at the entrance to the slot canyon. Turn left (northwest) on the Cave Loop Trail. The trail to the right (northeast) is the Slot Canyon Trail.

0.6 Reach the shelter cave on the right (north) side of the trail.

1.0 Descend a steep hill to a cluster of pointed tent rocks.

1.1 The loop portion of the hike ends. Turn right (southwest) and return to the trailhead.

1.2 Arrive back at the trailhead.

Area Info

Cochiti Visitor Center, 1101 NM 22, Cochiti Pueblo 87072; (505) 465-8535

Bandelier National Monument, 15 Entrance Rd., Los Alamos 87544; (505) 672-3861; www.nps.gov/band

Turquoise Trail National Scenic Byway, NM 14 from Albuquerque to Santa Fe; Turquoise Trail Association, PO Box 303, Sandia Park 87047; (505) 281-5233; www.turquoisetrail.org

Tetilla Peak Recreation Area, 82 Dam Crest Rd., Pena Blanca 87401; (505) 465-0274

22 Cerrillos Hills State Park Trails

This scenic 4.8-mile loop hike in Cerrillos Hills State Park northeast of Albuquerque explores arid volcanic hills and shallow valleys that were mined for silver, iron, and lead in an 1880s boom.

Distance: 4.8-mile loop
Hiking time: About 3 hours
Difficulty: Moderate
Best seasons: Year-round. Winter days are mild and warm.
Schedule: Open daily sunrise to 9 p.m. Visitor center open 2 to 4 p.m. daily.
Other trail users: Mountain bikers and horseback riders
Canine compatibility: Leashed dogs allowed

Fees and permits: Fee per vehicle
Maps: USGS Picture Rock and Madrid; trail map available at trailhead park office and park visitor center
Trail contact: Cerrillos Hills State Park, 37 Main St., Cerrillos 87010; (505) 474-0196; www.emnrd.state.nm.us/SPD/cerrilloshillsstatepark
Special considerations: Watch for rattlesnakes on the trails.

Finding the trailhead: From Albuquerque, take I-40 east to exit 175 toward NM 14 / Cedar Crest. Drive 31.9 miles on NM 14 to the turnoff for Cerrillos. Turn left (west) onto Main Street and drive 0.3 mile. Turn right (north) onto First Street and drive 0.6 mile to a fork in the road. Stay right at the fork onto CR 59 / Camino Turquesa. Continue for another mile on CR 59 to the Cerrillos Hills State Park entrance and a parking area on the left. GPS: 35.444802 N / -106.122389 W

The Hike

By linking several trails in Cerrillos Hills State Park, hikers can enjoy a 4.8-mile loop hike through rolling hills that were volcanoes almost thirty million years ago. Precious metals, including iron, lead, and silver, were deposited during volcanic periods. Native American and Spanish settlers later came and mined the area, during a brief mining boom in the 1880s. This hike visits several of the old mining claims and gives clues to the area's interesting human history. Read the many interpretive signs along the trails to learn more about mining in the Cerrillos Hills.

The park's high-desert ecosystem includes native grasses, diverse wildflowers, one-seed juniper, piñon pine, yucca, and several cactus species. Large mammals like mountain lions, bobcats, coyotes, and foxes roam across the hills, so look for tracks and scat along the trails. Tarantulas also call the area home and are most likely to be spotted in early fall.

Cerrillos Hills State Park became a state park in 2009 but was originally created by Santa Fe County in 2003 as Santa Fe County Cerrillos Hills Historic Park. The 1,116-acre park offers ten trails with 5 miles of hiking through dry hills and valleys. Before your hike, stop at the park visitor center in the town of Cerrillos south of the park for interpretive displays, trail maps, and ranger advice.

The Jane Calvin Sanchez Trail, the first mile-long leg of the hike, begins on the east side of the park entrance road, Camino Turquesa (CR 59). Follow the wide dirt path east and then north, climbing uphill past scattered junipers, yuccas, and cacti. At 0.4 mile the trail reaches the Christian Lode Historical Mine, then continues northwest to the Amsterdam Rotterdam Historical Mine at 0.6 mile. After 0.8 mile reach a Y-junction and turn left (west) on the JC Sanchez Trail. Reach Mineral Spring at 1.1 miles and continue southwest across Camino Turquesa.

The second leg of the hike, the Escalante Trail, begins on the opposite side of the road. This portion of the hike has steep grades, and hikers will be grateful to find two rest benches, at 1.2 miles and at 1.3 miles. After the second bench the trail curves sharply to the northeast. Reach an intersection with the Elkins Canyon Trail at 1.5 miles and continue north on the Escalante Trail.

The hike in Cerrillos Hills State Park passes through a piñon pine and juniper woodland.
EMILY RESSLER-TANNER

The junction with the Coyote Trail on the left is at 1.6 miles. Stay on the Escalante Trail and continue hiking north. The Escalante Trail intersects the Cortez Mine Trail after a short distance and continues north, then reaches another junction at 1.7 miles and again continues north. The trail bends to the left (southwest) at 1.9 miles near the park's northern boundary and becomes the Mirador Trail.

Take a right turn at 2.1 miles on a spur trail that leads to one of the best viewpoints in the park. The overlook offers breathtaking views of Mount Taylor, the Sandia Mountains, the Ortiz Mountains, Redondo Peak, the Jemez Mountains, and the southern end of the Sangre de Cristo Mountains. The 0.25-mile round-trip hike is worth the effort. After enjoying the views, return to the Mirador Trail at 2.4 miles.

GREEN TIP
Stay on established trails to avoid damaging vegetation and creating new social trails. Try to stay on durable surfaces that will be least affected by your passage, like rock, gravel, dry grasses, or snow.

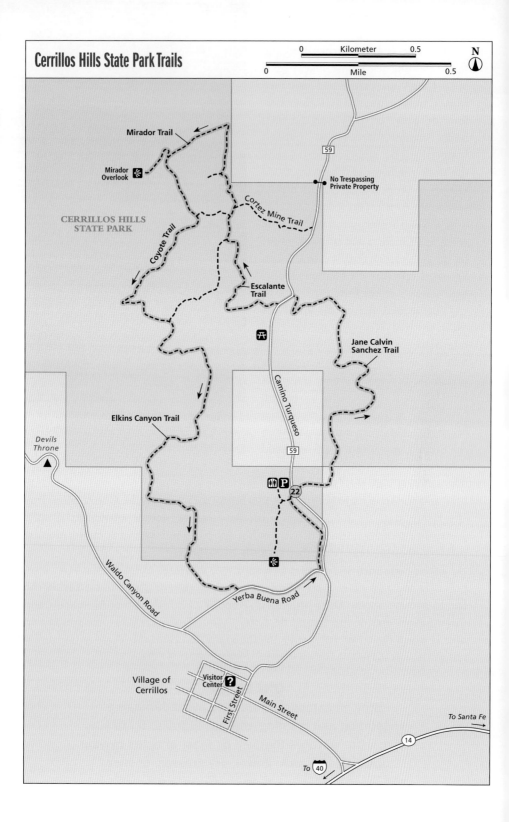

Cerrillos Hills State Park Trails

0 Kilometer 0.5

0 Mile 0.5

N

Mirador Trail

Mirador Overlook

No Trespassing Private Property

CERRILLOS HILLS STATE PARK

Cortez Mine Trail

Coyote Trail

Escalante Trail

Jane Calvin Sanchez Trail

Elkins Canyon Trail

Camino Turqueso

Devils Throne

Waldo Canyon Road

Yerba Buena Road

Village of Cerrillos

Visitor Center

First Street

Main Street

To Santa Fe

To 40

TARANTULAS

Tarantulas—large, hairy spiders—are incredibly fascinating creatures. During mating season in September and October, male tarantulas roam across the desert in search of a mate. While appearing creepy, tarantulas are relatively harmless. They may bite if handled, but their venom is weak and not likely to cause damage to humans.

Although some people claim that tarantulas eat birds and lizards, their main source of food are smaller insects. Tarantulas have a surprisingly long life expectancy, with females living to twenty years of age. Regardless of your fears of spiders, please treat tarantulas with respect, as they are an important part of this desert ecosystem.

The trail bends south here and reaches another old mine at 2.5 miles. Walk the footbridge over the top for a look into the depths of the mine. Be respectful of the historic site and don't throw anything into the open shaft. After 2.6 miles the Mirador Trail ends at an intersection with the Coyote Trail. Turn right (south) and follow the Coyote Trail past more historic mines and signs that interpret the area's colorful history.

After 0.5 mile of hiking, the trail ends at its junction with the Elkins Canyon Trail at 3.1 miles. Turn right (south) onto this trail and head south for a mile to short, narrow Elkins Canyon. Hike down the canyon and reach Yerba Buena Road at 4.3 miles. At this point the trail follows the road east for a short distance.

The last hike segment heads east for 0.2 mile on the road to an obvious dry wash next to Camino Turquesa, the park entrance road. Turn north and hike up the arroyo for 0.25 mile to the trailhead and parking lot after your 4.8-mile hike.

Miles and Directions

0.0 Begin at the trailhead on Camino Turquesa (GPS: 35.444802 N / -106.122389 W). Hike east on the Jane Calvin Sanchez Trail.

0.4 Reach the Christian Lode Historical Mine and continue northwest.

0.6 Reach the Amsterdam Rotterdam Historical Mine.

0.8 Reach a Y-junction (GPS: 35.451875 N / -106.120072 W) and turn left (west).

1.1 Reach Mineral Spring and Camino Turquesa (GPS: 35.451875 N / -106.120072 W). Go left and walk down the shoulder of Camino Turquesa to the Escalante Trail on the right (GPS: 35.451875 N / -106.120072 W).

1.2 Reach a rest bench.

1.3 Reach a second rest bench.

1.5 Reach a junction with the Elkins Canyon Trail (GPS: 35.454660 N / -106.125752 W). Go right and continue north on the Escalante Trail.

1.6 Reach a junction with the Coyote Trail (GPS: 35.455456 N / -106.125509 W). Continue north on the Escalante Trail.

1.7 Reach a junction with the Cortez Mine Trail (GPS: 35.455708 N / -106.125401 W). Continue north on the Escalante Trail.

1.9 Reach a junction with the Mirador Trail (GPS: 35.458966 N / -106.125591 W), an old road, near the park's northern boundary. Go left on the Mirador Trail.

2.1 Reach a junction with a spur trail to Mirador Overlook (GPS: 35.457750 N / -106.12842 W). Turn right on the spur trail to the overlook.

2.2 Reach Mirador Overlook (GPS: 35.457260 N / -106.129614 W). Return to the Mirador Trail.

2.4 Turn right and go south on the Mirador Trail.

2.5 Reach a Y-junction (GPS: 35.457398 N / -106.128519 W). Leave the old road and go left on the singletrack Mirador Trail.

2.6 Reach a junction and the end of the Mirador Trail (GPS: 35.455509 N / -106.127070 W). Keep right and hike south on the Coyote Trail.

3.1 Reach a Y-junction with the Elkins Canyon Trail (GPS: 35.451442 N / -106.128371 W) and the end of the Coyote Trail. Go right (south) on the Elkins Canyon Trail.

4.3 Reach Yerba Buena Road (GPS: 35.440689 N / -106.125897 W). Turn left (east) and walk beside the road.

4.5 Turn left (north) on a trail up an arroyo just before Camino Turquesa. Hike north up the arroyo.

4.8 Arrive back at the trailhead.

Area Info

Turquoise Trail National Scenic Byway, NM 14 from Albuquerque to Santa Fe; Turquoise Trail Association, PO Box 303, Sandia Park 87047; (505) 281-5233; www.turquoisetrail.org

GREEN TIP
If you're toting food, leave the packaging at home. Repack your provisions in self-locking bags that you can reuse and can double as garbage bags on your way home.

23 Sandia Cave Trail: Cibola National Forest

This short hike takes you to Sandia Cave, a controversial archaeological site that contained artifacts from some of the first people to inhabit North America between 9,000 and 11,000 years ago.

Distance: 1.0 mile out and back
Hiking time: About 1 hour
Difficulty: Moderate
Best seasons: Spring, summer, and fall
Schedule: Open year-round
Other trail users: None
Canine compatibility: Leashed dogs allowed
Fees and permits: None

Maps: USGS Placitas; trail map available at Sandia Ranger District and on website
Trail contact: Sandia Ranger District, 11776 NM 337, Tijeras 87059; (505) 281-3304; www.fs.usda.gov/cibola
Special considerations: NM 165 may be snowy, icy, and impassable in winter.

Finding the trailhead: From Albuquerque, take I-25 north to exit 242 toward NM 165E/ Placitas. Turn right (east) on NM 165 and drive 9.2 miles until the pavement ends. Continue another 2.5 miles on the gravel road to the Sandia Man Cave parking area on the left (east). GPS: 35.250269 N / -106.409882 W

The Hike

The Sandia Cave Trail (#72) climbs a half-mile to Sandia Cave, a grotto tucked into a limestone cliff on the eastern side of Las Huertas Canyon in the northern Sandia Mountains. The narrow, 381-foot-long cave, 4 miles east of Placitas, provided controversial evidence of early Native Americans that roamed New Mexico over 9,000 years ago. While the trail is easy to hike, it's not wheelchair accessible, with a concrete staircase, a fenced walkway along an exposed ledge, and finally a 12-foot staircase that spirals up to a metal platform at the cave entrance on the cliff face.

Although open year-round, the trail is best hiked from May through October since NM 165 becomes impassable in winter after heavy snow and in mud season when the snow melts. Cibola National Forest warns that when there is snow, driving a four-wheel-drive vehicle is not a guarantee to get in and out of the area. Four-wheel-drive vehicles have been known to get stranded and abandoned for a season after getting stuck in snow or mud.

Sandia Cave was initially explored in 1925 by a troop of Boy Scouts that dug in the dusty entrance but found only rocks. In 1936 Kenneth Davis, a University of New Mexico graduate student, visited the cave and sifted through the top layer of fine dust, uncovering a piece of antler, pottery shards, part of a coiled basket, and a projectile point. He put the objects in a cigar box and took them to university professor Frank Cummings Hibben, who promptly made plans to excavate the cave.

Hibben organized a crew of diggers, mostly archaeology students, and began the arduous excavation of the cave. The cave sloped downward and was some 10 feet wide and filled with dust and fallen rocks, which completely blocked the passage in places. The diggers labored with lanterns, trowels, shovels, and picks, slowly moving debris and breathing dust. Hibben was almost ready to give up the search until a chance discovery was made about 300 feet into the passageway.

One of the diggers found an unusual bone and brought it out of the cave. Hibben later described the fragment: "The object was . . . a piece of bone, but certain it was no ordinary bone from an ordinary animal. . . . It was the bony core of the claw of a giant ground sloth, which has been extinct these last 10,000 years."

Hibben's team excavated the cave between 1937 and 1941, uncovering a trove of bones and artifacts, including not only giant sloths but other Pleistocene mammals like mastodons and woolly mammoths as well as stone scrapers, bits of moccasins woven from yucca, and nineteen distinctive Sandia spear points, a slope-shouldered projectile point hafted onto a spear that was probably used to hunt ice age megafauna.

Beneath the surface, Hibben found a layer containing animal bones and artifacts from about 10,000 years ago that he believed belonged to a group of early hunter-gatherers called the Folsom culture, first found near Folsom, New Mexico, in 1926. In another deeper layer, Hibben discovered the remnants of an older unknown culture that he theorized was at least 25,000 years old. He dubbed these ancient big-game hunters the Sandia Cave people. The discovery cemented Hibben's reputation as an archaeologist, which was boosted when *Time* magazine wrote an article in 1940 about the Sandia Cave excavation and the ancient people believed to be the first Americans.

After Hibben hailed the Sandia Cave people as the oldest culture in the New World, other archaeologists began looking closely at the excavation, including radiocarbon dates that fluctuated from 15,000 to 33,000 years ago and spear points that appeared to be worked with modern tools. There were also problems with the stratigraphy, or layers, at the site, which include a layer of yellow ocher accurately dated to 300,000 years ago that lies above the much younger Sandia points. The Sandia projectile points are problematic for many archaeologists since there's a lack of broken points at the site; the points don't exhibit wear or weathering; some were made by percussion flaking and others by pressure flaking; and the points are found in only one other place, the Lucy Site in New Mexico.

GREEN TIP

For rest stops, step off-trail so others won't have to get around you. Head for hard surfaces like rock outcrops, bedrock, and boulders without vegetation.

The Sandia Cave Trail offers views past cliffs of Las Huertas Canyon.
EMILY RESSLER-TANNER

So many scientific inconsistencies have arisen since the initial excavation that many archaeologists now call Sandia Cave the most controversial early human site ever excavated in North America, while others say that the site is an outright hoax and fraud perpetuated by Frank Hibben, who planted the spear points and used charcoal samples from other sites for dating. The truth about Sandia Cave will never be known, since Hibben died in 2002.

Begin the hike from the parking lot and trailhead at 7,040 feet on the east side of NM 165, a dirt road that climbs Las Huertas Canyon to the Sandia Crest on the north slope of the Sandia Mountains. The marked dirt trail heads north, climbing slowly as it contours along the east side of the steep-walled canyon. Look north down the canyon to the distant Rio Grande Valley. The trail reaches the first of two sets of stone steps after 0.4 mile. At 0.5 mile the narrow trail, perched above a limestone cliff, arrives at the final obstacle, a metal spiral staircase that climbs a dozen feet to the entrance to Sandia Man Cave, a National Historic Landmark.

Your initial impression of the historic cave will likely be disappointing, since previous visitors have vandalized the inner walls with spray-painted graffiti and littered

MASTODONS AND MAMMOTHS

Mastodons and mammoths were huge North American mammals that once roamed fertile lands in New Mexico. Both extinct animals resembled modern elephants but were not closely related. While they wandered the earth over 10,000 years ago at the end of the last ice age, mammoths arose about 5.1 million years ago in Africa before expanding their range to Eurasia and North America. The woolly mammoth evolved about 250,000 years ago. Mammoths became extinct about 10,000 years ago, although a small population of dwarf mammoths continued to live on Wrangel Island off Siberia until 3,700 years ago. Mastodons, an older mammoth cousin, arose over 27 million years ago, living primarily in North and Central America before becoming extinct roughly 10,000 years ago.

While some people believe that widespread big-game hunting by early humans led to the extinction of both species, most scientists point to climate change and loss of habitat as the reason they vanished. Both species were between 7 and 14 feet tall, although mastodons were generally smaller than mammoths, and both had long tusks and the hallmark shaggy fur coats that enabled them to thrive in cold climates. The biggest difference between the two species is their teeth. Mastodons had cone-shaped cusps on their molars to pulverize vegetation like branches and leaves, while mammoths had corrugated molars like elephants, allowing them to munch about 400 pounds of grass and vegetation daily.

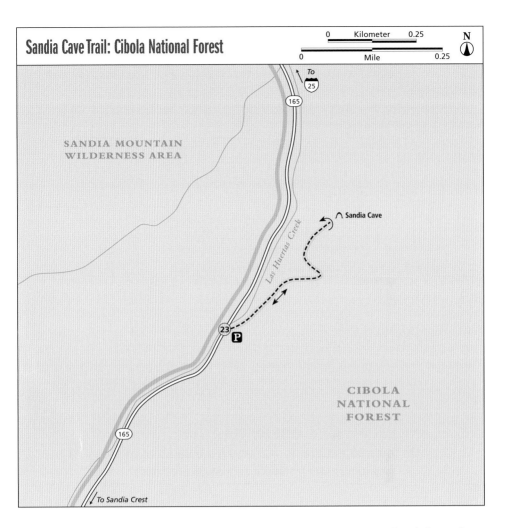

0   Kilometer   0.25

0   Mile   0.25

N

SANDIA MOUNTAIN
WILDERNESS AREA

To
25

165

Las Huertas Creek

⌂ Sandia Cave

23

P

CIBOLA
NATIONAL
FOREST

165

To Sandia Crest

the floor with trash. The cave entrance is also blackened from illegal fires. If you brought a trash bag, pick up whatever you can to tote back to the trailhead for proper disposal. The Sandia Grotto caving club, an Albuquerque chapter of the National Speleological Society, has been caretaker of the cave for several decades. Hats off to the club for removing most of the graffiti in 2014 and 2015 from the first two chambers in the cave.

Sitting in the entrance, imagine this dusty cave when it sheltered early Native Americans who hunted game and gathered edible plants in the Sandia Mountains. It's possible to explore farther into the cave at your own risk but bring multiple headlamps or flashlights and extra batteries. If you venture past the first 40 feet of the cave, bring caving equipment, including a helmet, three sources of light, kneepads, sturdy clothes, gloves, and a dust mask. The cave is extremely dry and dusty, and any movement stirs clouds of fine dust. Hikers with respiratory problems should not enter the cave. Most of Sandia Cave is explored on your hands and feet, since there are only a few spots where a spelunker can stand upright. Lastly, respect the archaeological significance of Sandia Cave and remember that it is culturally important to nearby Pueblo people.

After exploring the cave entrance, descend the staircase and hike back to the trailhead for a 1-mile round-trip hike.

Miles and Directions

0.0 Begin at the trailhead at the northeast corner of the parking area on NM 165 (GPS: 35.250269 N / -106.409882 W). Hike northeast on the dirt trail.

0.4 Reach the first set of stone steps. Continue north on the trail above a cliff.

0.5 Arrive at a spiral staircase. Climb 12 feet to the Sandia Man Cave entrance (GPS: 35.254706 N / -106.405679 W). Return to the parking area on the same trail.

1.0 Arrive back at the Sandia Man Cave trailhead and parking area.

Area Info

Santa Ana Pueblo, 2 Dove Rd., Bernalillo 87004; (505) 867–3301; www.santaana .org

Turquoise Trail National Scenic Byway, NM 14 from Albuquerque to Santa Fe; Turquoise Trail Association, PO Box 303, Sandia Park 87047; (505) 281–5233; www .turquoisetrail.org

GREEN TIP
On the trail eat grains and veggies instead of meat products, which have a higher energy cost.

Sandia Mountains

Looking south across the Sandias to the cloud-shrouded Manzano Mountains.
EMILY RESSLER–TANNER

24 Boundary Loop Trail: Cibola National Forest

The Boundary Loop Trail, a combo hike formed by the East Jaral Canyon Trail and the West Jaral Canyon Trail, explores arid Jaral Canyon in the Sandia foothills on the northeast side of Albuquerque. Expect fine views, few hikers, and plenty of sunshine during the cool months.

Distance: 2.6-mile lollipop
Hiking time: About 2 hours
Difficulty: Easy
Best seasons: Late fall through early spring. Summer days are hot.
Schedule: Trail open year-round
Other trail users: Mountain bikers
Canine compatibility: Leashed dogs allowed

Fees and permits: Day use / parking fee
Map: USGS Alameda
Trail contact: Sandia Ranger District, 11776 NM 337, Tijeras 87059; (505) 281-3304; www.fs.usda.gov/cibola
Special considerations: No shade or water along the trail. Carry water and sports drinks and wear a hat and sunscreen.

Finding the trailhead: From Albuquerque, take I-25 north to exit 234 toward NM 556 / Tramway Road. Turn right (east) onto NM 556 / Tramway Road and drive 4 miles to FR 333. Turn left (north) onto FR 333 and drive 0.2 mile to a fee station and parking area on the right (southeast) side of the road (GPS: 35.202524 N / -106.504096 W). The trailhead is on the opposite (northwest) side of FR 33 from the parking lot. Cross the road to the trailhead. GPS: 35.202784 N / -106.503945 W

The Hike

The Boundary Loop Trail is a fun and easy day hike in the western foothills of the Sandia Mountains on the northeast side of Albuquerque. The trail traverses a rough, arid landscape of steep, rocky slopes and scattered piñon pines, junipers, desert grasses, and cacti including cane cholla and prickly pear. The trail, following the East Jaral Canyon Trail (#204) and West Jaral Canyon Trail (#3A), lies outside the Sandia Mountain Wilderness Area, so mountain bikes are allowed on the trails. The hike passes many junctions with social trails, so follow the main trail to stay on course.

The best hiking seasons are spring and fall, although winter days are usually warm and sunny. Summers are hot and dry, with almost no shade found along the trail. Plan to hike early in the morning or in the evening to avoid summer heat. Also, wear a hat, use sunscreen, and carry plenty of beverages to stay hydrated.

Start the Boundary Loop Trail from the parking area on the right side of FR 333 just past the second cattle guard and national forest fee station. Cross the paved road to the trailhead on the north side of the road. Head up the marked rocky trail and reach a junction with a trail on the right after 425 feet. Keep straight and reach a ridge after 0.1 mile. Cross the blunt ridge and follow the mostly level trail to the right, contouring across a wooded slope into East Jaral Canyon. After 0.3 mile reach a Y-junction and the start of the hike's loop segment. Keep right on the East Jaral Canyon Trail. The left trail is the return West Jaral Canyon Trail. Continue hiking on slopes above the dry wash and at 0.35 mile descend into the wash.

Hike north up the wide, stony wash and after a couple bends, reach a dry waterfall over broken rocks at 0.55 mile. Scramble over boulders past the feature and continue north up the shallow canyon floor. Follow the sandy streambed up Jaral Canyon and near the head of the canyon, begin climbing north up the twisting canyon to bare slopes that lead to a viewpoint and trail junction at 1.4 miles on a high ridgeline at the top of the canyon. The deep slice of Juan Tabo Canyon stretches north below the overlook.

The return loop begins atop the ridge. Turn sharply southwest on the trail and follow the ridgeline for 0.2 mile to a five-way trail junction at a rounded saddle between two low peaks. Turn left at the saddle and hike south on the West Jaral Canyon Trail. The other trails follow nearby ridges and one drops west into Juan Tabo Canyon. The left fork follows a ridge that separates East and West Jaral Canyons. The preferred trail is the middle one, which descends into West Jaral Canyon.

Looking up East Jaral Canyon on the Boundary Loop Trail. EMILY RESSLER-TANNER

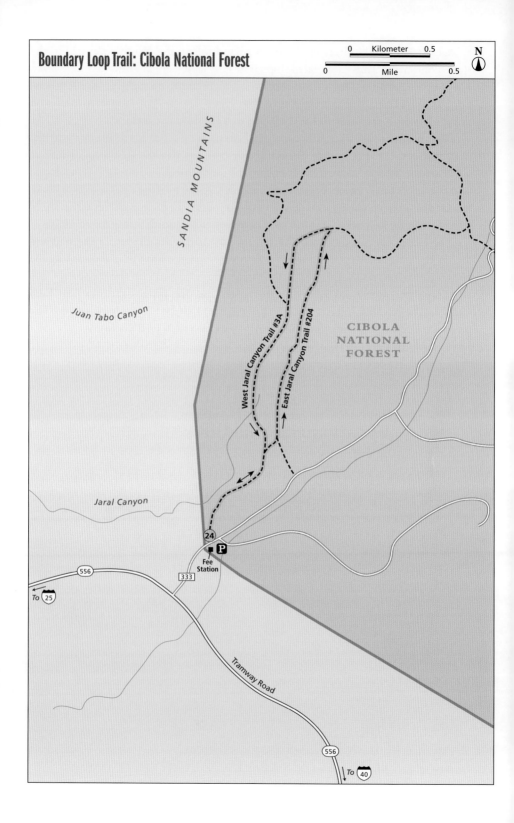

SANDIA MOUNTAINS

Juan Tabo Canyon

West Jaral Canyon Trail #3A

East Jaral Canyon Trail #204

CIBOLA
NATIONAL
FOREST

Jaral Canyon

24

P

Fee
Station

556

To 25

333

Tramway Road

556

To 40

Follow the trail down the canyon, twisting down the rocky arroyo and crossing open slopes above the floor. Keep right at the junction at 1.8 miles and continue south down the West Jaral Canyon Trail to another junction at 2.2 miles. Stay right here and descend to the bottom of East Jaral Canyon. Scramble up the opposite side of the canyon to the junction with the East Jaral Canyon Trail and the end of the loop section at 2.3 miles. Go right on the trail and return to the trailhead and parking lot for a 2.6-mile round-trip hike.

Miles and Directions

0.0 From the fee station and parking area on FR 333, cross the road to an obvious trail that climbs north up a rocky slope.

0.1 Reach the top of the rocky slope and follow the trail as it bends right (east).

0.3 Reach a Y-junction and start the hike's loop portion. Keep right on the east fork as the trail dips down into East Jaral Canyon and then heads north up the arroyo.

0.55 Reach a rocky waterfall-like section of the arroyo—an indicator you are on the right trail.

1.4 Hike out of the canyon onto a ridge that overlooks Juan Tabo Canyon (GPS: 35.217508, -106.497347 W). The trail bends sharply left (west) here and follows a broad ridge to the southwest.

1.6 Reach a saddle on the ridge. Turn left (south).

1.8 Reach a Y-junction. Stay right (south) on the West Jaral Canyon Trail.

2.2 The trail splits in three directions. All trails lead into East Jaral Canyon. Follow the trail to the right (westernmost) and drop into the canyon.

2.3 The loop portion of the trail ends at the East Jaral Canyon Trail. Go right.

2.6 Arrive back at the trailhead and parking area on FR 333.

Area Info

Elena Gallegos Open Space, 7100 Tramway Blvd. NE, Albuquerque 87122; (505) 768-5353; www.cabq.gov/openspace/elenagallegos.html

Sandia Peak Tramway and Ski Area, 30 Tramway Rd. NE, Albuquerque 87122; (505) 856-1532; www.sandiapeak.com

GREEN TIP

When you just have to use the toilet in an emergency situation, dig a hole 6 to 8 inches deep and at least 200 feet from all water sources, campsites, and trails. Bring a reclosable bag to carry out used toilet paper or use a natural substitute such as leaves, but not poison ivy! Don't burn the toilet paper—you don't want to start a forest fire. Fill in the cat hole with soil and other natural materials when you're done with business.

25 Tramway Trail: Cibola National Forest

The popular Tramway Trail begins near the Lower Tram Terminal and is often used as an access to La Luz Trail. Because of its lower elevation, it is a great choice for a winter hike when other Sandia trails are icy or snow-packed.

Distance: 5.2 miles out and back
Hiking time: About 3 hours
Difficulty: Moderate
Best seasons: Spring and fall
Schedule: Open year-round
Other trail users: None
Canine compatibility: Leashed dogs allowed
Fees and permits: Day use / parking fee

Maps: USGS Sandia Crest; trail map available at Sandia Ranger District
Trail contact: Sandia Ranger District, 11776 NM 337, Tijeras 87059; (505) 281-3304; www.fs.usda.gov/cibola
Special considerations: Hike early or late in the day during summer and carry plenty of water.

Finding the trailhead: From Albuquerque, take I-25 north to exit 234 toward NM 556 / Tramway Road. Turn right (east) onto NM 556 / Tramway Road and drive 4.9 miles, then turn left (east) to stay on Tramway Road NE. Drive 1 mile to the Tramway fee station and continue 0.1 mile to the parking area after paying the entrance fee. GPS: 35.191818 N / 106.479175 W

The Hike

The Tramway Trail (#82) is a popular hike that skirts the western base of the Sandia Mountains between a trailhead at the Sandia Peak Aerial Tramway and the La Luz Trail (#187) above the Juan Cabo Trailhead and Picnic Area to the north. The 2.6-mile-long trail connects the trailheads and is often used by hikers who ride the tramway to an observation deck at 10,378 feet on the crest of the Sandias and then hike down the La Luz Trail for a 10.3-mile loop hike or do it in reverse and ride the tram down the mountain.

The 5.2-mile round-trip hike on the Tramway Trail makes a fun half-day outing, passing suburban developments, dipping across shallow canyons, and passing many granite boulders. Get an early start during the warmer months, since the low-elevation trail receives plenty of sun, especially in the afternoon, and little shade is found. Bring water, use sunscreen, and wear a hat for sun protection. The shoulder months in spring and autumn offer ideal hiking conditions, with pleasant temperatures and usually calm weather.

Start the hike at the Tramway Trailhead on the north end of the parking lot for the Sandia Peak Aerial Tramway at the end of Tramway Road NE. The Tramway Trail passes a giant granite boulder on the left and then bends north across boulder-strewn slopes at the base of the Sandia Mountains. A development of large houses spreads across the bench west of the trail. After 0.05 mile the trail crosses into the Sandia

Mountain Wilderness Area and Cibola National Forest. Keep an eye on the trail and stay on the main path, since occasional social side trails head off the trail.

The trail dips and rolls across scrubby mountainsides covered with wild grasses, wildflowers, and various cacti including cane cholla and prickly pear cactus. A pygmy forest of piñon pines, junipers, and Gambel oaks scatters across the open slopes covered with boulders. After 0.6 mile the trail reaches the southern edge of a shallow rocky canyon and heads northeast across a terrace before dipping across a dry creek bed after 0.8 mile. Climb away from the stony wash onto a grassy terrace and after 0.9 mile reach a junction with the Rozamiento Trail on the left. Continue straight on the Tramway Trail. The Rozamiento Trail heads west for 0.1 mile to a dry wash and the ruins of Jaral Cabin, an old ranger cabin.

The hike continues north across a bench below steep slopes covered with jumbled boulders and small cliffs before dipping down to another trail junction at 1.5 miles. To reach an alternate trailhead and the historic La Cueva Picnic Grounds, hike west on this spur trail for 0.3 mile to La Cueva Road. The buildings at the picnic area were built by the Civilian Conservation Corps (CCC) in the 1930s. Past the junction, the Tramway Trail bends right and reaches another dry wash below Cañon la Cueva.

Fresh snow adorns shrubs and grass along the Tramway Trail. EMILY RESSLER-TANNER

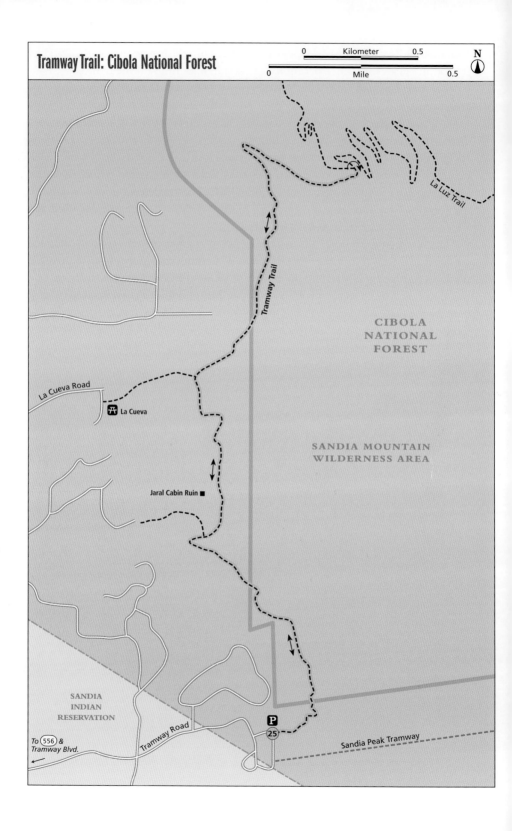

Cross the wash and begin traversing across rough slopes above another plush sub-urban development. After 2.3 miles reach the crest of a ridge above a deep canyon. The trail bends sharply right here and contours across a steep wooded slope to the bottom of the canyon and the junction of the Tramway and La Luz Trails at 2.6 miles. Cool down under a shady tree and catch your breath before following the Tramway Trail back south to the Tramway Trailhead for a 5.2-mile round-trip hike.

Alternatively, go left and descend for 0.9 mile to the La Luz Trailhead at the Juan Tabo Picnic Grounds or head right and climb the classic La Luz Trail for 5.7 miles to the Sandia Crest, the lofty summit of the mountain range. A 1.2-mile trail goes south from the crest to the top of the tramway and a quick ride in a gondola car down to the Tramway Trailhead and parking lot.

Miles and Directions

0.0 From the Tramway Trailhead at the north end of the parking lot for the Sandia Peak Aerial Tramway, hike north on the obvious Tramway Trail, crossing into the Sandia Mountain Wilderness Area.

0.8 Reach a junction with a spur trail. Continue north on the Tramway Trail.

0.9 Reach the junction with the Rozamiento Trail (GPS: 35.199817 N / -106.482433 W). Continue north on the Tramway Trail.

1.5 Reach a junction with a spur trail that goes west for 0.3 mile to La Cueva picnic area (GPS: 35.205592 N / -106.483448 W). Continue north on the Tramway Trail.

2.3 Reach the top of a ridge (GPS: 35.214407 N / -106.480697 W).

2.6 Reach the junction with the La Luz Trail (GPS: 35.213623 N / -106.475444 W). Return to the trailhead via the same route.

5.2 Arrive back at the Tramway Trailhead.

Area Info

Sandia Peak Tramway and Ski Area, 30 Tramway Rd. NE, Albuquerque 87122; (505) 856-1532; www.sandiapeak.com

GREEN TIP
Carry a reusable water container that you can fill at the tap. Bottled water is expensive, petroleum is used to make the plastic bottles, and they're a disposal nightmare.

26 Domingo Baca Trail: Cibola National Forest

The 2.4-mile Domingo Baca Trail climbs Cañon de Domingo Baca to a turn-around point below the site of a 1955 TWA plane crash. This 4.8-mile out-and-back hike begins at Elena Gallegos Open Space Park and ascends into a rugged, cliff-lined canyon on the western flank of the Sandia Mountains.

Distance: 4.8 miles out and back
Hiking time: 4 to 5 hours
Difficulty: Strenuous, with rocky terrain and route-finding
Best seasons: Spring and fall
Schedule: Open daily 7 a.m. to 9 p.m. Apr through Oct, 7 a.m. to 7 p.m. Nov through Mar
Other trail users: None
Canine compatibility: Leashed dogs allowed

Fees and permits: Day use / parking fee
Maps: USGS Sandia Crest; trail map available at Sandia Ranger District
Trail contact: Sandia Ranger District, 11776 NM 337, Tijeras 87059; (505) 281-3304; www.fs.usda.gov / cibola
Special considerations: Elena Gallegos Open Space Park may close in winter due to bad weather.

Finding the trailhead: From Albuquerque, take I-25 north to exit 232 toward NM 423 / Paseo del Norte. After exiting, turn right (east) and drive 4.8 miles to NM 556E / Tramway Boulevard NE. Turn right (south) on NM 556E / Tramway Boulevard NE and drive 1.2 miles to Simms Park Road NE. Turn left (east) on Simms Park Road NE and continue 1.4 miles to the Elena Gallegos Open Space fee station. Circle left around the fee station, following signs for the Cottonwood Springs Trailhead, and drive north for 0.3 mile to the parking area and trailhead. GPS: 35.165948 N / -106.473136 W

The Hike

The Domingo Baca Trail is a 4.8-mile out-and-back hike up steep and remote Cañon de Domingo Baca on the west flank of the Sandia Mountains above Albuquerque. The trail climbs from the Cottonwood Springs Trailhead at Elena Gallegos Open Space up the canyon until it divides. It then continues up the left fork to a turn-around point, while an Extra Credit Hike follows another unmaintained trail that scrambles up the rugged right fork for another 1.1 miles to the site of a TWA plane crash in 1955. The strenuous hike gains over 900 feet from the trailhead to trail's end, while the hike to the higher crash site is extremely strenuous, gaining 2,330 feet in 3.5 miles and requiring route-finding and rock-scrambling skills. The hike offers plenty of solitude, water in the upper canyon from perennial springs, and plenty of wildlife.

With pleasant temperatures, spring and fall are the best seasons to do the hike, especially if you plan to do the Extra Credit Hike to the crash site. Summers are also fine but expect hot temperatures in the lower elevations. The upper trail section is

Ruins of a stone cabin on the Domingo Baca Trail. EMILY RESSLER-TANNER

shaded by a canopy of trees along the creek. Winter isn't the ideal time to do the hike, since snowy and icy sections may be found. Don't plan on hiking to the crash site in winter with its short days.

The hike begins in the 640-acre Elena Gallegos Open Space, an Albuquerque-owned natural area that includes the Elena Gallegos Picnic Area and Albert G. Simms Park. The parkland has an extensive trail network that includes two trails, Domingo Baca and the Pino Trail (Hike 27), that access the Sandia Mountain Wilderness Area in Cibola National Forest. Most of the open space trails, except for Pino and the Cottonwood Springs Trail, are open to hikers, mountain bikers, and equestrians. The Domingo Baca Trail in the wilderness area is open only to hikers.

A minimal parking and day-use fee is charged to enter the open space. It's important to time your hike within the hours that the open space land is open so that your vehicle is not locked inside the gate at closing time. Restrooms are at the Cotton-wood Springs Trailhead and at the Elena Gallegos Picnic Area.

Start the hike at the 6,435-foot Cottonwood Springs Trailhead on the northwest side of Elena Gallegos Open Space. Two short trails run 325 feet from the trailhead on the west side of the parking lot to Trail #230A. Go right on #230A and hike north-east across open slopes below the mountain front to a junction with Trail #342 at 0.4

TWA FLIGHT 260

Flight 260, bound for Santa Fe, crashed in the Sandia Mountains on the morning of February 19, 1955. That night and the following day, members of the New Mexico Mountain Club and other volunteers assisted the New Mexico State Police in the recovery effort.

The wreckage was discovered high in Domingo Baca Canyon on the west flank of the Sandias. Sadly, there were no survivors and sixteen lives were lost. The wreckage burned for days. The official report stated that the plane had crashed into the Dragon's Tooth, a prominent rock spire on the northeast side of Domingo Baca Canyon, when it deviated from its flight plan, possibly due to compass trouble.

Many hikers visit the wreckage each year, and large pieces of the double-engine plane are still scattered about the rugged canyon. Those visiting the site should remember that this is a memorial site. Be respectful of the dead and leave all pieces of the wreckage in peace and in place.

mile. Continue straight on #230A, passing a junction with Trail #505 on the left, and after 0.6 mile reach a major three-way trail junction. Go left on the Domingo Baca Trail (#230) and head north along the mountain base. The right trail at the junction is #341, which heads southeast for 0.9 mile to the Pino Trail.

Hike north on the worn trail, keeping right at the first junction and crossing brushy slopes studded with juniper trees. The trail passes into the Sandia Mountain Wilderness Area, a 37,877-acre refuge on the western side of the Sandia Mountains, after 0.7 mile and swings past a shattered granite cliff and jumbles of giant boulders at 0.9 mile. Below the outcrop the trail meets a social trail on the right. Keep left on the main pathway and swing around a rounded hillock, then bend east on the south side of lower Cañon de Domingo Baca.

At 1.2 miles the trail drops across the usually dry wash and climbs onto a sloping bench on the north side of the canyon. Head east on the slowly rising trail on open slopes below steeper boulder-studded terrain. The canyon begins to narrow and at 1.6 miles, below slabby cliffs, the trail reaches the ruins of an abandoned stone shelter at about 7,000 feet.

The next 0.2-mile trail section follows the rocky canyon floor, shaded by tall trees. The spring-fed creek usually flows from here to the Sandia Crest, except during dry spells. The trail crosses the creek several times before reaching a trail junction where Cañon de Domingo Baca divides into two forks at 1.8 miles. The right trail heading up the main canyon to the east climbs sharply to the TWA crash site below the range crest. If you want to hike this trail, follow the directions in the Extra Credit Hike sidebar.

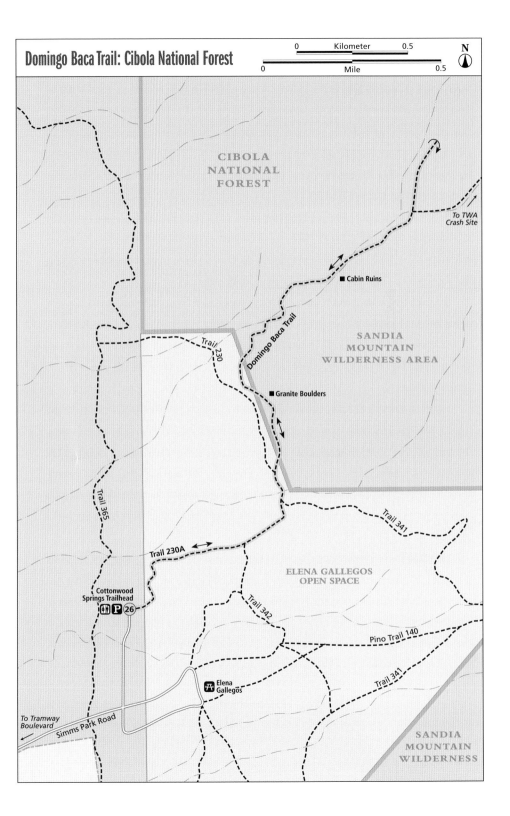

Domingo Baca Trail: Cibola National Forest

0 Kilometer 0.5

0 Mile 0.5

N

CIBOLA
NATIONAL
FOREST

To TWA
Crash Site

Cabin Ruins

Trail 230

Domingo Baca Trail

SANDIA
MOUNTAIN
WILDERNESS AREA

Granite Boulders

Trail 365

Trail 341

Trail 230A

ELENA GALLEGOS
OPEN SPACE

Cottonwood
Springs Trailhead

26

Trail 342

Pino Trail 140

Elena
Gallegos

Trail 341

To Tramway
Boulevard

Simms Park Road

SANDIA
MOUNTAIN
WILDERNESS

EXTRA CREDIT HIKE: DOMINGO BACA TRAIL TO TWA CRASH SITE

The 7.2-mile round-trip hike to the TWA crash site high in Cañon de Domingo Baca is one of the toughest hikes in this book. For experienced hikers only, the hike requires route-finding skills on an unmaintained trail, scrambling up boulders, bushwhacking through underbrush, and excellent physical condition since the hike gains over 2,300 feet from the trailhead to the crash area below the Sandia Crest. The humbling reward is the wreckage of a TWA commercial flight that crashed in 1955.

Bring plenty of water, food, and trekking poles. Long pants and a long-sleeved shirt are also advisable for diving through thick brush covered with stickers and thorns. Watch for poison ivy. It's a good idea to also bring a GPS unit and load the waypoints below to ensure that you find the site. Allow six to nine hours to do the hike.

Start the hike from the Cottonwood Springs Trailhead in Elena Gallegos Open Space and follow the Domingo Baca Trail description above until the canyon forks at 1.8 miles (GPS: 35.181433 N / -106.459909 W). The trail up the right fork is difficult to find here and steep, gaining 1,400 feet in a mile and a half. Don't follow the good trail up the left fork, which is described above.

From the streambed, scramble up a steep slope and find a trail that heads up the canyon bottom. Hike the trail past a couple usually dry waterfalls over cliffs at 2.5 and 2.7 miles. The trail and canyon begin bending left past the upper falls. Aim for a couple large pointed buttresses to the northeast. The crash site is below them. The trail continues uphill, passing under the tramway cables, and at 3.45 miles reaches a broken cliff. Scramble up the cliff and boulders and head up the ravine to the plane's debris field below the cliffs at 3.5 miles (GPS: 35.194944 N / -106.442497 W).

Take time to remember the sixteen lives lost in the plane crash and remember that this is a memorial site. Please do not take any souvenirs. Hundreds of pieces of aluminum and metal are scattered across the steep slopes, including rubber tires, a large piece of fuselage with the number 416 painted on it, and pieces of a propeller, landing gear, and seats. A marker commemorates the people who died. After a moment of silence and remembrance, descend back down the trail and canyon to the trailhead.

The hike heads up the easy-to-follow trail in the brushy left-fork canyon, following slopes on the right side above the clear tumbling creek. While it's possible to hike all the way to the top of the range above, the trail and described hike end at 2.4 miles at a granite wall that blocks the narrow canyon. Stop here in the shade for a snack and drink of water before turning around and descending back to the trailhead on the same route.

Miles and Directions

0.0 Begin at the trailhead for Trail #230A on the west side of the Cottonwood Springs Trailhead parking lot (GPS: 35.165948 N / -106.473136 W). Hike north on Trail #230A for 325 feet to a Y-junction and go right on #230A.

0.4 Reach a junction with Trail #342 on the right (GPS: 35.168190 N / -106.468349 W). Continue northeast on the Domingo Baca Trail (#230). Trail #342 is an alternative start to the hike and runs 0.37 mile north from the Pino Trail (#140).

0.6 Reach a junction with Trail #341 (GPS: 35.169982 N / -106.466451 W). Continue north on the Domingo Baca Trail. A right turn on Trail #341 heads southeast for 0.9 mile to the Pino Trail.

0.65 Reach a Y-junction (GPS: 35.171035 N / -106.466837 W). Keep right on the Domingo Baca Trail. The left trail is also labeled #230.

0.7 Enter the Sandia Mountain Wilderness Area.

0.9 Pass a large outcrop of granite boulders.

1.2 Cross a usually dry wash in the bottom of Cañon de Domingo Baca (GPS: 35.176814 N / -106.467357 W).

1.6 Reach stone cabin ruins on the left (GPS: 35.180098 N / -106.461981 W).

1.8 Reach the junction with the spur trail to the TWA crash site in upper Cañon de Domingo Baca (GPS: 35.181433 N / -106.459909 W). Go left on a good trail and hike northeast up the left-hand canyon.

2.4 Reach the end of the hike. Turn around and return to the trailhead on the same trail.

4.8 Arrive back at the Cottonwood Springs Trailhead and parking area.

Area Info

Sandia Crest House Gift Shop and Restaurant, 701 Sandia Crest Rd., Sandia Park 87047; (505) 243-0605; www.sandiacresthouse.com

Sandia Peak Tramway and Ski Area, 30 Tramway Rd. NE, Albuquerque 87122; (505) 856-1532; www.sandiapeak.com

EXTRA CREDIT HIKE: FOOTHILLS TRAIL (#365)

This 13-mile trail in Cibola National Forest runs north to south along the western slope of the Sandia Mountains. Popular with hikers, runners, and mountain bikers, the trail can be accessed from several points, including Elena Gallegos Open Space Park, the Sandia Peak Aerial Tramway lower parking area, and the Embudito Trailhead parking area.

27 Pino Trail: Cibola National Forest

The challenging 4.7-mile Pino Trail, one of the most popular hikes in the Sandia Mountains, climbs from Elena Gallegos Open Space on the eastern edge of Albuquerque to the range crest and then returns to the trailhead for a 9.4-mile round-trip hike. The well-traveled trail offers cool temperatures, dense evergreen woods, and spacious views on its upper section.

Distance: 9.4 miles out and back
Hiking time: 5 to 6 hours
Difficulty: Strenuous, with 2,828 feet of elevation gain
Best seasons: Spring and fall
Schedule: Open daily 7 a.m. to 9 p.m. Apr through Oct., 7 a.m. to 7 p.m. Nov through Mar
Other trail users: Hikers only on Pino Trail in open space and wilderness area
Canine compatibility: Leashed dogs allowed

Fees and permits: Day use / parking fee
Maps: USGS Sandia Crest; trail map available at Sandia Ranger District and on website
Trail contact: Sandia Ranger District, 11776 NM 337, Tijeras 87059; (505) 281-3304; www.fs.usda.gov/cibola
Special considerations: Elena Gallegos Open Space may close early in the winter due to weather. Summer days are hot in the lower elevations.

Finding the trailhead: From Albuquerque, take I-25 north to exit 232 toward NM 423 / Paseo del Norte. After exiting, turn right (east) and drive 4.8 miles to NM 556E / Tramway Boulevard NE. Turn right (south) onto NM 556E / Tramway Boulevard NE and drive 1.2 miles to Simms Park Road NE. Turn left (east) on Simms Park Road NE and continue 1.4 miles to the Elena Gallegos Open Space fee station. Turn right at the fee station on a one-way road and drive 0.4 mile to the Pino Trail parking lot and trailhead. GPS: 35.163297 N / -106.470104 W

The Hike

The challenging 4.7-mile Pino Trail (#140), one of the best scenic hikes in the Sandia Mountains, climbs 2,828 feet from Elena Gallegos Open Space on the eastern edge of Albuquerque to the turn-around point at its junction with the Crest Trail atop the range. The out-and-back, 9.4-mile hike is easy to follow, climbs through three distinct ecological zones, and offers excellent views across the city and Rio Grande Valley below. Despite its popularity, the Pino Trail is a strenuous day hike with substantial elevation gain and distance. Plan on a long trail day and carry plenty of water and snacks. Lower Pino Trail, as well as the trails at Elena Gallegos Open Space, are usually busy with hikers on weekends and holidays.

Many hikers prefer doing an abbreviated version of the Pino Trail, hiking 2 to 3 miles from the trailhead to a turn-around point before the trail steepens in Pino Canyon. The distance and elevation gain vary depending on how far you hike up the canyon, but plan on 3 to 5 miles round-trip and 700 to 900 feet of elevation gain. A shorter, easy, out-and-back, 1.6-mile hike follows the Pino Trail to a bench just before

The Pino Trail threads past cholla cacti to the Sandia Mountain Wilderness boundary.

the fenced Sandia Mountain Wilderness Area boundary on the east side of Elena Gallegos Open Space.

Alternatively, if you want the full-value Pino Trail experience without the uphill hiking pain, consider riding the Sandia Peak Tramway to the tram station below Sandia Crest. After rising 2.7 miles in 15 minutes, enjoy a coffee at the station and then hike down the South Crest Trail (#130) for 3.4 miles to its junction with the Pino Trail. Take a right turn and quickly descend 4.7 miles down Pino to the trailhead for an 8.1-mile downhill hike. If you arranged a car shuttle, leave from Elena Gallegos or hike north on the easy Foothills Trail (#365) to the Tramway parking lot.

The best season to hike the Pino Trail is in the spring and fall months. While summer days are hot on the first trail section, the temperature cools as the trail begins climbing Pino Canyon toward the Sandia Crest and shady pines and firs line the path. If you hike during monsoon season in July and August, bring a raincoat and watch for heavy thunderstorms accompanied by lightning, especially on the upper trail and range crest.

The best winter hike is doing the short version of the Pino Trail described above, since the lower trail is often snow-free and temperatures warm. The upper trail is often snow-packed and icy from November until April, and there are several spots where a slip could result in serious injury. Only experienced hikers should attempt the Pino Trail in winter and carry microspikes or other foot traction devices, snowshoes if deep snow is on the crest, trekking poles, a headlamp, and warm clothes. Winter days are short, so plan on being back at your vehicle by 7 p.m., when the area gate is locked, if you parked inside Elena Gallegos Open Space.

Begin at the 6,472-foot Pino Trailhead on the east side of the Elena Gallegos Picnic Area. Hike east on the marked asphalt-paved trail past a dog poop bag station, a drinking fountain, and an information board with a map and trail details. Reach a Y-junction and signpost after 160 feet. Keep right on the dirt Pino Trail. A left turn goes east on a paved, wheelchair-accessible trail to a series of abstract sculptures called *The Five Stones of Elena Gallegos*, a grouping of sculpted granite boulders created by artist Billie Walters. The memorial sculptures honor Phillip B. Tollefsrud, a local conservationist who helped preserve Albuquerque's natural areas, including the former Elena Gallegos Land Grant. This side trail rejoins the Pino Trail past the sculptures and makes a fun variation to the hike.

Continue east on the wide, well-traveled trail and reach a junction with Trail #342 after 0.25 mile. Continue straight on the hiker-only Pino Trail, passing through a fence intended to keep mountain bikers from straying onto the trail. Arid vegetation,

The Sandia Crest towers above hikers on the Pino Trail in Elena Gallegos Open Space.

THE ELENA GALLEGOS LAND GRANT

An official State Historic Marker at the start of the Pino Trail explains the life of Doña Elena Gallegos (1680–1731), an early Hispanic colonist. Her parents, Antonio Gallegos and Catalina Baca, left New Mexico in 1680 with newborn Elena after the Pueblo Revolt. Her uncle returned to New Mexico in 1693 with thirteen-year-old Elena and her two brothers. She married Frenchman Jacques Santiago Gurulé, a member of the ill-fated La Salle Expedition on the Mississippi River, at age nineteen. After his death in 1711, Elena ran a stock business, becoming the first New Mexican woman to record her own brand in 1712.

Around 1716 Elena acquired the Jesus Maria Grant from Captain Diego Montoya, a huge area that stretched from the Rio Grande to the Sandia Crest. Rumor has it that Diego was fond of Señora Gallegos, and despite having five sons as heirs, he chose to allow the land to become her property. Over the next couple of centuries, the land grant, including most of north Albuquerque, was divided and sold. A large section was given by Albert G. Simms in the 1930s to the Albuquerque Academy. Later the City of Albuquerque purchased 7,630 acres from the school, exchanging some with the US Forest Service and using 640 acres in 1984 to create today's Elena Gallegos Open Space and Albert G. Simms Park.

including scrubby grasses, spiky yuccas, cholla cacti, and scattered juniper trees, line the dusty trail as it slowly climbs east across a broad outwash plain below the mouth of Pino Canyon.

At 0.75 mile the trail passes through a gate and reaches a junction with Trail #341, a hiking and mountain-biking trail that loops around the east side of the open space land. Continue east past a rest bench and pass through a gate in a fence marking the Sandia Mountain Wilderness Area boundary at 0.8 mile. An information sign with Cibola National Forest regulations and a wilderness trail map is just beyond the boundary fence. The trail from here to its junction with the Crest Trail is open only to hikers and equestrians, no mountain bikes.

The next 3.9-mile trail section heads east from the wilderness boundary, slowly gaining elevation and contouring across wooded slopes on the south side of the canyon above the trickling creek. At 1.3 miles the trail swings by a huge granite boulder, a good turn-around point if you're doing the short version of the Pino Trail. As the trail climbs, the vegetation changes from desert plants to a shady mature forest of ponderosa pine, Douglas fir, and spruce. The upper trail is also quiet, with few other hikers since most turn around near the wilderness boundary. Watch for mule deer, coyotes, and other mammals and birds in the woodland along the trail.

After passing Pino Springs at 3.2 miles, the trail begins to steepen at about 7,600 feet and climbs into a drainage in a side canyon below the crest. After crossing a trickling creek, the trail swings across open mountain slopes covered with dense thickets

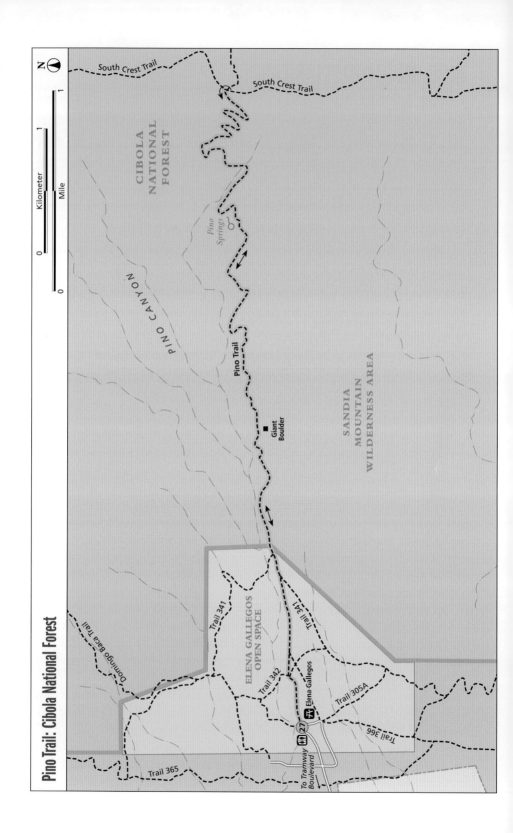

Pino Trail: Cibola National Forest

of scrub oak and occasional groves of quaking aspen. The final 0.6-mile trail section switchbacks up a shaded north-facing slope to the top of the Sandia Mountains and a four-way junction with the Crest Trail (#130) and Cienega Trail (#148) at 9,211 feet after 4.7 miles of hiking.

This lofty trail junction marks the end of the trail but not the hike. After catching your breath, enjoy spacious views down the canyon to sprawling Albuquerque and distant mountain ranges. To the south stretch the lower Manzanita Mountains and the long ridge of the Manzano Mountains, while humped Ladron Peak pokes above the southwestern horizon. For extra credit views, scramble up the two ranked but unnamed peaks—Point 9,627 and Point 9,579—on the north and south sides of the trail junction, respectively.

When you're ready to hit the trail again, return back down the Pino Trail to the trailhead for a 9.4-mile round-trip hike. Allow about two-thirds of the time for the ascent to get back to the trailhead. Several other options are also available at the upper junction. See the Extra Credit Hike sidebar to hike 2.2 miles down the Cienega Trail on the east side of the Sandias. If you're ambitious, hike 3.4 miles north on the Crest Trail to the Upper Tramway Terminal and take a fast gondola ride down the Sandia Peak Tramway and then follow the Foothills Trail (#365) back to Elena Gallegos.

Miles and Directions

0.0 Start at the Pino Trailhead at the Elena Gallegos Picnic Area (GPS: 35.163297 N / -106.470104 W). Hike east on the marked paved trail for 160 feet to a junction. Keep right on the main trail. The left trail goes to a sculpture garden.

0.1 The Nature Trail breaks off to the north. Continue east on the Pino Trail.

0.25 Reach the junction with Trail #342. Continue east on the Pino Trail.

0.8 Enter the Sandia Mountain Wilderness Area. Continue east on the Pino Trail.

1.3 Pass a giant granite boulder.

3.2 Reach Pino Springs. Continue ascending the slopes above the canyon floor.

4.7 Reach the Crest Trail at the top of a ridge (GPS: 35.168987 N / -106.414306 W). Return to the trailhead and parking area via the same route.

9.4 Arrive back at the trailhead and parking area.

Area Info

Sandia Crest House Gift Shop and Restaurant, 701 Sandia Crest Rd., Sandia Park 87047; (505) 243-0605; www.sandiacresthouse.com

Sandia Peak Tramway and Ski Area, 30 Tramway Rd. NE, Albuquerque 87122; (505) 856-1532; www.sandiapeak.com

GREEN TIP

Observe wildlife from a distance. Don't interfere in their lives—both of you will be better for it. Bring binoculars or a spotting scope to get up-close and personal.

28 South Crest Trail–Sandia Crest to Upper Tram Terminal: Cibola National Forest

A 3-mile out-and-back hike along the ridge of the Sandia Mountains. Beginning at the Crest House and ending at the Sandia Tramway, highlights include 100-mile views, a spur trail to the historic Kiwanis Cabin, and wildlife in Kiwanis Meadow.

Distance: 3.0 miles out and back
Hiking time: About 2 hours
Difficulty: Moderate
Best seasons: Spring, summer, and fall
Schedule: Open year-round
Other trail users: Mountain bikers and horse-back riders; skiers in winter
Canine compatibility: Leashed dogs allowed
Fees and permits: Day use/parking fee

Maps: USGS Sandia Crest; trail map available at Sandia Ranger District
Trail contact: Sandia Ranger District, 11776 NM 337, Tijeras 87059; (505) 281-3304; www.fs.usda.gov/cibola
Special considerations: Trail may be snowy and icy in winter. NM 536 may be closed after heavy snow.

Finding the trailhead: From Albuquerque, take I-40 east to exit 175 toward NM 14 / Cedar Crest. After exiting to the right, stay left on NM 14 and drive north 6 miles to NM 536. Turn left (west) on NM 536 / Sandia Crest Road and continue 14 miles until the road dead-ends at the visitor center and parking area. GPS: 35.210616 N / -106.449525 W

The Hike

This hike follows a scenic 1.5-mile section of the upper South Crest Trail (#130S), a 16-mile trail that begins at a trailhead in Tijeras off I-40 and runs north to the Sandia Crest House and the 10,678-foot summit of the Sandia Mountains. This high hike, a 3-mile out-and-back trek, offers spectacular views, mostly easy hiking, and cool summer weather. The trail, connecting Sandia Crest House and the tramway terminal, is often busy with crest visitors and hikers, especially on weekends. Plan a weekday adventure for more solitude. Food, water, and restrooms are available at the Sandia Crest House near the trailhead.

The best hiking temperatures and weather is from early May through October, with usually stable weather patterns and sunny days. Summer days can be warm but watch for approaching thunderstorms and lightning in the afternoon. Winter brings cold and snow, so plan your hike accordingly and be prepared with warm clothes, trekking poles, microspikes, and even snowshoes if there's fresh snow. Temperatures on the crest are usually 20 to 40 degrees cooler than in Albuquerque.

Begin the hike at the trailhead at the south end of the summit parking lots and southeast of the Sandia Crest House, a gift shop and restaurant perched on the range

The Sandia Crest Trail offers stunning views across the western escarpment of the Sandia Mountains. WIKIMEDIA COMMONS © SAMAT JAIN, USED CC-BY-SA 2.0

crest. Sandia Crest House makes a good stop before or after your hike if you want to pick up souvenirs or eat lunch at the Two-Mile-High Café. Restrooms and interpretive signs are at the trailhead.

Hike south on the South Crest Trail, also labeled Trail #130S, along the western rim of the Sandia Crest past a spectacular overlook. This first trail section is wheelchair accessible. After 0.1 mile reach a trail junction. Go left (southeast) at the fork on the South Crest Trail, marked with green-and-silver trail markers. Groves of quaking aspen, subalpine fir, and Engelmann spruce trees line the wide trail.

The trail reaches a junction with the Crest House Nature Trail (#95) after 0.25 mile. Continue south on the South Crest Trail, following signs that point the way to the Upper Tramway Terminal. The trail gently descends the east side of Sandia Crest ridge and at 0.5 mile reaches a junction with Kiwanis Cabin Road (#94), a closed road that leads south to the Kiwanis Cabin. An interpretive sign at the junction displays an area map with the Sandia trail system.

To see the historic Kiwanis Cabin, go right at the junction on Kiwanis Cabin Road and hike 0.75 mile south to the cabin perched on the crest. Return to the South Crest Trail on the 0.5-mile Kiwanis Cabin Trail (#93). The Kiwanis Cabin, named for the Kiwanis Club, was built in the early 1930s by the Civilian Conservation Corps (CCC). The ruins of the stone cabin perch on bedrock on the western edge of the Sandia Crest, with cliffs and steep wooded slopes falling 4,000 feet to the base of the mountains at the tramway's lower station. The cabin site offers broad views

HIKING WITH DOGS

We all love hiking with our dogs. It's not only great exercise for dogs, but they are arguably the best hiking partners: They never complain and are always ready to explore a new trail. If you hike with your dog, please be a responsible pet owner by always cleaning up after your dog and keeping him under control at all times. Pet waste is smelly, unsightly, and a health hazard for humans and wildlife, and it pollutes waterways. Keeping your dog on a leash and under voice control is the best way to ensure that your pet is safe and not a nuisance to other hikers and wildlife. With these simple actions, you are doing your part to ensure that trails remain open to hikers and their four-legged friends.

across central New Mexico from Albuquerque below to distant mountains, including Mount Taylor and the Jemez Mountains.

Return to the South Crest Trail by hiking back north on Kiwanis Cabin Road or going east on the Kiwanis Cabin Trail. From the original junction of Kiwanis Cabin Road and the South Crest Trail, head southeast and briefly hook up with the Challenge Trail (#233) before bending south around the eastern edge of spacious 16.5-acre Kiwanis Meadow. The open grassland was closed for public use in 2012 to allow the area to recover from decades of public use and abuse, including social trails and dispersed campsites, which caused serious erosion and damage. The meadow,

The Kiwanis Cabin, perched on the Sandia Crest, is reached by a spur trail from the South Crest Trail. EMILY RESSLER-TANNER

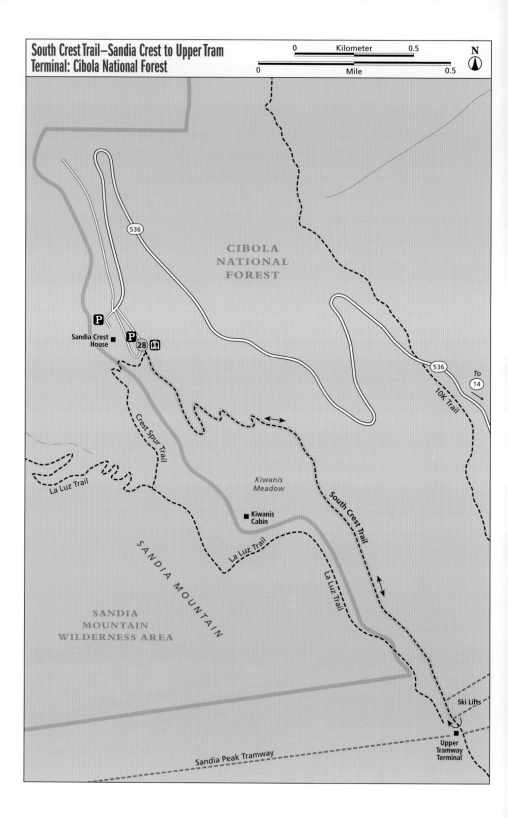

South Crest Trail–Sandia Crest to Upper Tram Terminal: Cibola National Forest

0   Kilometer   0.5
0   Mile   0.5

N

CIBOLA
NATIONAL
FOREST

536

536

To
14

10K Trail

P

Sandia Crest
House

P

28

Crest Spur Trail

La Luz Trail

Kiwanis
Meadow

Kiwanis
Cabin

La Luz Trail

South Crest Trail

La Luz Trail

SANDIA MOUNTAIN

SANDIA
MOUNTAIN
WILDERNESS AREA

Ski Lifts

Upper
Tramway
Terminal

Sandia Peak Tramway

bordered by a split-rail fence, is a great spot to glimpse wildlife, including mule deer. The area also offers fine bird watching. Look for calliope hummingbirds migrating south in late summer, ruby-crowned and golden-crowned kinglets, yellow-rumped warblers, green-tailed towhees, and American three-toed woodpeckers, as well as finches, chickadees, nuthatches, robins, and ravens.

The trail continues south from the meadow, passing a couple more trail junctions, and forks at 0.7 mile. Hikers keep right; the left trail is open to mountain bikes. Trail #130 intersects the Gravel Pit Trail (#339) at 0.8 mile. Continue south, returning to the crest ridge and spectacular views across Albuquerque and the Rio Grande Valley to the west. Stop on the ridge for a good view north to the Kiwanis Cabin sitting on the cliff edge. Farther south on the trail is a junction with the Four Seasons Nature Trail (#97) in a grove of quaking aspens. The 0.5-mile loop, beginning north of the tramway terminal, educates visitors about the unique natural history and geology of the Sandia Mountains.

Hike south on Trail #130 along the ridgeline, passing through Gambel oaks, quaking aspens, and New Mexico maples. Note flagged trees along the ridgeline that are almost bare on their windward west side. Most of the trees' growth is on the eastern leeward side, giving them the appearance of a windblown flag. Persistent high winds shape the trees, especially during the winter months.

Continue down the trail and reach the upper terminal for the Sandia Peak Aerial Tramway and the top of Sandia Peak Ski Area after 1.5 miles. The popular tramway hauls passengers up the western flank of the Sandias in 15 minutes, rising over 4,000 feet in 2.7 miles from the terminal at the mountain base. The ski area offers fine skiing on thirty-nine trails on the eastern slope of the Sandias. The area, with an average snowfall of 125 inches, is easily accessed by the tramway or by driving up NM 536 to the mountain base. The Upper Tramway Terminal offers restrooms and the Ten 3 Restaurant with fine dining and finer views.

EXTRA CREDIT HIKE: CREST HOUSE NATURE TRAIL (#98)

The Crest House Nature Trail is an easy 0.5-mile loop trail that begins at the trailhead for the South Crest Trail at the south end of the parking areas and by the Sandia Crest House. Restrooms and information signs are at the trailhead. Hike south from the trailhead and parking area on the paved South Crest Trail (#130) for 300 feet to a dramatic viewpoint overlooking Albuquerque and the Rio Grande Valley to the west. This first trail section is wheelchair accessible. Continue hiking south on the cliff-edge trail (watch children here) and after 0.25 mile the trail bends east toward Kiwanis Meadow. Hike 50 or so feet on the trail to a junction with the Crest House Nature Trail (#98). Go left on the trail and hike north back to the overlook through a spruce, fir, and pine forest. Continue north on Trail #130 to the trailhead.

After visiting the terminal, reverse the hike back to the trailhead and parking lot at the Sandia Crest House. The 1.5-mile return hike gains about 300 feet of elevation.

Miles and Directions

0.0 Start at the trailhead at the south end of the parking area by the Sandia Crest House (GPS: 35.209406 N / -106.448457 W). Hike south on the South Crest Trail (#130).

0.1 Reach a trail junction. Take the left (southwest) fork for the South Crest Trail.

0.25 Reach a junction with the Crest House Nature Trail. Continue south on the South Crest Trail.

0.5 Reach a junction with the closed Kiwanis Cabin Road. Go right on the closed road for 0.75 mile to the Kiwanis Cabin or continue southeast on the South Crest Trail around the east side of closed Kiwanis Meadow.

0.6 Reach Kiwanis Meadow and a junction with the Ellis Trail (#202). Continue south on the South Crest Trail.

0.7 Keep right at a trail fork.

0.8 Reach a junction with the Gravel Pit Trail. Keep right on South Crest Trail toward the Upper Tramway Terminal.

1.4 Enter a grove of Gambel oaks.

1.5 Reach the Upper Tramway Terminal and the top of Sandia Peak Ski Area. Return to the trailhead by hiking up the South Crest Trail.

3.0 Arrive back at the trailhead and parking area at Sandia Crest House.

Area Info

Sandia Crest House Gift Shop and Restaurant, 701 Sandia Crest Rd., Sandia Park 87047; (505) 243-0605; www.sandiacresthouse.com

Sandia Peak Tramway and Ski Area, 30 Tramway Rd. NE, Albuquerque 87122; (505) 856-1532; www.sandiapeak.com

GREEN TIP
Stay on the trail. Cutting switchbacks destroys fragile plant life and creates unwanted washes that erode the trail.

29 Tree Spring Trail: Cibola National Forest

The popular Tree Spring Trail is a 3.7-mile out-and-back hike that climbs the eastern flank of the Sandia Mountains to the 10K Trail. From the junction of the two trails, return down the Tree Spring Trail, explore the 10K Trail, or hike the South Crest Trail to the tramway station.

Distance: 3.7 miles out and back
Hiking time: 2 to 3 hours
Difficulty: Moderate, with 1,040 feet of elevation gain
Best seasons: Spring, summer, and fall
Schedule: Open year-round
Other trail users: Mountain bikers and horseback riders; snowshoers in winter
Canine compatibility: Leashed dogs allowed

Fees and permits: Day use / parking fee
Maps: USGS Sandia Crest; trail map available at Sandia Ranger District
Trail contact: Sandia Ranger District, 11776 NM 337, Tijeras 87059; (505) 281-3304; www.fs.usda.gov/cibola
Special considerations: Trail may be snowy and icy in winter. Parking area may be closed after heavy snow.

Finding the trailhead: From Albuquerque, take I-40 east to exit 175 toward NM 14 / Cedar Crest. After exiting to the right, stay left on NM 14 and continue north 6 miles on NM 14 to NM 536. Turn left (west) onto NM 536 / Sandia Crest Road and continue 6.3 miles to the Tree Spring Trailhead parking area on the left (west). GPS: GPS: 35.193659 N / -106.404691 W

The Hike

The nearly 2-mile Tree Spring Trail (#147) is a popular out-and-back hike that begins at a trailhead on the Sandia Crest National Scenic Byway (NM 536) and climbs the eastern slope of the Sandias to a junction with the 10K Trail and another junction a little higher with the South Crest Trail. From the junction, hikers can either reverse the path back down or explore the upper mountain by following the South Crest Trail to the Upper Tramway Terminal and expansive views west across Albuquerque and the Rio Grande Valley.

The easy-to-follow trail, one of the best easier hikes in the Sandia Mountains, has a good surface, although it's rocky and eroded in places. The trail gains about 950 feet from the trailhead at 8,398 feet to the junction with the South Crest Trail. Trail use is heavy in spring, summer, and fall, especially on weekends, so plan your hike on a weekday for more elbow room. It's a multiuse trail shared with equestrians and mountain bikers. The Tree Spring Trail is also one of the best trails near Albuquerque for snowshoeing in winter. The trail is named for a spring that flows from beneath a tree stump 0.4 mile below the trailhead on NM 536.

Start the hike from the Tree Spring Trailhead, marked with a highway sign, on the west side of the road. The parking area offers sixteen designated spots. All parked

The Tree Spring Trail ascends the eastern flank of the Sandias to the range crest. JD TANNER

vehicles must display a valid forest recreation pass. The trailhead on the south end of the parking lot has a picnic table and information kiosk. The lot is often busy on summer weekends, but most days parking isn't an issue. In the winter, heavy snow sometimes forces plows to move snow onto the parking area.

Tree Spring Trail: Cibola National Forest

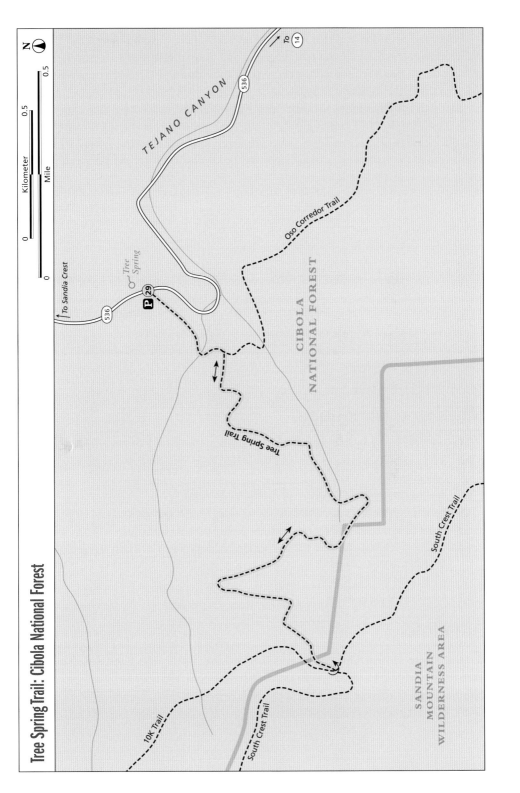

Tejano Canyon

To 14

536

To Sandia Crest

Tree Spring

536

P 29

Oso Corredor Trail

CIBOLA NATIONAL FOREST

Tree Spring Trail

South Crest Trail

South Crest Trail

10K Trail

South Crest Trail

SANDIA MOUNTAIN WILDERNESS AREA

N

Kilometer

Mile

0   0.5   0.5

Hike west on a dirt trail that steadily climbs the gentle eastern slope of the Sandia Mountains. At 0.3 mile the trail reaches a junction with the Oso Corredor Trail (#265), which heads left for 2.75 miles to the Faulty Trail (#195). Keep right on the Tree Spring Trail and hike southwest.

The trail steadily climbs to a rest spot with boulders and Sandia views on the right after 0.5 mile. After catching your breath, continue slowly ascending for another 0.5 mile through a mixed forest of long-needled ponderosa pine and spruce. At the 1-mile point, the trail bends sharply right and heads northwest up steeper terrain to another rest stop at 1.2 miles.

The Tree Spring Trail continues climbing to a junction with the 10K Trail (#200) at 1.85 miles and then the junction with the South Crest Trail (#130), the major trail that follows the crest of the Sandia Mountains. Hikers can turn around here and return back down the trail for a 3.7-mile hike or continue their adventure on the upper trails.

For good views of the Sandias, Albuquerque, the Rio Grande Valley, and distant Mount Taylor to the west, go left on the South Crest Trail and hike a short distance to an overlook on the range crest. The preferred alternative is to head right on the South Crest Trail and hike 1.6 miles to the upper station for the Sandia Peak Aerial Tramway. Here you can sit down for lunch or buy a Sandia souvenir before trekking back down the South Crest Trail to the Tree Spring Trail and returning to the highway trailhead for a 6.9-mile round-trip hike.

Miles and Directions

0.0 Leave the Tree Spring Trailhead (GPS: 35.193659 N / -106.404691 W) and hike west.

0.3 Reach a junction with the Oso Corredor Trail (#265). Keep right (southwest) on the Tree Spring Trail.

0.5 Reach a resting spot with views of the Sandias on the right (north).

1.0 The trail makes a sharp right (northwest) turn. Continue on steeper terrain.

1.2 Reach another opening with views across the eastern flank of the Sandias.

1.85 The Tree Spring Trail meets the 10K Trail (#200) and South Crest Trail (#130). Turn around and return to the trailhead via the same route or go right on South Crest Trail for 1.6 miles to the upper tramway station.

3.7 Arrive back at the trailhead.

Area Info

Sandia Crest House Gift Shop and Restaurant, 701 Sandia Crest Rd., Sandia Park 87047; (505) 243-0605; www.sandiacresthouse.com

Sandia Peak Tramway and Ski Area, 30 Tramway Rd. NE, Albuquerque 87122; (505) 856-1532; www.sandiapeak.com

30 Cienega Trail: Cibola National Forest

The 2.2-mile Cienega Trail, accessing the Crest Trail, passes through meadows and forests on the eastern slope of the Sandias.

Distance: 4.4 miles out and back
Hiking time: About 3 hours
Difficulty: Moderate, with 1,659 feet of elevation gain
Best seasons: Spring, summer, and fall
Schedule: Open year-round
Other trail users: Horseback riders
Canine compatibility: Leashed dogs allowed
Fees and permits: Day use/parking fee

Maps: USGS Sandia Crest; trail map available at Sandia Ranger District and on website
Trail contact: Sandia Ranger District, 11776 NM 337, Tijeras 87059; (505) 281-3304; www.fs.usda.gov/cibola
Special considerations: Trail is snowy and icy in winter. Road from NM 536 to trailhead parking area is closed in winter.

Finding the trailhead: From Albuquerque, drive east on I-40 to exit 175 toward NM 14/Cedar Crest. After exiting to the right, go left on NM 14 and continue north for 6 miles to NM 536. Turn left (west) onto NM 536/Sandia Crest Road and drive 1.7 miles to a side road that goes left to the Sulphur Spring and Cienega picnic areas. Turn left (west) on the road and make an immediate left (south) onto an asphalt road to the Cienega Canyon Picnic Site. Drive 0.5 mile to a T-junction and keep right on the road for another mile to the picnic area at the end of the road and the Cienega Trailhead. GPS: 35.169652 N / -106.384136 W

The Hike

Located on the eastern slope of the Sandia Mountains, the 2.2-mile Cienega Trail (#148) offers a challenging hike up Cienega Canyon to the crest of the range. The singletrack trail is an ideal hike for warm days, with plenty of shade. The trail, one of the best in the Sandias, crosses wildflower-studded meadows and offers broad views across central New Mexico at the top.

The trail is a quiet winter trek, but hikers should be prepared for snowy and icy conditions by carrying snowshoes, trekking poles, and microspikes or other boot traction devices. The trail also requires route-finding skills in winter, since it's often snowbound from late November until early spring. The gates to the trailheads at Sulphur Spring and Cienega picnic areas are closed by snow in winter. To hike the Cienega Trail in winter once the entrance gate is closed, park outside the gate off NM 536 and walk 1.5 miles on the access road to the Cienega Trailhead, adding an additional 3 miles round-trip to the hike's distance.

The Cienega Trail is a fun hike that also accesses other Sandia Mountain trails, including the Faulty Trail (#195), Crest Trail (#130), and Pino Trail (#140), which descends the west side of the Sandias to a trailhead at Elena Gallegos Open Space on the eastern edge of Albuquerque. The Cienega Canyon Interpretive Trail is a short

The Cienega Trail reaches the crest of the Sandia Mountains. EMILY RESSLER-TANNER

paved trail, accessible to wheelchairs and strollers, that starts at the picnic area and loops through meadows and along a trickling creek. The trail, built by the US Forest Service in cooperation with the New Mexico Association for the Blind, offers raw nature to children, senior citizens, disabled hikers, and those with limited mobility.

Begin the Cienega Trail at the west side of a large parking lot at the road's end. Follow brown markers west along a paved pathway past picnic sites and Cienega Spring for 0.05 mile to the trail, which leaves the sidewalk and heads west to a kiosk at the trailhead.

The trail travels west up stone steps and crosses wooden bridges over a creek to a large boulder and rest bench at 0.3 mile. After catching your breath, hike west to the junction with the Faulty Trail at 0.4 mile on the border of the Sandia Mountain Wilderness Area, a 37,877-acre wilderness area that protects most of the range. The Faulty Trail goes south for 2.3 miles to the Cañoncito Trail or north for 0.5 mile to the Sulphur Springs Trail.

Continue straight on the Cienega Trail and begin steadily climbing along the south side of a creek in Cienega Canyon. After 2.3 miles the trail passes a grove of Gambel oaks and reaches a junction with the Crest Trail and the Pino Trail atop the Sandia Crest, the spine of the range. This junction is the turn-around point for the out-and-back hike. If you arranged a car shuttle, hike down the Pino Trail for 4.7

Cienega Trail: Cibola National Forest

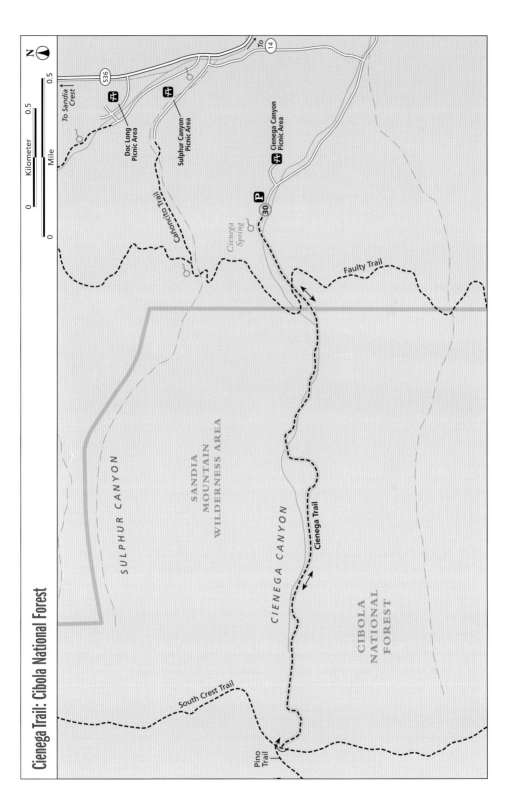

Bring snowshoes to hike the Cienega Trail in winter. EMILY RESSLER-TANNER

miles on the opposite west side of the range to a trailhead at Elena Gallegos Open Space. Otherwise, enjoy the view and then return to the trailhead on the Cienega Trail for a 4.4-mile round-trip hike. It's quick to descend since it's all downhill.

Miles and Directions

0.0 Start at the Cienega Trailhead at the end of the access road (GPS: 35.169652 N / -106.384136 W). Hike west from the parking lot on a paved sidewalk. After 250 feet, reach the trailhead kiosk on the left and continue west.

0.3 Pass a boulder and wooden bench. Continue west.

0.4 Pass the junction with the Faulty Trail.

0.5 Enter the Sandia Mountain Wilderness Area. Continue west on the Cienega Trail.

2.2 Reach the junction with the Crest Trail and Pino Trail at the ridgetop (GPS: 35.168984 N / -106.414307 W). After resting, return to the trailhead via the same route.

4.4 Arrive back at the trailhead and parking lot.

Area Info

Sandia Peak Tramway and Ski Area, 30 Tramway Rd. NE, Albuquerque 87122; (505) 856-1532; www.sandiapeak.com

31 Three Gun Spring Trail: Cibola National Forest

The Three Gun Spring Trail climbs 4 miles up a wide valley to high ridges at the southern end of the Sandias. The 8-mile round-trip hike offers bird watching, seclusion, diverse ecosystems, and stellar views across the Sandia Mountains, Albuquerque, and the Manzanita Mountains.

Distance: 8.0 miles out and back
Hiking time: 4 to 6 hours
Difficulty: Strenuous due to length and climb
Best seasons: Spring, fall, and winter
Schedule: Trail open year-round
Other trail users: Horseback riders
Canine compatibility: Leashed dogs allowed
Fees and permits: Day use / parking fee

Maps: USGS Tijeras; trail map available at Sandia Ranger District and on website
Trail contact: Sandia Ranger District, 11776 NM 337, Tijeras 87059; (505) 281-3304; www.fs.usda.gov/cibola
Special considerations: Upper trail is snowy and icy in winter. Hot in summer, with little shade.

Finding the trailhead: From Albuquerque, take I-40 east to exit 170 toward NM 333 / Historic Route 66. After exiting, drive 1.6 miles east on NM 333 and turn left (north) onto Monticello Drive in the Monticello Subdivision. Continue 0.6 mile on Monticello Drive to Alegre Road and turn left (west) onto Alegre Road. After 0.1 mile turn right (north) on Siempre Verde Drive. Drive 0.2 mile on Siempre Verde to the Three Gun Spring Trailhead and parking area. GPS: 35.076493 N / -106.444200 W

The Hike

The 4-mile Three Gun Spring Trail (#194), also called Tres Pistolas Trail, is a superb winter hike with plentiful sunshine on the southern slopes of the Sandia Mountains. Legend says that three pistols left by early Spanish soldiers were found in the canyon, giving Three Gun Spring and the trail their names. The trail runs up a broad south-facing canyon, sometimes called Three Gun Spring Canyon, that acts like a heat sink during the winter. Plentiful sunshine keeps the trail and mountain slopes free of snow and ice, making the Three Gun Spring Trail an ideal winter hike. Pick a different trail for a summer hike, since the sun bakes the canyon, making temperatures uncomfortably hot. The spring and autumn shoulder seasons also offer good hiking temperatures. The trail lies along a raptor migration route, so bring binoculars, especially in spring, to spot twenty different species, including black-shouldered kites, golden eagles, and zone-tailed hawks.

The trailhead and parking lot are at the northern end of a small subdivision off I-40 and old Route 66 east of Albuquerque. Don't leave valuables, including cameras, purses, and wallets, in your vehicle at the trailhead, since vandalism and break-ins have

The Three Gun Spring Trail heads up a broad valley on the southern edge of the Sandias.
EMILY RESSLER-TANNER

occurred at the parking lot. The trailhead is at the north end of the parking lot at the end of dirt Tres Pistolas Trail, the northernmost road in the subdivision. The trailhead is also the starting point of the Hawk Watch Trail (Hike 32).

The Three Gun Spring Trailhead area is open space land that was purchased by the City of Albuquerque, Bernalillo County, and the federal government to protect it from development as luxury home sites and to provide continued public access to the southern Sandia Mountains and the famed Sandia Hawk Watch site on the ridge to the east.

From the trailhead at the northern end of the parking area, hike north up a wide valley on the Three Gun Spring Trail. The easy-to-follow trail follows a sandy wash for 150 feet and then trends left onto a humped ridge. Continue north for 0.5 mile to a Cibola National Forest sign with a trail map and interpretive information. Past the sign the trail enters the 37,822-acre Sandia Mountain Wilderness Area. The Hawk Watch Trail (#215) busts right here and climbs 1.2 miles to the ridgeline. Continue north from the boundary on the Three Gun Spring Trail.

The trail slowly ascends the steepening canyon, passing a sparse woodland of piñon pine, juniper, gray oak, and desert live oak. Wild grasses, including beargrass, and various prickly pear, barrel, and cholla cacti are scattered across the dusty ground. Keep your binoculars handy to spot typical birds like the curve-billed thrasher, spotted towhee, black-chinned hummingbird, and black-headed grosbeak.

After 1.5 miles and about 850 feet of elevation gain, the trail reaches a Y-junction. Keep left on the signed Three Gun Spring Trail. A right turn heads up a shallow canyon for 600 feet to Three Gun Spring, a spring that usually flows after wet winters. Continue north on the Three Gun Spring Trail and after another 0.1 mile, reach a second sign that directs hikers to go left up a set of steep switchbacks that zigzag up a long blunt ridge at the head of the canyon. Near the top the trail passes granite outcroppings and the angle begins to ease. Take in spacious views of the southern Sandia Mountains and the Manzanita Mountains south of I-25. The switchbacks get plenty of sun, so plan on taking your time on hot days or time your hike for early morning or evening during the summer.

After trudging up the switchbacks, the trail winds north beneath shady ponderosa pines and reaches a wide ridge and the 7,910-foot-high junction with the Embudo Trail at 2.5 miles. The Embudo Trail (#193), beginning on the eastern edge of Albuquerque, climbs 3.2 miles to this junction. This is a good stop for a rest and snack. Some hikers turn around here to shorten the hike or, if they've arranged a car shuttle, descend west down the Embudo Trail.

For the last 1.5-mile-long trail segment, keep right on the Three Gun Spring Trail from the trail junction and head northeast across wooded slopes. After climbing steeply from the warm lower valley, this trail section is delightful as it dips and rolls across shady slopes before climbing the last 0.5 mile up a steeper ridge to the end of

Tall stands of rabbitbrush line the Three Gun Trail. EMILY RESSLER-TANNER

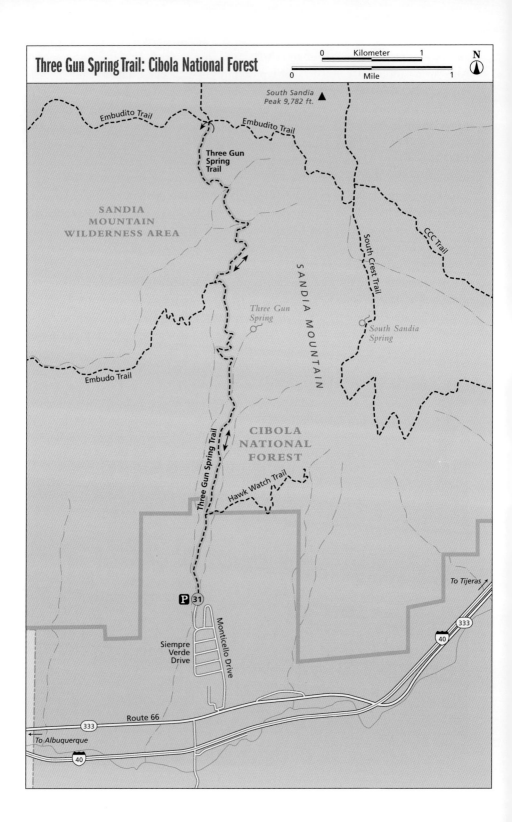

Three Gun Spring Trail: Cibola National Forest

0   Kilometer   1

0   Mile   1

N

South Sandia Peak 9,782 ft. ▲

Embudito Trail

Embudito Trail

Three Gun Spring Trail

SANDIA
MOUNTAIN
WILDERNESS AREA

CCC Trail

South Crest Trail

Three Gun Spring

South Sandia Spring

S A N D I A   M O U N T A I N

Embudo Trail

Three Gun Spring Trail

CIBOLA
NATIONAL
FOREST

Hawk Watch Trail

To Tijeras

P 31

Monticello Drive

Siempre
Verde
Drive

333

40

Route 66

333

To Albuquerque

40

the hike at Oso Pass, an 8,500-foot saddle below South Sandia Peak, and the junction with the Embudito Trail (#192) after 4 miles of hiking. The Embudito Trail begins off Tramway Boulevard to the west and climbs 4.1 miles to this junction, then continues up another 1.5 miles to the South Crest Trail, which heads north to the Sandia Crest, the range's high point. This last trail section usually has snow and ice in winter, so bring microspikes or other boot traction as well as trekking poles for safe footing.

After resting in the piney woods, shoulder your pack and return 4 miles back to the Three Gun Spring Trailhead for an 8-mile round-trip hike. The hike back is mostly downhill, so it goes fast. The rule of thumb is that a mountain descent takes about one-third of the total hiking time, while the ascent usually takes about two-thirds of the time.

Miles and Directions

0.0 Begin at the Three Gun Spring Trailhead (GPS: 35.076493 N / -106.444200 W) and hike north on the Three Gun Spring Trail.

0.5 Reach a junction with the Hawk Watch Trail and a Sandia Mountain Wilderness Area information sign (GPS: 35.082639 N / -106.443611 W). Continue hiking straight (north) on the Three Gun Spring Trail.

1.5 Reach a sign directing hikers to keep left on the Three Gun Spring Trail. For a side trip, go right up a canyon for 500 feet to Three Gun Spring.

1.6 Reach a second sign and keep left (west) and begin hiking steep switchbacks out of the canyon.

2.5 Reach a wide ridge and a junction with the Embudo Trail on the left. Stay right (northeast) and continue hiking on the Three Gun Spring Trail.

4.0 Reach the trail's end at a junction with the Embudito Trail on Oso Pass (GPS: 35.117729 N / -106.443191 W). Turn around and return to the trailhead via the same route.

8.0 Arrive back at the Three Gun Spring Trailhead.

Area Info

National Museum of Nuclear Science & History, 601 Eubank Blvd. SE, Albuquerque 87123; (505) 245-2137; www.nuclearmuseum.org

Tijeras Pueblo Archaeological Site, 11776 NM 337, Tijeras 87059; (505) 281-3304; www.friendsoftijeraspueblo.org

Turquoise Trail National Scenic Byway, NM 14 from Albuquerque to Santa Fe; Turquoise Trail Association, PO Box 303, Sandia Park 87047; (505) 281-5233; www.turquoisetrail.org

32 Hawk Watch Trail: Cibola National Forest

The Hawk Watch Trail climbs steep slopes from the Three Gun Spring Trail in the southern Sandia Mountains to a scenic overlook that is one of Albuquerque's best bird-watching sites, with thousands of migrating raptors, including hawks and eagles, soaring past in the springtime.

Distance: 3.4 miles out and back

Hiking time: 2 to 3 hours

Difficulty: Strenuous, with 1,400 feet of elevation gain

Best seasons: Spring and fall

Schedule: Trail open year-round

Other trail users: Horseback riders on first 0.5 mile; hikers only on Hawk Watch Trail

Canine compatibility: Leashed dogs allowed

Fees and permits: None

Maps: USGS Tijeras; trail map available at Sandia Ranger District and on website

Trail contact: Sandia Ranger District, 11776 NM 337, Tijeras 87059; (505) 281-3304; www.fs.usda.gov/cibola

Special considerations: Trail may be snowy and icy in winter. Summer days are hot and sunny.

Finding the trailhead: From Albuquerque, take I-40 east to exit 170 toward NM 333 / Historic Route 66. After exiting, drive 1.6 miles east on NM 333 and turn left (north) onto Monticello Drive. Continue 0.6 mile on Monticello Drive to Alegre Road and turn left (west) onto Alegre Road. After 0.1 mile turn right (north) onto Siempre Verde Drive. Drive 0.2 mile on Siempre Verde to the Three Gun Spring / Hawk Watch Trailhead and parking area. GPS: 35.076493 N / -106.444200 W

The Hike

The Hawk Watch Trail (#215), a 3.4-mile out-and-back hike, is an excellent spring outing to a lofty overlook on the southern edge of the Sandia Mountains. The viewpoint is a renowned spot for birders to see migrating raptors during the peak spring migration season from late February until early May and the fall migration from late August to mid-November. The trail, gaining 1,400 feet of elevation, is short and steep, with gravelly sections and occasional loose footing. Bring trekking poles or a walking stick for balance, especially on the descent. Don't forget a bird identification guide and binoculars to spot hawks, falcons, and eagles.

Spring and autumn are the best times to hike the trail to see migrating raptors. Winter usually offers warm temperatures on open west-facing slopes, but summer days are hot and sunny. Hike early in the day in summer, carry plenty of water, and wear a hat and sunscreen for sun protection.

The trail was constructed by the US Forest Service for HawkWatch International, an organization that studies raptors and raptor migration in the western United States. HawkWatch's mission is to provide raptor education, monitor raptor migrations, and support scientific research. The organization started annual migration counts in the Sandia Mountains in 1985 and began banding raptors here in 1990. These projects ended in 2010 when HawkWatch decided to focus their raptor research efforts at a more remote site 25 miles to the south in the Manzano Mountains.

While the Sandia HawkWatch site was active, the annual raptor count in spring ranged between 3,200 and 6,500 migrating birds from eighteen species. The Sandia project monitored raptor population trends by migrating birds using the southern Rocky Mountain Flyway, as well as tracked raptors banded in the Sandia and Manzano Mountains with satellites to study raptor migrations, breeding areas, and wintering sites. HawkWatch International continues to use the trail for guided hikes to the overlook during the peak spring migration. Visit their website at www.hawkwatch .org for more information and scheduled field trips.

The hike starts at 6,320 feet from the Three Gun Spring Trailhead on the north side of a parking lot at the end of Tres Pistolas Trail NE in the Monticello Subdivision. The first half-mile of the hike follows the marked Three Gun Spring Trail (#194) up a wide canyon lined with yuccas, junipers, cholla and prickly pear cacti, and dry desert grasses. Hike north on the sandy trail for 175 feet to a junction. Go

Looking south from the Hawk Watch Trail to the Manzanita Mountains.
EMILY RESSLER-TANNER

Red-tailed hawks are often seen soaring in the sky above the Hawk Watch Trail.
WIKIMEDIA COMMONS © LARRY LAMSA, USED CC ATTRIBUTION 2.0

left on the trail and continue for 0.5 mile on a humped ridge, passing a pile of granite boulders, to the boundary of the Sandia Mountain Wilderness Area. A right turn will also reach the boundary, but that trail is hard hiking up a sandy wash. At the wilderness boundary is an information sign and Sandia trail map. Walk 25 feet north from the boundary and go right on the Hawk Watch Trail.

The next hike section, heading northeast, follows the steep Hawk Watch Trail for 1.2 miles to a viewpoint for spotting migrating raptors in the sky overhead. The trail heads east across the valley floor, dipping across dry washes and scrambling over low gravel ridges. After 0.2 mile the trail bends northeast and begins climbing and contouring across steeper slopes, passing boulders and scattered piñon pines and junipers. After a series of switchbacks, the trail edges between several large granite boulders atop a ridge at 1.3 miles from the trailhead and bends northeast along the ridgetop.

The trail begins climbing steeply again and reaches wooden steps and a handrail on a rocky section at 1.4 miles before bending around the east side of a high ridge studded with jumbled white boulders. Follow the trail up steep slopes to an overlook and the hike's end on the north end of the bouldery ridge at 1.7 miles. Numerous boulders at the overlook provide front-row seats for the raptor flyby in spring.

Brushy slopes rise above the 7,700-foot overlook to the cliff-lined crest of the southern Sandia Mountains. These remote cliffs and others in the area provide summer habitat and nesting sites for raptors stopping here between the spring and fall migrations. While the hike ends at this overlook, the trail continues another half-mile up the slopes to a higher viewpoint that was once used by Hawk Watch International as a research site to trap and band passing raptors.

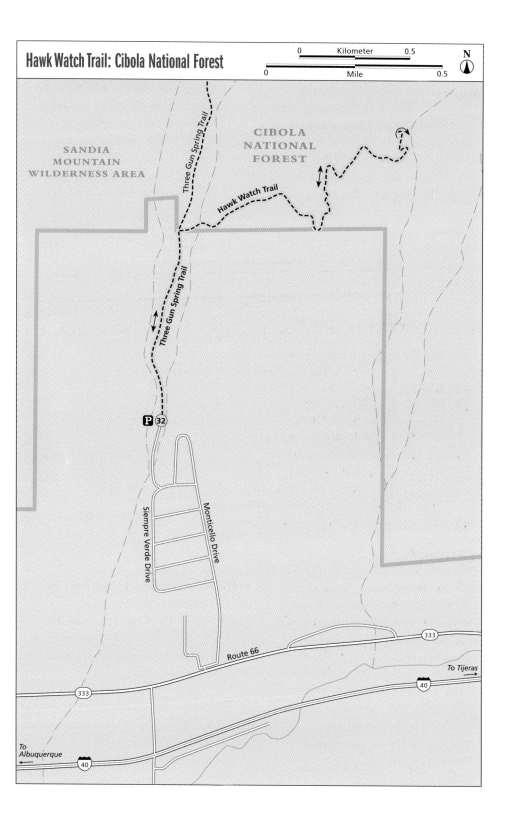

Hawk Watch Trail: Cibola National Forest

0 — Kilometer — 0.5
0 — Mile — 0.5

N

SANDIA
MOUNTAIN
WILDERNESS AREA

CIBOLA
NATIONAL
FOREST

Three Gun Spring Trail

Hawk Watch Trail

Three Gun Spring Trail

P 32

Siempre Verde Drive

Monticello Drive

Route 66

333

To Tijeras

40

333

To
Albuquerque

40

If you visit the overlook during the prime raptor migration, get out your bird book and binoculars and start scanning the sky for soaring birds. As many as twenty different raptor species have been spotted here. Commonly seen hawks include Cooper's hawk, sharp-shinned hawk, northern goshawk, Swainson's hawk, red-tailed hawk, rough-legged hawk, and ferruginous hawk. Other raptors are peregrine and prairie falcons, American kestrel, osprey, golden and bald eagles, and turkey vulture. HawkWatch research here and at the Manzano Mountains site indicates that roughly 5,000 raptors soar through here in spring; that American kestrel, a small falcon, numbers are declining; and that bald eagles and peregrine falcons, once endangered species, are increasing in number.

After enjoying the spacious views and adding some raptors to your lifetime bird list, pack your binoculars and start back down the trail. The first mile of the descent is steep and gravelly, with uneven footing. Use poles or a walking stick for balance. After rejoining the Three Gun Spring Trail, return south to the trailhead for a 3.4-mile round-trip hike.

Miles and Directions

0.0 Start from the Three Gun Spring Trailhead at the north end of the parking lot (GPS: 35.076493 N / -106.444200 W). Hike north on the obvious gravel trail.

0.1 At the sign for the Three Gun Spring Trail, continue north on that trail.

0.5 Enter the Sandia Mountain Wilderness Area and pass an information sign with a Sandia trail map. Just past the wilderness boundary, turn right (northeast) on the Hawk Watch Trail (GPS: 35.082639 N / -106.443611 W).

1.3 Pass between large granite boulders.

1.4 Reach wooden steps and a handrail.

1.7 Reach the top of a ridge and the Hawk Watch overlook (GPS: 35.086925 N / -106.432601 W). Return to the trailhead via the same route.

3.4 Arrive back at the Three Gun Spring Trailhead.

Area Info

National Museum of Nuclear Science & History, 601 Eubank Blvd. SE, Albuquerque 87123; (505) 245-2137; www.nuclearmuseum.org

Tijeras Pueblo Archaeological Site, 11776 NM 337, Tijeras 87059; (505) 281-3304; www.friendsoftijeraspueblo.org

Turquoise Trail National Scenic Byway, NM 14 from Albuquerque to Santa Fe; Turquoise Trail Association, PO Box 303, Sandia Park 87047; (505) 281-5233; www.turquoisetrail.org

Manzanita and Manzano Mountains

The Mission Ruins at Quarai have stood for almost 400 years.

33 Tunnel Canyon Trail: Cibola National Forest

The Tunnel Canyon Trail, in the northern Manzanita Mountains southeast of Albuquerque, offers a 4.4-mile out-and-back hike on a multiuse trail. The popular trail follows a scenic canyon into wooded hills and links with other trails for longer loop hikes.

Distance: 4.4 miles out and back
Hiking time: 2 to 3 hours
Difficulty: Moderate
Best seasons: Apr through Nov
Schedule: Open year-round
Other trail users: Mountain bikers, motorcyclists, and horseback riders
Canine compatibility: Leashed dogs allowed
Fees and permits: None

Maps: USGS Sedillo; Manzanita Mountains Trail System Map on Cibola National Forest website
Trail contacts: Sandia Ranger District, 11776 NM 337, Tijeras 87059; (505) 281-3304. Cibola National Forest, 2113 Osuna Rd. NE, Albuquerque 87113; (505) 346-3900; www.fs .usda.gov/cibola.
Special considerations: Trail borders military property in places. Stay on the trail, as the military property is patrolled.

Finding the trailhead: From Albuquerque, take I-40 east for about 15 miles to exit 175 toward NM 337/ NM 333 to Tijeras. Turn right (south) onto NM 337 and drive 2.5 miles to the dirt Tunnel Canyon Trailhead parking area on the right (west) side of the highway. GPS: 35.046556 N / -106.383165 W

The Hike

The 2.2-mile Tunnel Canyon Trail (#05145), a 4.4-mile out-and-back hike, is a popular hiking and mountain-biking trail that threads through the northern Manzanita Mountains a few miles south of I-40 and Tijeras. The trail, beginning at 6,592 feet in Cedros Canyon, gains 481 feet as it ascends the canyon to a high point of 7,064 feet in ponderosa pine woods before descending to the Otero Canyon Trail. The upper part of the trail skirts a military base, so make sure that you don't wander off the trail onto Department of Defense property, which is regularly patrolled by military police.

The Tunnel Canyon Trail is a fine year-round hike with plenty of shade trees during the summer and generally light snowfall in the winter, although hikers should carry microspikes and trekking poles if it's snowy or icy. The canyon is also sheltered from the wind, making it a good spring hike.

Start the hike at the Tunnel Canyon Trailhead on the south side of a large dirt parking lot on the west side of NM 337. An information board is at the trailhead, but no restrooms or water. The trail heads southwest above a dry wash on the right side of Tunnel Canyon, passing through a pygmy forest of piñon pines and junipers amid low, rounded hills. After 325 feet is a junction. Keep right on the Tunnel Canyon Trail.

The canyon narrows as the trail continues southwest, and at 0.7 mile it reaches a creek crossing that is usually dry except after rainstorms or from snowmelt. Past a footbridge over the creek at 1.0 mile, the trail bends sharply left and then right as it begins to climb east from the bottom of Tunnel Canyon across mountain slopes. At 1.2 miles the trail swings past a prominent rock outcropping. Stop here to catch your breath and admire the southern escarpment of the rugged Sandia Mountains to the north. The trail continues to climb, curving around an east-facing ridge before leveling out. Look for a T-junction with the West Ridge Trail (#05268). To make a loop hike following the West Ridge Trail and Birdhouse Ridge Trail back to the trailhead and parking lot, consult the Extra Credit Hike directions.

At 1.8 miles the trail begins to descend east down gentle wooded slopes with wide, sweeping turns and at 2.2 miles reaches a T-junction with the Otero Canyon Trail (#05056) in the bottom of steep-sided Otero Canyon. If you've arranged a car shuttle, walk north on the Otero Canyon Trail for 0.3 mile to its trailhead on NM 337. Otherwise, turn around at the trail junction and return north on the Tunnel Canyon Trail to the trailhead for a 4.4-mile out-and-back hike.

The Tunnel Canyon Trail offers spacious views across the Manzanita Mountains.
EMILY RESSLER-TANNER

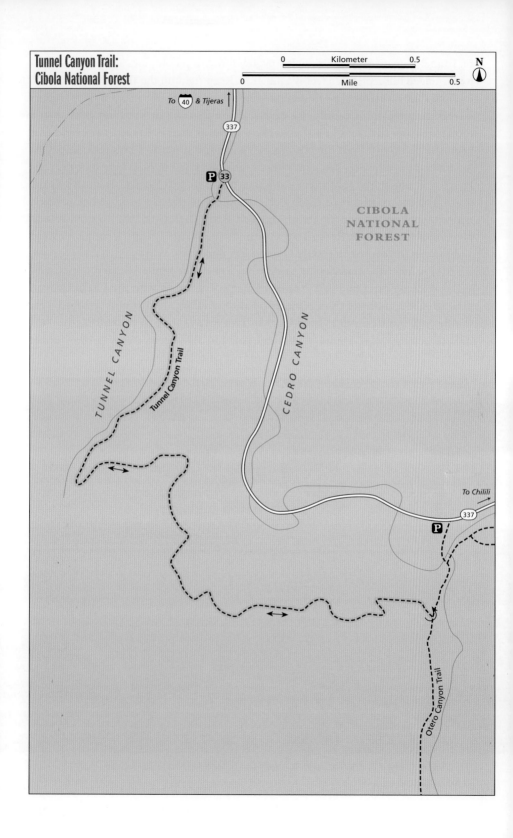

Tunnel Canyon Trail:
Cibola National Forest

0   Kilometer   0.5

0   Mile   0.5

N

To 40 & Tijeras

337

P 33

CIBOLA
NATIONAL
FOREST

TUNNEL CANYON

CEDRO CANYON

Tunnel Canyon Trail

To Chilili

337

P

Otero Canyon Trail

EXTRA CREDIT HIKE

Combine the Tunnel Canyon Trail with the West Ridge Trail (#05268) and Birdhouse Ridge Trail (#05411) for a lightly trafficked 4.7-mile loop hike that begins and ends at the Tunnel Canyon Trailhead. Hike the Tunnel Canyon Trail for 1.8 miles to its junction with the West Ridge Trail (GPS: 35.032223 N / -106.378973 W). Turn right (west) on the West Ridge Trail and hike 0.3 mile to its junction with the Birdhouse Ridge Trail (GPS: 35.029652 N / -106.382207 W). Turn right (north) on the Birdhouse Ridge Trail and follow it north for 2.6 miles across mountain slopes to a broad ridge before descending back to the trailhead.

Miles and Directions

0.0 Start at an information sign at the Tunnel Canyon Trailhead and parking area on the west side of NM 337 (GPS: 35.046556 N / -106.383165 W). Hike southwest on the trail.

0.1 Reach a "Tunnel Canyon Trail" sign. Keep right on the Tunnel Canyon Trail and hike southwest up the canyon.

0.7 Reach a creek crossing and continue hiking south as the trail begins to climb.

1.0 Cross a wooden footbridge before the trail makes a sharp left turn to the north and then turns right. Begin hiking east out of Tunnel Canyon onto wooded slopes.

1.2 Reach a rock outcropping on the left (north) that provides a view of the Sandia Mountains to the north.

1.8 The trail begins to descend into Otero Canyon.

2.2 Reach a trail junction with the Otero Canyon Trail (GPS: 35.030566 N / -106.373612 W). Turn around and return to the trailhead via the same route.

4.4 Arrive back at the Tunnel Canyon Trailhead and parking area.

Area Info

Tinkertown Museum, 121 Sandia Crest Rd., Sandia Park 87047; (505) 281-5233; www.tinkertown.com

Tijeras Pueblo Archaeological Site, 11776 NM 337, Tijeras 87059; (505) 281-3304; www.friendsoftijeraspueblo.org

34 Cedro Creek Nature Trail: Cibola National Forest

The 0.9-mile-long Cedro Creek Nature Trail, a family-friendly hike, follows a rich riparian zone along Cedro Creek in the Manzanita Mountains southeast of Albuquerque. The 1.8-mile round-trip hike crosses meadows and woodlands filled with wildlife and vegetation in an arid landscape.

Distance: 1.8 miles out and back
Hiking time: About 1 hour
Difficulty: Easy
Best seasons: Spring, summer, and fall. Winters can be cold and snowy.
Schedule: Open year-round
Other trail users: None
Canine compatibility: Leashed dogs allowed
Fees and permits: None

Maps: USGS Sedillo; trail map available at Sandia Ranger District office and on website
Trail contact: Sandia Ranger District, 11776 NM 337, Tijeras 87059; (505) 281-3304; www.fs.usda.gov/cibola
Special considerations: This area is a sensitive riparian habitat. Stay on the trail and practice Leave No Trace principles while hiking.

Finding the trailhead: From Albuquerque, take I-40 east for about 15 miles to exit 175 toward NM 337/NM 333 to Tijeras. Turn right (south) onto NM 337 and drive 3.8 miles to the Otero Canyon Trailhead parking area on the right (south) side of the highway. GPS: 35.034645 N / -106.374292 W

The Hike

The 0.9-mile Cedro Creek Nature Trail (#05236), a 1.8-mile round-trip hike, explores the riparian ecosystem along Cedro Creek on the south side of NM 337 in Cedro Canyon. The easy trail, perfect for children and families, has minimal elevation gain and offers fun hiking by the trickling creek. The best time to hike the trail is in late spring and early summer, with wildflowers, wetlands alive with birds and insects, and pleasant mountain temperatures. The creek often dries up later in the summer. While the trail may be hiked in winter, the landscape is dormant, with few birds and animals.

Cibola National Forest offers an educational brochure for the nature trail that is tied to eleven numbered, knee-high markers scattered along the pathway. Pick up a copy of the brochure on your way to the trail at the Sandia Ranger Station between 8 a.m. and 4 p.m. from Monday to Friday. The station is located a half-mile south of I-40 on the left (east) side of NM 337 on the south side of Tijeras.

Riparian ecosystems, the most species-rich plant and animal communities in New Mexico, form long, sinuous bands of vegetation near creeks, rivers, and lakes. Riparian zones are rare in arid New Mexico, occurring on only 2 percent of the state's land.

The trail follows a lush riparian zone along Cedro Creek. JD TANNER

By contrast, about 65 percent of the state's wildlife lives near riparian zones. Since Cedro Creek doesn't flow year-round, it's called an "interrupted" stream. Parts of the creek dry up during part of the year, usually in late summer's hot weather, while other parts are wet most of the time.

Riparian zones are often disrupted by human activities, including diversion of upstream water, loss of native plants, introduction of invasive species that crowd out native plants, and runoff from roads and highways. This trail, exploring the riparian ecosystem along a state highway, showcases a mature life zone with few invasive species and roadside plants and shrubs that deter quick highway runoff.

Begin the hike at the Otero Canyon Trailhead on the south side of a large parking lot lined with big boulders along NM 337. The Otero Canyon Trail (#05056) also begins here and heads south up Otero Canyon in the Manzanita Mountains. From the parking lot, walk between a couple boulders to an interpretive sign and map. Hike south on the Otero Canyon Trail for 0.07 mile to the trailhead for the Cedro Creek Nature Trail on the left.

Go left (east) on the trail and hike along the south side of the creek. A hillside thickly covered with piñon pines and scrub oaks rises south of the trail, and scattered cottonwoods dot the canyon floor. The trail crosses an open meadow and continues east past marshes and shady trees. Cedro Creek ripples over cobbles in its streambed to the left. Reach the first creek crossing after 0.5 mile and skip across the water. Unless the creek is swollen after heavy rain, hikers won't get their feet wet in the

A GOOD RULE OF THUMB

Approaching wildlife is *never* a good idea. A rule of thumb is that if the wildlife changes its behavior in any way, you are too close or getting too close.

A fun way to teach children this rule is by using their thumbs. Have your kids hold a thumb up an arm's distance in front of their faces. If they cannot cover up the animal they are looking at with their thumbnail, they are probably too close and should back up. The technique helps kids learn to slow down and think about how close they are to wild animals.

three stream crossings. Hike east to the next crossing at 0.6 mile and then the third crossing at 0.8 mile.

Watch for wildlife along the creek, including water striders on glassy ponds, tiger salamanders hiding among rocks, birds flitting in the cottonwoods and box elders on the floodplain, and desert cottontail rabbits and mule deer grazing in grassy meadows.

Reach the end of the trail at 0.9 mile, where a sign, directing hikers to turn around, marks the hike's end point. The Big Block climbing area, a limestone cliff

The Cedro Creek Nature Trail begins at a trailhead on NM 337. JD TANNER

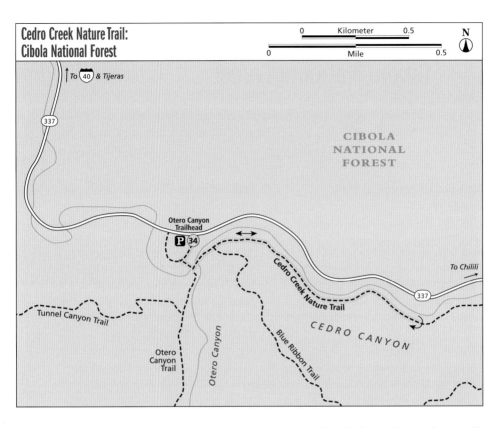

band and a pyramid-shaped rock block, tucks into a bend above the creek at trail's end. Return to the trailhead on the same path for a 1.8-mile round-trip hike.

Miles and Directions

0.0 Start at the Otero Canyon Trailhead and parking lot (GPS: 35.034645 N / -106.374292 W). Go south on the Otero Canyon Trail.

0.07 Reach the Cedro Creek Nature Trail and trailhead sign on the left (east). Hike east on the Cedro Creek Nature Trail.

0.5 Reach a creek crossing and continue hiking east.

0.6 Make a second creek crossing.

0.8 Make a third creek crossing.

0.9 Reach the end of the trail (GPS: 35.031360 N / -106.361968 W). A sign directs hikers to turn around and return to the trailhead on the same trail.

1.8 Arrive back at the trailhead and parking area.

Area Info

Tijeras Pueblo Archaeological Site, 11776 NM 337, Tijeras 87059; (505) 281–3304; www.friendsoftijeraspueblo.org

35 Fourth of July Trail: Cibola National Forest

The 1.4-mile Fourth of July Trail, climbing to the crest of the Manzano Mountains southeast of Albuquerque, offers a spectacular out-and-back hike up a canyon decorated with colorful fall foliage, including gold, scarlet, and orange bigtooth maple trees.

Distance: 2.8 miles out and back

Hiking time: About 2 hours

Difficulty: Moderate, with over 900 feet of elevation gain

Best seasons: May through Oct

Schedule: Open year-round; Fourth of July Campground open Apr through Oct

Other trail users: Horseback riders

Canine compatibility: Leashed dogs allowed

Fees and permits: No fee for day use; overnight camping fee is charged

Maps: USGS Bosque Peak; trail maps available on national forest website

Trail contact: Mountainair Ranger District, 40 Ranger Station Rd., Mountainair 87036; (505) 847-2990; www.fs.usda.gov/cibola

Special considerations: Mountain lions and black bears are present in the area. Access road may be impassable in winter.

Finding the trailhead: From Albuquerque, take I-40 east for about 15 miles to exit 175 toward NM 337/NM 333 to Tijeras. Turn right (south) onto NM 337 and drive 29.1 miles to NM 55. Turn right (west) on NM 55 and continue to the village of Tajique. On the south side of town, turn right (west) at 32.9 miles on Torreon Tajique Loop Road / FR 55. Drive 7 miles on dirt FR 55 to the Fourth of July Campground on the right. Park outside the gate during the winter, or drive through the gate and park in the picnic area or designated parking if the campground is open. Walk to the trailhead at the northwest end of the campground's Gallo Loop (GPS: 34.790367 N / -106.382555 W). Alternatively, drive 6.9 miles on FR 55 and park on the road's shoulder at the Albuquerque Trail (#78) trailhead, about a half-mile from the campground entrance.

The Hike

The popular 1.4-mile Fourth of July Trail (#173), an out-and-back 2.8-mile hike, ascends a wooded valley to the crest of the Manzano Mountains southeast of Albuquerque. The eastern slope of the Manzano Mountains is famed as one of New Mexico's best places to view October's fiery blaze of color. The Fourth of July Trail is ground zero for autumn's amazing colors, with one of the state's largest groves of bigtooth maple trees glowing pumpkin orange, crimson, and gold along the dirt path. Besides the vivid colors of the bigtooth maple, other trees including the Rocky Mountain maple, scrub oak, and box elder, add more hues to the Manzano palette. The area, popular with Albuquerque leaf-peepers, offers more color variation to fall's firewall than the Sandia Mountains and Jemez Mountains to the north, where golden groves of quaking aspen reign supreme.

The moderate Fourth of July Trail, one of the best trails for autumn hikes, is easy to follow up a shallow canyon to the crest of the Manzanos and a junction with the Cerro Blanco Trail (#79). Rather than turning around at the junction, hikers can extend their trek by jogging south to the summit of 8,388-foot Cerro Blanco or heading north to the Crest Trail and then descending the Mosca (#58) and Albuquerque (#78) Trails down Cañon de la Gallina to the Mosca Loop at the Fourth of July Campground for a 5.8-mile loop hike. Consult a detailed trail map to plan the longer hike.

Besides autumn, it's best to hike the Fourth of July Trail in late spring and summer when wildflowers speckle mountain meadows and temperatures are cooler than the lowlands. Watch for thunderstorms accompanied by lightning on July and August afternoons, especially if you venture onto the range crest or isolated peaks like Cerro Blanco or Mosca Peak. The prime leaf-viewing season is from mid-September until late October, but the actual dates vary from year to year, depending on mountain temperatures. The colder the temperatures, the earlier the leaves will change. Watch the weather ahead of time and check with Cibola National Forest's Mountainair Ranger District (505-847-2990) for color updates. The peak date for the Manzano blaze of glory is usually around October 10. To avoid the autumn color crowds, it's best to hike the trail during the week rather than on busy weekends.

The trail is open in winter, but it is difficult to reach the trailhead since the road may be impassable without chains and a four-wheel-drive vehicle, and the trail is snowbound and icy. Bring microspikes or other boot traction devices as well as trekking poles.

After parking at the Albuquerque Trailhead on FR 55 or at designated day-use parking near the Fourth of July Campground entrance, walk on the campground road through Gallo Loop to the Fourth of July Trailhead on the left (west) side of the road just before a loop at the road's end. The trailhead is about a quarter mile from the parking area. Hike northwest on the marked Fourth of July Trail on an old road that

THE MANZANO MOUNTAINS

The Manzano Mountains, a 30-mile-long range southeast of Albuquerque, is one of New Mexico's best-kept secrets. The rugged range, topped by 10,098-foot Manzano Peak, is rarely visited compared to the Sandia Mountains on Albuquerque's eastern doorstep. Those who venture into the Manzanos will find the 36,875-acre Manzano Mountain Wilderness Area, the 22-mile Crest Trail, Manzano Mountains State Park with trails and camping, and scattered groves of bigtooth maples, which offer some of New Mexico's best autumn colors. Besides a wealth of wildlife, including black bears, mountain lions, mule deer, and wild turkeys, the Manzanos are also a prime spot to view raptors like hawks, eagles, and falcons during the spring and fall migrations.

becomes a singletrack trail up a wide canyon. After 0.1 mile reach a junction with the Spring Loop Trail. Stay straight on the Fourth of July Trail along the trickling creek. Tall ponderosa pines and Douglas firs along with bigtooth maples tower above the trail.

After 0.2 mile of hiking, the trail is surrounded by bigtooth and Rocky Mountain maples, many arching over the trail and creating a corridor of color. Continue hiking up the trail and at 0.4 mile pass a junction with the Fourth of July Spur Trail, which goes right to the campground's Mosca Loop, and a circular water box for wildlife (bring water rather than drinking here). Past here the trail becomes rocky and steepens as the canyon narrows down.

The steep section ends after 0.7 mile and the trail passes Upper Fourth of July Spring on the left. Horsetails and yellow monkeyflowers adorn the seeping spring in summer, but also watch for poison ivy with its shiny leaves. Past the spring is a junction with the Albuquerque Trail, which goes right and contours north across shady slopes before descending Cañon de la Gallina for 2.5 miles to the Fourth of July Campground.

Continue west up the main trail before it bends left and heads south across slopes, slowly climbing to a T-junction with the Cerro Blanco Trail and trail's end at 1.4 miles. This is the turn-around point for the Fourth of July Trail. Return down the trail for a 2.8-mile round-trip hike.

The Fourth of July Trail is one of the best spots for autumn color near Albuquerque.
EMILY RESSLER-TANNER

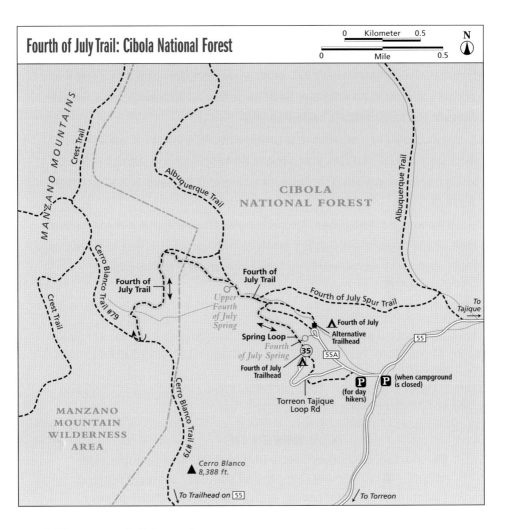

Fourth of July Trail: Cibola National Forest

Miles and Directions

0.0　Start at the Fourth of July Trailhead on the west side of Gallo Loop in Fourth of July Campground (GPS: 34.790367 N / -106.382555 W). Hike northwest on the wide trail.

0.1　Reach a junction with the Spring Loop Trail. Continue straight on the Fourth of July Trail, passing a Manzano Mountain Wilderness Area sign.

0.4　Reach a junction with the Fourth of July Spur Trail, which goes right. Continue straight and begin climbing up a rocky canyon.

0.7　Pass Upper Fourth of July Spring on the left and reach a junction with the Albuquerque Trail (#78), which heads right. Continue straight.

1.4　Reach the trail's end at a junction with the Cerro Blanco Trail (#79) (GPS: 34.792451 N / -106.396555 W). Turn around here to return to the trailhead on the same route.

2.8　Arrive back at the Fourth of July Trailhead.

EXTRA CREDIT HIKES

From the end of the Fourth of July Trail, go left on the Cerro Blanco Trail for 0.3 mile to an overlook across the eastern Manzano Mountains or hike 1.3 miles southeast on the trail, descending to the Cerro Blanco Trailhead on FR 55.

Another option for a longer hike is to go right on the Cerro Blanco Trail and hike 0.6 mile to the Crest Trail (#170). Follow it for a mile to the Mosca Trail (#58), which descends 0.8 mile to the Albuquerque Trail (#78). Follow it for 2.2 miles to the Fourth of July Campground and FR 55.

If you want to climb 9,508-foot Mosca Peak, one of the highest mountains in the Manzanos, hike to the junction of the Crest and Mosca Trails and scramble west for 0.5 mile up brushy slopes to the pointed summit and forever views across central New Mexico.

Area Info

Manzano Mountains State Park, CR B062, Mile Marker 3 on NM 131, Mountainair, 87036; (505) 469-7608; www.emnrd.state.nm.us/SPD/manzanomountains statepark.html

Salinas Pueblo Missions National Monument, PO Box 517, Mountainair 87036; (505) 847-2585; www.nps.gov/sapu

GREEN TIP

Be courteous of other hikers and visitors. Many people visit natural areas for quiet, peace, and solitude, so avoid making loud noises, playing music, and intruding on others' privacy.

36 Mission Ruins Loop and Spanish Corral Trail: Salinas Pueblo Missions National Monument

The Quarai unit of Salinas Pueblo Missions National Monument in central New Mexico offers a 1.5-mile loop hike on two trails that explore ancient Puebloan ruins and one of the best-preserved seventeenth-century Spanish mission ruins in New Mexico.

Distance: 1.5-mile double loop
Hiking time: 1 to 2 hours
Difficulty: Easy; Mission Ruins Loop Trail is wheelchair accessible
Best seasons: Spring, summer, and fall
Schedule: Open daily 9 a.m. to 6 p.m. Memorial Day through Labor Day, 9 a.m. to 5 p.m. the rest of the year. Closed Thanksgiving Day, Christmas, and New Year's Day.
Other trail users: None

Canine compatibility: Leashed dogs allowed; clean up after your pet
Fees and permits: None
Maps: USGS Punta de Agua; trail map available at visitor center and on park website
Trail contact: Salinas Pueblo Missions National Monument, PO Box 517, Mountainair 87036; (505) 847-2585; www.nps.gov/sapu
Special considerations: Some park areas may be closed in spring due to high winds.

Finding the trailhead: From Albuquerque, drive east on I-40 for about 15 miles to exit 175 toward NM 337 / NM 333 to Tijeras. Turn right (south) onto NM 337 and drive 29.1 miles to NM 55. Turn right (west) onto NM 55 and continue 16.9 miles to CR B076. Take a right (southwest) onto CR B076 and drive 1.1 miles to the Quarai parking lot, visitor center, and trailhead. GPS: 34.595124 N / -106.297650 W

The Hike

The Mission Ruins Loop and Spanish Corral Trails, a 1.5-mile double-loop hike, explore the 90-acre Pueblo of Quarai ruins unit of Salinas Pueblo Missions National Monument on the eastern flank of the Manzano Mountains southeast of Albuquerque. Quarai, formerly a New Mexico State Monument, was combined with two other large Native American and Spanish mission archaeological sites, Abó and Gran Quivira, in 1981 to form today's national monument. Gran Quivira, with multiple ruins, was originally designated Gran Quivira National Monument in 1909.

The monument preserves the best existing examples of seventeenth-century Spanish Franciscan architecture in the United States and the ruins of three of the largest Pueblo villages. All three units are easily visited in a day. Abó lies 17 miles southwest of Quarai on NM 55, while Gran Quivira, with the largest ruins, is 33 miles south of Quarai off NM 55.

The Quarai ruins are the remains of a Puebloan and later Spanish settlement in the Estancia Basin east of 10,098-foot Manzano Peak, the range high point. Archaeological evidence indicates that the pueblo was settled in the 1300s, probably due to nearby springs. Spanish explorers first visited the flourishing trade community in the early 1580s, and in 1598 conquistador Don Juan de Oñate, a controversial New Mexican figure who brutally massacred most of the inhabitants of Acoma in 1599, stopped at the pueblo to obtain an oath of allegiance to the King of Spain. A few years later, Franciscan priests arrived here and at the nearby pueblos to establish missions and convert the Native people to Christianity.

The Salinas pueblos of Quarai, Abó, and Gran Quivira depict the cultural contact between the Puebloan people and the invading Spanish and the subsequent changes from that contact, including long-lasting cross-cultural influences, the effect of Native people on Spanish culture, and the impact of Spanish missions on the Pueblos.

The Franciscans arrived in the early 1600s, planting apple orchards that probably gave the name Manzano to the mountains, derived from the Spanish word for apple, *manzana*. The Quarai Mission and Convento, large red stone buildings, were established in 1626, and construction of the mission Nuestra Señora de la Purísima

The prosperous Spanish mission at Quarai was built between 1627 and 1632.

Concepción de Cuarac began in 1627 and was completed in 1632. An enduring Quarai mystery is that a square kiva, a Pueblo religious structure, was built in the convento at the same time the mission buildings were constructed.

The pueblo and mission prospered through the mid-1600s, until attacks by marauding Apaches, called "The Red Death," and a severe drought led to the abandonment of the area by 1675. Other factors included deteriorating relations between the Puebloan people and the Franciscans; smallpox and other diseases introduced by the Spanish; and widespread famine with little rain to raise vital crops. One priest noted that no crops were harvested for three years and that over 450 Natives died of starvation in Las Humanas pueblo at Gran Quivira in 1868. The Quarai people moved west and settled in pueblos along the Rio Grande south of Albuquerque. The site was later used in the 1820s by ranchers Juan and Miguel Lucero, who used the convento as a sheep pen and built an irrigation system with stone from the mission ruins.

The thick stone walls at the Quarai church still rise almost 40 feet.

They abandoned Quarai after an Apache raid in 1830.

Now Quarai is a quiet and remote site with low visitation. The two trails are a wonderful way to explore New Mexico's rich history and discover the pleasure of ruins. Hikers on the 0.5-mile Mission Ruins Loop Trail learn about the Franciscan and Spanish influence by strolling through the church ruins and learning about the convento functions and the unique square kiva within its walls. The 1-mile Spanish Corral Trail loops across open grasslands and a scattered piñon pine and juniper woodland. Bring binoculars and a field guide for excellent bird watching. After your hike, pull out the picnic basket and dine under rustling cottonwood trees in the park picnic area.

Salinas Pueblo Missions National Monument is also a designated Dark Sky Park, although all units are closed at night. Ask at the visitor center for details on the occasional dark sky interpretive programs and ranger-led star parties at the different national monument units.

Start your hike at the visitor center on the west side of Quarai by exploring exhibits detailing the history of the site, getting park information, and shopping at the gift store. Also pick up a Quarai Trail Guide, keyed to numbered markers along the trail. The center has restrooms and water. The monument parking lot is too small for RVs and vehicles pulling trailers. Oversize units must park in the overflow parking area north of the entrance gate.

Begin the hike by walking through the breezeway in the visitor center to the wheelchair-accessible Mission Ruins Loop Trail and a Y-junction. Go right on the paved trail and hike 0.15 mile, passing several heaped mounds of soil and rock that are the remains of ancient Pueblo buildings, to a trail junction. Go right to start the Spanish Corral Trail, a mile-long loop hiked counterclockwise.

The trail crosses a footbridge over a usually dry wash and reaches a Y-junction after 115 feet. Go right on the dirt Spanish Corral Trail and ascend a gentle hillside covered with a pygmy forest of piñon pine and juniper south of broad Cañon Sapato, which drains east onto the plains. After 0.4 mile the trail makes a sharp left turn and continues to interpretive signs at 0.65 mile and a bench that overlooks the valley and the mission ruins to the north.

The trail bends west here and skirts the edges of the old Spanish Corral, stone walls and foundations that were possibly used by nineteenth-century settlers for corralling sheep or as holding pens for sheep shearing. The rocky trail begins descending north to the creek's floodplain and then turns west to the trail junction at the start of the loop at 1.2 miles. Go right and cross the footbridge to the Mission Ruins Loop Trail, then go right again on the paved trail.

The next hike section explores the main mission site. Follow the trail beneath shady cottonwood trees for 525 feet to the South Convento ruins and the mission cemetery on the left. The next trail section explores the mission ruins, winding through the convent and church of Nuestra Señora de la Purísima Concepción de Quarai. While the church was the heart of the mission, the convento, built around a central plaza, provided a living area for the Franciscan priests as well as kitchens, storage areas, and livestock corrals.

The first Franciscans came in early 1626, when Fray Juan Gutiérrez de la Chica rode into Quarai with wagons of supplies and tools. He encountered little resistance to conversion to Christianity from the village's people and elders and designed the mission. Construction began in 1627 atop a leveled pueblo mound and continued until 1632. The convento is now mostly low walls dwarfed by the towering church walls.

Quarai's magnificent church as well as nearby Abó church are considered among the best remaining examples of wall-and-lintel construction, with their high vertical walls and flat roofs once supported by massive wooden beams. About 80 percent of the Quarai church and 40 percent of the convent still survive after four centuries of erosion. The church ruin is particularly imposing, with its solid bell towers rising almost 40 feet high and thick walls of quarried red sandstone bonded with adobe

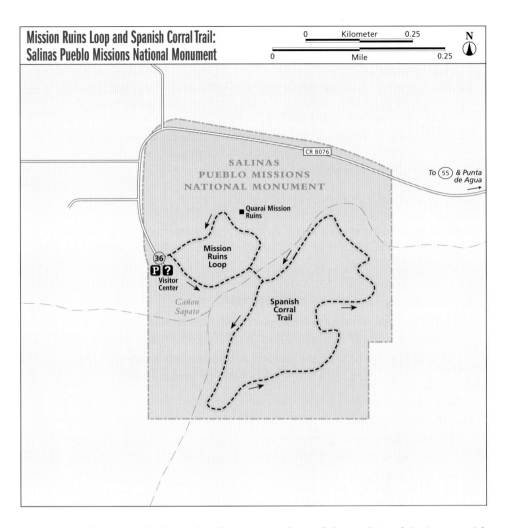

Mission Ruins Loop and Spanish Corral Trail:
Salinas Pueblo Missions National Monument

0   Kilometer   0.25   N

0   Mile   0.25

CR B076

SALINAS
PUEBLO MISSIONS
NATIONAL MONUMENT

To 55 & Punta de Agua

Quarai Mission Ruins

36

Mission Ruins Loop

Visitor Center

Cañon Sapato

Spanish Corral Trail

---

mortar. The church's floor plan forms an outline of the traditional Latin cross. It's a marvel to walk through the ancient church, its looming walls lending a sense of reverence to this still-remote outpost. Also check out the almost perfect acoustics in the sacred space.

After exploring the mission ruins, exit the church and turn right on the paved trail. Hike 0.15 mile past unexcavated ruin mounds back to the visitor center and the end of the hike at 1.5 miles.

Miles and Directions

0.0   Begin at the breezeway at the park's visitor center. Hike southeast on the paved Mission Ruins Loop Trail behind the center.

0.15   Cross a footbridge and turn right (southeast) onto the Spanish Corral Trail (GPS: 34.594712 N / -106.294991 W). Hike southeast through a piñon-juniper forest.

0.4 The trail makes a sharp left turn and heads east.

0.65 Reach an interpretive sign and bench that overlooks the Spanish Corral and the mission ruins to the north.

1.2 The loop Spanish Corral Trail ends. Go right across the footbridge over a wash and reconnect with the Mission Ruins Loop Trail. Turn right (northeast) on the Mission Ruins Loop Trail and pass the South Mound ruins.

1.3 Reach the Quarai mission ruins. Turn right (north) to enter the convent and church ruins. After exiting the church ruin, turn right (southwest) on the Mission Ruins Loop Trail.

1.5 Arrive back at the visitor center.

Area Info

Manzano Mountains State Park, CR B062, Mile Marker 3 on NM 131, Mountainair 87036; (505) 469-7608; www.emnrd.state.nm.us/SPD/manzanomountains statepark.html

GREEN TIP
Don't take souvenirs from your hike home with you. This means natural materials like plants, rocks, fossils, shells, and driftwood as well as historic artifacts such as potsherds, corn cobs, and projectile points or arrowheads.

37 Mesa View Trail: Sevilleta National Wildlife Refuge

The 3.2-mile Mesa View Trail makes a lollipop–loop hike across a dry mesa in Sevilleta National Wildlife Refuge, a wild desert area 50 miles south of Albuquerque. The moderately difficult trail, an ideal winter hike, offers spectacular views of the rugged Sierra Ladrones and Rio Grande Valley.

Distance: 3.2-mile lollipop
Hiking time: 2 to 4 hours
Difficulty: Moderate
Best seasons: Oct through May. Summers are hot.
Schedule: Trails open daily sunrise to sunset. Park outside the gate and hike in after hours. Front gate and visitor center open 8 a.m. to 4:30 p.m. Mon through Sat.
Other trail users: None

Canine compatibility: Leashed dogs allowed
Fees and permits: None
Maps: USGS San Acacia; trail map available at visitor center and on website
Trail contact: Sevilleta National Wildlife Refuge, PO Box 1248, Socorro 87801; (505) 864-4021; www.fws.gov/refuge/sevilleta
Special considerations: Flash floods occur during the monsoon season from early July through Sept.

Finding the trailhead: From Albuquerque, drive south on I-25 for about 50 miles to exit 169, the exit for Sevilleta National Wildlife Refuge. After exiting, turn right (west) and follow an unsigned road for 0.3 mile to the visitor center and parking area. GPS: 34.351481 N / -106.882279 W

The Hike

The Mesa View Trail makes a 3.2-mile circuit across open desert to the top of a broad mesa that offers spacious 360-degree views across central New Mexico. The well-marked trail, rated moderately difficult with a short climb onto the mesa, threads across the western sector of 230,000-acre Sevilleta National Wildlife Refuge, one of the largest refuges outside of Alaska. While the loop section of the trail can be hiked in either direction, it's best to go clockwise to avoid a steep climb up the east flank of the 5,000-foot-high mesa. Several rest benches are scattered along the trail so you can catch your breath and eat a snack.

While the Mesa View Trail can be hiked year-round, the ideal season is from October through May. Winter offers excellent hiking weather with brisk, clear days and a rare dusting of snow. Expect wind on spring afternoons. Summer days are usually hot, with daily high temperatures climbing to 100 degrees. Hike the trail in the early morning or late afternoon when temperatures cool. Heavy monsoon thunderstorms regularly occur on July and August afternoons. Watch the weather and make sure you're off high places to avoid lightning strikes. Little shade is found on the trail, so wear a hat, use sunscreen, and carry plenty of water and sports drinks to stay hydrated.

The Sevilleta National Wildlife Refuge, established in 1973, is a mostly wild desert landscape filled with wide plains, pygmy forests of piñon pine and juniper, dry washes, cliff escarpments, and the Rio Grande, central New Mexico's river of life. The refuge is divided into two segments: a large area of brushy hills and the Los Pinos Mountains east of the Rio Grande, and more hills and the Rio Salado's dry bed sweeping west to the rugged Sierra Ladrones.

Sevilleta, closed to recreational uses except for hiking and seasonal waterfowl hunting, protects this swath of almost pristine land for animal habitat and research. The refuge's Chihuahuan Desert ecosystem supports over 1,200 plant species and a diversity of wildlife, including 80 mammal species, 251 bird species, 58 reptile species, and 15 amphibian species. Resident wildlife includes large mammals like black bear, mule deer, pronghorn, coyote, and desert bighorn sheep, as well as birds like golden eagle, falcon, red-tailed hawk, burrowing owl, great blue heron, black-crowned night heron, sandhill crane, and killdeer.

Begin the hiking adventure at the refuge's visitor center next to the parking lot and trailhead. The center offers educational exhibits about the area's natural history, geology, cultural history, and the refuge's ongoing scientific research. The park staff can also answer any questions about the trails and conditions. The visitor center is also the trailhead for the Mesa View Trail, the 0.25-mile Wildflower Loop Trail, the 1.1-mile Nature Loop Trail, and the 1.9-mile Ladrones Vista Trail. The paved Wildflower Loop east of the visitor center is an excellent wheelchair-accessible trail to discover native plants, wildflowers, and scenic views across the Rio Grande Valley.

If the visitor center is closed and the gate at the refuge's entrance is locked, park in a large gravel lot by the gate and walk 0.25 mile up the paved road to the center. If you're getting a late hiking start, check at the visitor center before leaving to see if the gate will be open when you return. The area's open hours are usually sunrise to sunset.

The Mesa View Trail begins on the north side of the visitor center. Walk 25 feet north on a paved trail past interpretive signs on the area's plants and birds to a trail junction. Go left (west) on the rock-lined gravel trail and hike 500 feet to a dirt service road. Follow the trail west and northwest across low hills and washes toward the

MEXICAN GRAY WOLF REINTRODUCTION PROGRAM

Sevilleta National Wildlife Refuge plays a critical role in the Mexican Gray Wolf Reintroduction Program. The refuge, with its remote location and large size, allows the program to foster wild behavior in captive wolves by isolating them from contact with humans. Wolves at the Sevilleta facility are eventually released into the wild in eastern Arizona and western New Mexico.

Hikers follow the Mesa View Trail across barren ridges below the mesa top. JD TANNER

Sunset light reddens Ladron Peak. US FISH AND WILDLIFE SERVICE

eroded east face of a high mesa. Look for scattered piñon pines, one-seed junipers, Mormon tea bush, and scrub live oaks along the trail.

After passing a rest bench, the trail drops into a dry wash at 0.4 mile marked with a cairn, a stack of rocks used to designate the trail. Turn west and hike up the wash

YOUTH CONSERVATION CORPS

The Youth Conservation Corps (YCC) constructed the Mesa View Trail from 2010 to 2012. Administered by the New Mexico Energy, Minerals and Natural Resources Department, the YCC was created in 1992 to employ young New Mexicans in public projects. Participants learn skills as well as a healthy work ethic, self-discipline, and self-esteem. The program's mission is to promote the education, success, and well-being of the youths through the conservation and enhancement of the state's natural resources and community benefits.

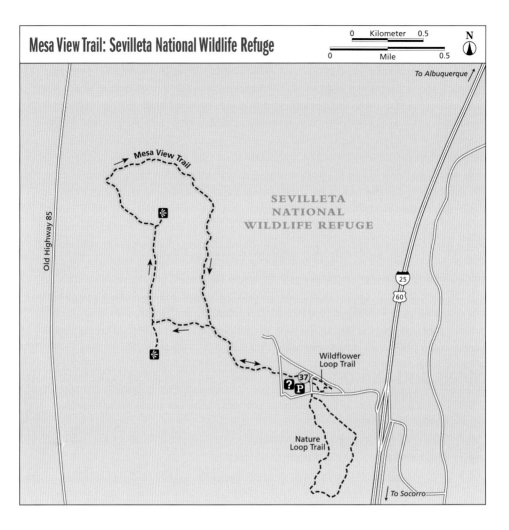

0   Kilometer   0.5

N

0   Mile   0.5

To Albuquerque

Mesa View Trail

SEVILLETA
NATIONAL
WILDLIFE REFUGE

Old Highway 85

25
60

Wildflower
Loop Trail

37
P

Nature
Loop Trail

To Socorro

for 0.05 mile until the trail exits right and climbs a hill past another bench to a trail junction at 0.5 mile. Go left on the main trail and reach another junction in a couple hundred feet at 0.6 mile. This is the start of the loop section of the trail. Keep left to hike the loop clockwise.

The trail heads west and slowly climbs along the rim of a deep wash to the left. After 0.75 mile the trail scampers up a steep set of rock and wood steps on the mesa's broken east face to the top and a trail junction at 0.8 mile. For great views, take a left turn here and hike south for 0.1 mile to a scenic overlook and rest bench at 5,096 feet on the mesa's eastern edge. The viewpoint looks across the Rio Grande Valley to the Los Pinos Mountains on the east side of the wildlife refuge; south to the Magdalena Mountains near Socorro; and northwest to Sierra Ladrones, a wild and rugged mountain range topped by 9,141-foot Ladron Peak. Return north to the trail junction to continue the hike. This segment to the overlook adds 0.2 mile to the length of the hike. For a shorter 1.6-mile hike, go right and return down the trail to the visitor center.

The next 0.3-mile trail section runs north along the edge of the mesa, offering stunning views across the face of the escarpment to distant mountains. Watch for wildlife on the flat mesa top, including fleet-footed pronghorns, the second-fastest mammal in the world, wily coyotes, jackrabbits, rattlesnakes, and horned lizards. The roadbed of old Highway 85, once the main north–south route through New Mexico, lies a few hundred feet west of the trail. Look for a side trail that heads east for 0.05 mile to an overlook for an 0.1-mile round-trip side hike.

After 1.5 miles the trail goes right and descends sharply down a steep draw on the mesa's eastern face. Past the initial steep section, the trail begins gently descending an open ridge between barren badlands. At 1.7 miles the trail reaches the bottom of a dry wash below the escarpment. Continue straight for 0.1 mile on the trail down the sandy wash until it exits right into low rocky hills. Several large cottonwood trees along the wash provide welcome shade on warm days.

The next 0.8-mile trail segment heads southeast, dipping across washes and climbing dry hillsides, below the eastern mesa escarpment. After 2.6 miles the trail reaches the first junction and the end of the loop. Go left and hike 0.6 mile back to the visitor center and trailhead for a 3.2-mile hike.

Miles and Directions

0.0 Start at the north side of the visitor center and walk 25 feet on a paved trail to a junction. Go left on a dirt trail.

0.1 Cross a dirt service road and hike northwest.

0.3 Reach a rest bench. The trail turns to the northwest.

0.4 Reach a dry wash marked by a cairn and hike west up the wash for 0.05 mile. Leave the wash on the right side and climb a hill to a bench.

0.6 Pass a junction and continue to a major trail junction. Go straight west to hike the loop clockwise. The right-hand trail is the return loop of the hike.

0.75 Climb steep rock and wood-plank steps on the eastern flank of the mesa.

0.8 Reach the mesa top and a trail junction. The hike goes right (north) here. To reach a scenic overlook, turn left (south) at the T-junction and follow a trail south along the mesa's edge for 0.1 mile to the overlook and two benches. Return to the junction to continue the hike. This spur adds 0.2 mile to the total hike mileage.

1.2 Hike north on the trail along the edge of the mesa, passing a short 0.05-mile spur trail to an overlook, until the trail goes right down the east face of the mesa.

1.5 Descend the trail in a steep draw. Continue down a broad ridge to a wash.

1.7 Reach the bottom of a wide dry wash. The trail goes east down the sandy wash.

1.8 The trail exits the wash on the right at several large cottonwood trees. Hike southeast across arroyos and low hills.

2.6 Return to the first major trail junction. Go left to the visitor center.

3.2 Arrive back at the trailhead and visitor center.

EXTRA CREDIT HIKES

Besides the Mesa View Trail, three other trails begin at the visitor center. The paved, wheelchair-accessible 0.25-mile Wildflower Loop Trail explores the desert east of the center. The 1.1-mile Nature Loop Trail begins at the visitor center and makes a loop through a Chihuahuan Desert ecosystem, passing five benches and offering scenic views and wildlife. The 1.9-mile Ladrones Vista Trail, connecting the Mesa View and Nature Loop Trails, is a moderate hike through arroyos and over hills southwest of the visitor center.

Farther south is the spectacular 2.35-mile San Lorenzo Trail, an out-and-back hike that threads through strangely eroded sandstone cliffs, mesas, and hoodoos. Take exit 163 on I-25 to reach the trailhead.

Area Info

Bosque del Apache National Wildlife Refuge, 1001 NM 1, San Antonio 87832; (575) 835-1828; www.fws.gov/refuge/bosque_del_apache

Appendix A: Land Management Agencies

Bureau of Land Management

New Mexico State Office, 301 Dinosaur Trail, Santa Fe, NM 87508; (505) 954-2000; www.blm.gov/office/new-mexico-state-office

Albuquerque District Office, 100 Sun Ave. NE, Pan American Building, Ste. 330, Albuquerque, NM 87109; (505) 761-8700; www.blm.gov/office/albuquerque-district-office

National Parks and Monuments

Bandelier National Monument, 15 Entrance Rd., Los Alamos, NM 87544; (505) 672-3861, ext. 517; www.nps.gov/band

Kasha-Katuwe Tent Rocks National Monument, BLM Rio Puerco Field Office, 100 Sun Avenue NE, Ste. 330, Albuquerque, NM 87109; (505) 331-6259; www.blm.gov/visit/kktr

Petroglyph National Monument, 6001 Unser Blvd. NW, Albuquerque, NM 87120; (505) 899-0205, ext. 335; www.nps.gov/petr

Salinas Pueblo Missions National Monument, PO Box 517, Mountainair, NM 87036; (505) 847-2585; www.nps.gov/sapu

Valles Caldera National Preserve, PO Box 359, Jemez Springs, NM 87025; (575) 829-4100, ext. 3; www.nps.gov/vall

USDA Forest Service

Cibola National Forest, 2113 Osuna Rd. NE, Albuquerque, NM 87113; (505) 346-3900; www.fs.usda.gov/cibola

Cibola National Forest, Sandia Ranger District, 11776 NM 337, Tijeras, NM 87059; (505) 281-3304; www.fs.usda.gov/detail/cibola/about-forest/districts/?cid=fsbdev3_065706

Santa Fe National Forest, 11 Forest Lane, Santa Fe, NM 87508; (505) 438-5300; www.fs.usda.gov/santafe

Santa Fe National Forest, Jemez Ranger District, PO Box 150, 051 Woodsy Lane, Jemez Springs, NM 87025; (575) 829-3535; www.fs.usda.gov/detail/santafe/about-forest/districts/?cid=fsbdev7_021072

US Fish and Wildlife Service

Sevilleta National Wildlife Refuge, PO Box 1248, Socorro, NM 87801; (505) 864-4021; www.fws.gov/refuge/Sevilleta

New Mexico State Parks

Cerrillos Hills State Park, 37 Main St., Cerrillos, NM 87010; (505) 474-0196; www.emnrd.state.nm.us/spd/cerrilloshillsstatepark

Rio Grande Nature Center State Park, 2901 Candelaria Rd. NW, Albuquerque, NM 87107; (505) 344-7240; www.emnrd.state.nm.us/spd/riograndenaturecenter statepark

New Mexico Game & Fish

NM Game & Fish, NW Area Office, 7816 Alamo Rd. NW, Albuquerque, NM 87120; (505) 222-4700; www.wildlife.state.nm.us

Albuquerque Open Spaces

Open Space Division, Parks and Recreation, 3615 Los Picaros SE, Albuquerque, NM 87105; (505) 452-5200; www.cabq.gov/parksandrecreation/open-space

Open Space Visitor Center, 6500 Coors Blvd. NW, Albuquerque, NM 87199; (505) 897-8831; www.cabq.gov/parksandrecreation/open-space/open-space-visitor -center

Appendix B: Outdoor Recreation and Environmental Protection Organizations

Amigos de la Sevilleta, PO Box 1248, Socorro, NM 87801; (505) 864-4021, ext. 102; www.amigosdelasevilleta.org

The Nature Conservancy, 212 E. Marcy St., #200, Santa Fe, NM 87501; (505) 988-3867; www.nature.org

New Mexico Mountain Club, 3754 Uptown Station, Albuquerque, NM 87190-3754; nmmtclub@gmail.com; www.nmmountainclub.org

Sierra Club–Rio Grande Chapter, 2215 Lead Ave SE, Albuquerque, NM 87106; (505) 243-7767; www.riograndesierraclub.org

Appendix C: Outdoor Outfitters

Cabela's
5151 Lang Ave. NE
Albuquerque, NM 87109
(505) 336-2700
www.cabelas.com/stores/New_Mexico/Albuquerque/084.jsp

Charlie's Sporting Goods
8908 Menaul Blvd. NE
Albuquerque, NM 87110
(505) 293-5290

Dick's Sporting Goods
3550 NM 528
Albuquerque, NM 87114
(505) 899-0355
www.stores.dickssportinggoods.com/nm/albuquerque

Eddie Bauer
2240 Q St. NE, #10H
Albuquerque, NM 87110
(505) 881-8400
www.eddiebauer.com

The North Face
2240 Q St. NE
Albuquerque, NM 87110
(505) 872-0134
www.stores.thenorthface.com/nm/albuquerque

Recreational Equipment Incorporated (REI)
1550 Mercantile Ave. NE
Albuquerque, NM 87107
(505) 247-1191
www.rei.com/stores/albuquerque.html

Sportz Outdoor
6915 Montgomery Blvd.
Albuquerque, NM 87109
(505) 837-9400

Hike Index

About the Author

Stewart M. Green is a freelance writer, editor, and photographer for FalconGuides, Globe Pequot Press, and other publications. He's written over forty-five hiking, travel, and climbing books, including *Best Hikes Colorado Springs*, *Best Easy Day Hikes Carlsbad Caverns and Guadalupe Mountains National Parks*, *Rock Climbing Colorado*, *Scenic Driving Colorado*, *Best Easy Day Hikes Moab*, and *Rock Art: The Meanings and Myths Behind Ancient Ruins in the Southwest and Beyond*. Stewart has hiked hundreds of miles and climbed many mountains in New Mexico. He's also a rock-climbing guide with Front Range Climbing Company. Visit him at http://green1109.wixsite.com/stewartmgreenphoto.

THE TEN ESSENTIALS OF HIKING

American Hiking Society

American Hiking Society recommends you pack the "Ten Essentials" every time you head out for a hike. Whether you plan to be gone for a couple of hours or several months, make sure to pack these items. Become familiar with these items and know how to use them. Learn more at **AmericanHiking.org/hiking-resources**

1. Appropriate Footwear

6. Safety Items (light, fire, and a whistle)

2. Navigation

7. First Aid Kit

3. Water (and a way to purify it)

8. Knife or Multi-Tool

4. Food

9. Sun Protection

5. Rain Gear & Dry-Fast Layers

10. Shelter